FLOYD PATTERSON

BOOKS BY W. K. STRATTON

Floyd Patterson: The Fighting Life of
Boxing's Invisible Champion

Dreaming Sam Peckinpah

Boxing Shadows

Chasing the Rodeo: On Wild Rides and
Big Dreams, Broken Hearts and Broken Bones,
and One Man's Search for the West

Splendor in the Short Grass:
The Grover Lewis Reader (coeditor)

Backyard Brawl: Inside the Blood Feud
between Texas and Texas A&M

FLOYD PATTERSON

THE FIGHTING LIFE OF BOXING'S INVISIBLE CHAMPION

W.K. STRATTON

MAINSTREAM
PUBLISHING

EDINBURGH AND LONDON

First published in USA in 2012 by
Houghton Mifflin Harcourt Publishing Company
215 Park Avenue South, New York, New York 10003

First published in Great Britain in 2012 by
MAINSTREAM PUBLISHING COMPANY
(EDINBURGH) LTD
7 Albany Street
Edinburgh EH1 3UG

ISBN 9781845963323

A catalogue record for this book is available
from the British Library

The author is grateful for permission to quote from the following sources: Letter
from Archie Moore to Floyd Patterson, reprinted by permission of J'Marie
Moore. "The Fight: Patterson vs. Liston" © 1963 by James Baldwin. Originally
published in *Nugget*. Copyright renewed. Collected in *The Cross of Redemption:
Uncollected Writings by James Baldwin*, published by Pantheon Books. Reprinted
by arrangement with the James Baldwin Estate

Book design by Brian Moore

Printed in Great Britain by
Clays Ltd, St Ives plc

1 3 5 7 9 10 8 6 4 2

For Richard Lord and John Schulian

CONTENTS

Prologue: Nothing Short of Miraculous   xi

1. I Don't Like That Boy!   1

2. Taken Up with Boxing   13

3. Floyd Patterson Is Out of This World   26

4. Cus Answers the Questions   34

5. Do I Have to Fight Floyd?   53

6. Youngest King of the Mountain   64

7. A Black Champion in America   73

8. Lightning and Toonder   94

9. Not the Time to Quit   106

10. Standing at the Peak   126

11. Camelot Denied   136

12. Confronting a Certain Weakness   156

13. A Title for America   167

14. A Boxing Man   189

Epilogue: Invisible Champion   213

Acknowledgments and Sources   219

Notes   229

Floyd Patterson's Boxing Record   245

Index   253

Brother,
This is advice from a friend who has been watching you closely. *Do not go too fast.* Keep working for the people but remember that you are one of *us* and do not forget if you get too big *they* will cut you down. You are from the South and you know that this is a *white man's world.* So take a friendly advice and go easy so that you can keep on helping the colored people. *They* do not want you to go too fast and will cut you down if you do. Be smart . . .

— RALPH ELLISON, *Invisible Man*

◆

Nothing Short of Miraculous

T HE THERMOMETERS IN midtown Manhattan registered a near-record high as dusk approached, but heat was not the worst meteorological malady afflicting New Yorkers that September day. Sulfur-based clouds floated eerily down the streets. A peculiar set of weather conditions had combined with the ever-present smoke belching from chimneys and exhaust pipes — common in the days before widespread pollution control. Calls from panicked city dwellers, their eyes burning and throats scratchy, tied up phone lines to police stations and newspaper offices. But neither cops nor reporters knew what to do about the noxious air, though there was a new word to describe this troublesome phenomenon: smog. Officials recommended that people stay inside until the situation improved.

That was not an option for seventeen-year-old Floyd Patterson. The newsreel announcers of the day might have pronounced Friday, September 12, 1952, as Patterson's date with destiny. At the very least, it marked the beginning of the prizefighting career he had dreamed of since elementary school. No way would toxic billows set him back.

Besides, the sulfurous air smelled sweet compared to what Floyd found inside the St. Nicholas Arena, where thick cigarette and cigar smoke all but obscured the boxing ring. Though not as famous as Madison Square Garden, St. Nick's had hosted thousands of fights over the previous fifty years. In fact, privately staged matches were held there even before boxing could be legally presented as a public event in New York, and it had become a favorite venue for Manhattan fight fans. Novelist and boxing aficionado Budd Schulberg lovingly recalled it as a place where "Damon Runyon's guys and dolls were all around ringside, and the balcony was full of blue-collar holler guys ready to fight themselves."[1] On this night, they were all out in force despite the smog, the swells and the working stiffs alike sweating in the unseasonable heat, to watch Olympic phenom Floyd Patterson box professionally for the first time.

Patterson's manager, Cus D'Amato, had matched Floyd against a nobody from Harlem named Eddie Godbold for this first fight. The newspaper writers scoffed at the choice. Lewis Burton, a longtime boxing writer at William Randolph Hearst's *New York Journal-American*, dismissed Godbold as nothing more than a "sacrificial lamb," a "guaranteed knockout."[2]

Still, Patterson was anything but confident before the fight. Earlier in the day, as he fretted about the outcome, his mother had tried calming him by listing all he'd accomplished as an amateur. But her efforts were to little avail. Floyd remained nervous as he ate his typical breakfast — a chocolate bar — at the subway station, and he grew even more anxious at the New York State Athletic Commission offices and the prefight weigh-in. There, gravel-voiced reporters lobbed questions while photographers aimed their cameras at him, flashbulbs popping like punctured balloons. Floyd hated it. He didn't feel comfortable on public display like this, and he preferred having D'Amato answer questions for him. He was happy to flee when the weigh-in was over. Floyd ate lunch, and D'Amato checked him in to a hotel, which was blessedly cool. Despite his nerves, he napped for most of the afternoon before departing for St. Nick's. He found it easy to fall asleep.

Floyd's nap did nothing to relieve his prefight jitters. He continued to worry about how well he would perform in the ring as his trainer, Frank Lavelle, wrapped his hands and laced on his gloves. When it was time for his bout, Patterson climbed into the ring, wearing the robe he'd earned as a member of the US Olympic team. The scene could have come straight from a Warner Bros. film noir popular at the time. Sportswriters, press cards stuck in the bands of their fedoras, crowded around the platform. Photographers with their ever-present Graflexes jockeyed for position along the ring apron. Stocky made-men with their ladies of the moment lounged in the expensive seats just behind the press. In the smoky darkness beyond them were the shouting stevedores and longshoremen in the cheap seats.

The bell rang, and Patterson delivered his first punches as a professional boxer, quickly making it clear that the prognosticators had been right. It was no contest. Godbold made it only to the fourth round before Floyd knocked him out. Patterson collected $300 for his night's work. He cared about the money, but the important thing was that he was now in the books as a prizefighter. He sensed a whole world of possibilities opening up for him.

Virtually no one who stepped out of St. Nick's into the foul vapors of that New York night could have fully known what had just been witnessed — the beginning of a two-decades-long career that would change sports in general and boxing in particular. A career that set records, earned Floyd Patterson millions of dollars, and made him one of the most famous people in the world, at least for a time. A career that thrust him to the forefront of the civil rights movement, gave him access to the most powerful American politicians of the day, and set the mold for athletes desiring to speak out about social causes. A career that would be wrapped in controversy, winning him both devoted fans and harsh critics.

Young men on the bottom rungs of American society have long turned to boxing to climb toward a better life. No one had a greater distance to scale than Floyd, a troubled kid who befuddled even those closest to him. "He's a kind of a stranger," D'Amato had said.[3] He was a walking contradiction. At times he was astonishingly well spoken, given his education. "Indeed, among contemporary boxers," novelist Joyce Carol Oates once observed, "no one is so articulate as Floyd Patterson."[4] But mostly he was quiet, disengaged from what was occurring around him. Muhammad Ali, who would become one of his great rivals, listed Patterson with legends Sonny Liston, Joe Frazier, and George Foreman as the best prizefighters he had battled. "Floyd Patterson was the most skilled as a boxer," Ali would say.[5] But Floyd also endured countless blows to the head over his long career, often winding up on the mat. No important boxing champ was knocked down more during vital contests than Patterson. Yet he possessed an extraordinary ability to get up after those knockdowns and battle on to claim victory.

Patterson was an overachiever who bootstrapped his way to the top, an all-American success story. As happens with many, perhaps most, such American heroes, he fell from popular favor as his skills waned and the nation's tastes changed. But on this smoggy New York night, he had no notion what fate awaited him. As he rode the subway home, he had money in his pocket and the prospect to make more, in a sport he loved. Such good fortune was beyond the fantasies of poor kids from Brooklyn's Bedford-Stuyvesant. For people who had known Floyd Patterson as an invisible ghetto child — a child indistinguishable from thousands of others trapped in urban poverty — his becoming a professional boxer was nothing short of miraculous. Just a few years earlier, it seemed unlikely he'd turn out to be anything at all.

1

I Don't Like That Boy!

ONE THING YOU could always say about Thomas Patterson:[1] he worked hard. People in Waco, North Carolina, bore witness to that fact as Thomas put in long, brutal hours on the Seaboard Air Line Railway line crew. But, like nearly all black Americans in the South, Thomas never saw much in return for his labor. In 1936 he had a growing family — including his one-year-old baby, Floyd, who had been born on January 4 of the previous year — and could have used some extra dollars. But there was not much opportunity to make money in Waco, a poor hamlet in a poor part of a nation suffering through the Great Depression. He and his wife, Annabelle,[2] heard from relatives that things were better up north. So they decided to depart North Carolina, with its poverty and its segregation, and seek out a better life elsewhere.

In the years following World War I, black Americans like the Pattersons began abandoning the rural South by the hundreds of thousands to flee racism and seek jobs in the industrialized Northeast and upper Midwest. Eventually, some seven million people took part in this Great Migration, forever changing the cultural landscape of the United States. American popular music would never be the same because of the demographic shift, nor would politics, cuisine, literature, fashion, or sports.

Thomas chose the Bedford-Stuyvesant area of Brooklyn as the new home for his family. Although blacks had lived in Brooklyn for more than two hundred years, Bedford-Stuyvesant, with its graceful brownstones and tree-lined streets, had been off-limits to them for decades. But in the early 1900s blacks began moving into Bed-Stuy as New York's burgeoning population forced the breakdown of old barriers. It became one of the first urban areas in the United States to experience white flight, as property speculators used the growing black population to convince whites to sell their homes at prices far below even the depressed market values of the 1930s. The once stately houses in Bed-Stuy were then gutted and reoutfitted as cheap apartment houses. In 1930 fewer than thirty thousand nonwhite residents lived in the neighborhood, but that changed quickly with wave after wave of black immigrants. Soon, Bed-Stuy was a large African American ghetto.

What Thomas Patterson found for his family in Bed-Stuy was different from what he'd known in North Carolina, but it would be hard to make the case that it was much of an improvement, at least as far as the family's livelihood was concerned. The Pattersons had simply traded small-town poverty for urban poverty. In Bed-Stuy, the sidewalks were crowded, and discarded newspapers took flight with each gust of wind. The buildings were dingy, rapidly falling into disrepair, and infested with roaches and other vermin. Crime was commonplace, and the family was forced to contend with street hustlers and gang members, something unheard of back in Waco. Yet Bed-Stuy was a place where blacks were free to speak much more openly than they could back in North Carolina. The Pattersons would have been exposed to the progressive concepts of W. E. B. Du Bois and the National Association for the Advancement of Colored People (NAACP), and to the street-corner preachments of radicalized followers of Marcus Garvey, something that would have been unheard of in the South of the 1930s and 1940s. However, the family's struggle to keep a roof overhead and food on the table overshadowed the lofty idealism surrounding them.

The Pattersons fell into a pattern of frequent moves within Bed-Stuy as the family grew larger. Floyd remembered six or seven apartments from his childhood, but there might have been more. All were four- or five-room dwellings known as railroad flats — apartments whose rooms are in a line with doors between them, not dissimilar to shotgun shacks in the South — with no running hot water, heated by coal or oil-fired stoves. "The only windows were in the rooms in the front and the back, and it was always too hot in the summer, too cold in the winter, and never big enough," Patterson recalled in his autobiography, *Victory over Myself*.[3]

To pay the rent on these shabby dwellings, Thomas Patterson worked long hours on construction crews, for the city sanitation department, as a longshoreman, and at the mob-controlled Fulton Fish Market on the East River waterfront in lower Manhattan. He was in his forties, and the harsh physical requirements of these jobs took everything out of him. He came home at night exhausted and frustrated. Sometimes he skipped dinner and went straight to the bedroom, where he collapsed into sleep, still wearing his work clothes. Every Friday he handed all his pay to Floyd's mother for household expenses. But his workweek wasn't over. He took odd jobs on weekends to bring in a little more cash. "I felt very, very sorry for my father," Floyd remembered. "I'd see him go out to work at six in the morning and come home sometimes at one the next morning. Some days he'd take a drink when it was cold outside, after he got home. I was the one who would take off his shoes and clean his feet. I enjoyed it."[4]

Annabelle also worked, first as a maid, then later at a bottling plant. With both parents employed, the Patterson children were on their own for most of the day. They, like other neighborhood children, had plenty of opportunity for getting into trouble on the streets. Fights, often involving clubs and knives, were common. Fruit carts and stores provided temptation for shoplifting. But the young Floyd Patterson had problems beyond those of a typical ghetto kid, problems that mystified his parents, his teachers, and ultimately himself.

A photograph hanging on a wall in the Patterson home showed Floyd at age two, during a trip to the Bronx Zoo with his brothers Frank and Billy. As Floyd grew older, he frequently stared at the picture, silent rage building inside him. He would point to the photo and shout to his mother, "I don't like that boy!" Annabelle Patterson had no idea what caused these outbursts. Her son's obsession with the image eventually took a darker turn when Floyd carved an X over his face in the photo, shocking his mother, who could not understand what would provoke such a destructive act.

Nor could she understand her son's odd nighttime behavior. Nightmares and screaming fits were regular occurrences. He also began sleepwalking, sometimes strolling the busy sidewalk outside the apartment house in his pajamas. The sleepwalking alarmed his parents so much that they took Floyd to a doctor, something that would not have been undertaken lightly given the family finances. The doctor charged the office-visit fee but offered no remedy.

When Floyd started elementary school, his troubles only increased. He was convinced the other kids were making fun of him. He saw himself as the perfect butt for jokes — a tall, skinny, gawky kid with a grimy face. His hand-me-down clothes were oversized: shoes too big for his feet, cuffed trousers with a waistband drawn tight with a belt to keep them from falling down, a shirt so large it flapped in the breeze. Beyond his appearance, Floyd knew there were other reasons for people to ridicule him. His social skills were all but nonexistent. He couldn't bring himself to talk to other people, nor could he look anyone in the eye.

Floyd quickly fell behind the other students. He went from one year to another without learning how to read or write, though later IQ tests showed him to be of average intelligence. Even when he knew the answer, Floyd did not raise his hand in class, not wanting to call attention to himself. Teachers had little opportunity to get to know him. He once estimated that he attended as many as ten Brooklyn elementary schools because of the family's frequent address changes. "The schools he went to in the area," Jimmy Breslin once wrote in his popular newspaper column, "have old, faded record cards showing he attended nine days in one of them, a couple of weeks in another. The rest of the time he ran the streets, a strange, illiterate kid who would stick his chin on his chest and look at the ground when anybody tried to talk to him."[5]

Floyd didn't care about schoolwork or whether he was promoted to the next grade. At the same time, he despised himself for not caring. He sought out dark places to hide whenever he had the chance. Frequently he hid in the school's cellar and stayed there until class was dismissed. The teachers became accustomed to his vacant desk. Eventually, he started skipping school altogether — especially Fridays, assembly day.

School rules required him to wear a white shirt and tie on Fridays, and his only dress clothes were hand-me-downs from his father that were much too large for him. Floyd believed he looked like a character straight from a comic book. The other kids laughed at him, even more so than usual. Or so it seemed to Floyd. Plenty of Bed-Stuy kids had it just as tough as he did, but Floyd was blind to them. On those Fridays, he could see only the kids who were better off, and register humiliation because he was not among them.

As Floyd's truancies became more frequent, he began prowling the streets of Brooklyn, finding alleys or shadowy corners where he could be by himself. If he had the eighteen cents for admission, he slipped into the comforting darkness of second-run Brooklyn movie houses like the Banco, the Regent, or the Apollo. If he didn't have the eighteen cents, he sneaked in. He might remain in the theater all day and into the evening, staring raptly at the giant images on the screen before him. The white actors represented to him what "normal" life should be: people who lived in comfortable houses, families with well-mannered children, a father who didn't come home completely used up by his job.

Sometimes he boarded the Eighth Avenue subway and rode it all day. One day he discovered a little room off the tracks near the High Street station. When no one was looking, he'd climb the metal ladder leading to it and push open the door. The tiny enclosure housed tools used by subway crews. He'd step inside and close the door. Suddenly, he'd be in complete darkness. And it was silent in that room, except when a train roared past. Floyd felt safe there, no eyes peering at him, no voices talking about him. This tool closet became his refuge from the real world, a place where he'd spread old newspapers on the floor, lie down, and drift into dreams of candy, nice clothes, and money.

But he couldn't stay in his hole in the wall forever. Skipping school was a serious offense, and Floyd drew the attention of truancy officers. He tried hiding from them, but they caught him often enough. He became familiar with courtrooms and judges. He pleaded with his mother to let him just quit school altogether. He fantasized that he could get a job, do a man's work, and supply badly needed income for the family. His mother would hear nothing of it. She adhered to the adage that staying in school meant staying out of trouble, so his fantasies of becoming a full-time worker evaporated. But he still skipped class as often as he could. And, as his mother feared, he found trouble.

He regularly snatched fruit from delivery trucks as well as from the Ess & Eff stores and Sam's Grocery. One night, he burglarized a shop to steal food. He took his booty to a corner two blocks away and began eating while sitting on a curb, convinced he'd pulled off his crime undetected. But he was wrong. A policeman soon nabbed him. Floyd was off to juvenile court yet again, where authorities added the incident to what was becoming a growing record of truancy offenses and petty crimes. Once, he stole for his mother. He saw female teachers wearing pretty clothes but never Annabelle. He resented this, so he broke into a store at two in the morning, grabbed an armload of dresses, and ran out the front door. "I carried them all the way home," he said, "taking special care when I had to jump over a wall. When my mother asked where I got the dresses . . . I told her I found them."[6] His mother grew suspicious about the mounting number of things young Floyd "found," but there was little she could do to stop him. His daring escalated. He even managed to steal a truck from the Sheffield Farms milk company and take it for a short joy ride, though his legs were hardly long enough to reach the pedals. He ran home after abandoning the truck, with no one pursuing him. But he knew this act, like his other misdeeds, would catch up with him at some point.

One day, the Bishops, a group of Bed-Stuy toughs, cornered Floyd on the street and tried to steal his pocket change. Outnumbered and smaller than his assailants, Floyd nonetheless flailed at them wildly until someone pulled a knife. Fortunately for Floyd, his older brother Frank happened along at that moment. Frank grabbed a stick in the gutter and threatened the thugs, who fled — without Floyd's money. In fighting back, Floyd had tapped into a familiar well of rage within himself. It proved effective against the Bishops. But when it surfaced during a confrontation with a cop, Patterson's whole life changed.

It started when Floyd snatched a case of soda from a bottling plant. As he hurried away, a police car pulled up.[7] A whole case of soda was too much for a ten-year-old boy like Floyd to carry while running, so he dropped it, snatched two bottles, then took off again. But even those two bottles were too much to handle. He threw one aside. Then, after a few more steps, he tossed the other one away. He made it all of a half block before the policeman from the patrol car collared him.

"You just robbed the factory down the street," the officer declared. "I saw you. Let's go."

The patrolman led him back to the soda plant, where he tried to make Patterson fess up. Floyd refused, claiming some other boy had given him the sodas, so the officer started slapping him around. The policeman also accused Floyd of hurling soda bottles at him. When Patterson began crying, the patrolman picked up an empty wooden crate and smashed it over Floyd's head. In that moment everything changed: Floyd went from the reclusive, shy, quiet kid to being "crazy mad," as he later described it.[8] Snatching up a crate himself, he attacked the officer. The patrolman later told Annabelle he'd never seen anything like it. Floyd had become a miniature wild man, screaming and fighting. It took two or three more cops to subdue him.

The incident sent Floyd back to juvenile court, where he went before a judge who knew him all too well from previous appearances. Patterson stared at the floor as he listened to the judge tell Annabelle that he feared Floyd was headed toward more serious crimes. It was time to take some action, the judge said. The boy needed a more regulated life. Annabelle agreed. Ten-year-old Floyd left the courtroom certain he was bound for prison.

Patterson had good reason to assume he was going to jail. Where else could he have been headed? Government-funded social services were all but unknown to Bed-Stuy denizens. The service providers that were prevalent had affiliations with churches and benevolent groups, and most chose not to deal with troubled African American youths. But one alternative existed, one Annabelle Patterson learned about from the courts. It sounded unreal: a facility in upstate New York where boys could find plenty of open spaces, woods, fresh air, and, most important, teachers dedicated to inner-city kids who battled internal demons. But the Wiltwyck School for Boys was real, and that was Floyd's destination as he departed Brooklyn in September 1945, riding in a car driven by a school counselor named Clarence Cooper.

Cooper attempted conversation during the ninety-mile drive to Esopus, the small town near Wiltwyck, but Patterson kept his eyes closed and his lips locked, fuming to himself and angry at his mother. Cooper tried to reassure Floyd, telling him that he was traveling to a place that would help him. But Patterson would have none of it. He gave every indication that he planned to fight whatever awaited him to the very end.

With his eyes clamped shut in the car — eventually he fell asleep — Patterson missed the startling changes in landscape as Clarence Cooper drove from Brooklyn up to Poughkeepsie, then across the bridge to Esopus. Had he been looking, Floyd would have taken in things he'd never seen before: mountains, forests, rivers, open fields, pastured horses. When the car finally came to a stop and he opened his eyes, Floyd saw four stone buildings trimmed with wood painted white. Behind them wooded hills stretched into the distance. As he stepped out of the car, he was impressed by what he didn't see: bars, barbed-wire-crowned fences, guards with guns. He did see a lot of other boys, mostly his age, mostly black. The kids seemed to be dressed better than he — he was still in his outsized hand-me-downs — but from the very beginning he felt like he could relate to them.

"One thing really astounded me," he said years later, reflecting on life at the school. "I found it didn't make any difference that I was colored, the way it did in Brooklyn where white boys called me names. There were about thirty white boys, and forty to fifty Negro boys at Wiltwyck, and they all got along. I never heard one remark about the color of a boy's skin, or his religion."[9] Other Wiltwyck boys had different memories, but the school's equitable treatment of residents probably served to minimize racial tensions.

As he settled in, Patterson learned that the standard form of corporal punishment common in public schools of the time was discouraged at Wiltwyck — although some staff members were known to beat unruly students, and plenty of ten-year-old thugs were on campus to challenge the staff's authority. Each residential cottage had a counselor and a trained social worker. A public school administered by the New York City Board of Education functioned on the grounds, and all the boys were required to attend. But the classroom atmosphere was far different from what was typical at a city school. The class size was smaller, allowing the teachers to devote more time to each of their students. The teachers themselves had made a conscious decision to work with emotionally troubled children, so they did not consider boys like Floyd to be a disruption or something to be endured. They had chosen to work with kids like him.

Many of the teachers had remarkable backgrounds. Art instructor Edith Kramer had learned painting from masters in Vienna, where she had been born and reared. She befriended a number of the early psychoanalysts in Vienna and underwent therapy herself. In Prague in the late 1930s, she taught art for children of Jewish and Communist refugees fleeing Nazi persecution. There, she helped pioneer the idea of art therapy for traumatized children. She eventually fled Hitler-controlled Europe herself and wound up at Wiltwyck, where she employed on the street kids from New York techniques she'd first used with refugees in Prague.

Miss Vivian Costen did not boast an exotic pedigree along the lines of Kramer's. But she became one of the most important people in Floyd's life. Almost nothing exists in public records about Costen. She was African American and had never married. Census records indicate she may have been born in North Carolina in 1901 and lived in Connecticut before her Wiltwyck days. According to Patterson, she died sometime during the mid-1950s. Other than that, she's unknown. But there is one thing about which there is no mystery: her influence on Patterson lasted a lifetime.

Working with just seven or eight boys at a time in the classroom, Costen patiently attempted to bring them out of their shells and convince them that they could learn. One day she asked a question of the class, but Floyd's lack of confidence kept him from responding. When Costen announced the answer and Floyd discovered he had been right, he leaped from his chair and darted out of the classroom, furious with himself for not speaking up. When Costen caught up with him in the hallway and saw the tears streaming down his cheeks, she told Floyd she knew he'd known the answer. She said she wanted him to overcome his fear of speaking out, that he was no different from any other boy his age.

From that point onward, Patterson began to risk speaking out in class. He was often wrong with his answers at the beginning, but newly engaged with his studies, he started to catch on. Soon, as a reward,

Costen invited him to spend a weekend at her house — a candy-sweetened honor she gave to the boy who had done the best academic work for the week. She also bought Floyd clothes and other small gifts.

Patterson soon proved himself to be among the bright lights at Wiltwyck. As such, he developed key friendships with two prominent adults. Ernst Papanek, who later became the school director, was a well-known man of the world who'd once been a member of the Vienna city council and the executive committee of the Socialist Youth International as well as a groundbreaking psychiatrist. He was best known for the work he'd done to protect Jewish children from Nazi persecution during World War II. After the war, he moved to the United States, where he became associated with the Children's Aid Society and the Unitarian Universalist Service Committee. His work brought him to Wiltwyck, where he met Patterson. The two stayed in touch for the remainder of Papanek's life, with Papanek, an unlikely fight fan, writing Patterson letters supporting his pro boxing career.

Floyd also befriended Eleanor Roosevelt, the president's widow. Wiltwyck, located just across the Hudson River from her Val-Kill home, existed only because of her ability to raise money for it. Justine Wise Polier, the first woman to serve as a judge in New York City and Roosevelt's friend, had convinced the Episcopalian Mission Society to create the Wiltwyck School for Boys at Esopus in 1936. Wiltwyck began accepting "disturbed" boys referred from New York City, with the city paying the private school for its services. Most of the students were like Floyd Patterson — poor and black, with criminal records and symptoms of mental illness. The school had its share of failures, and violence was fairly common among the students. Sometimes the staff reacted in kind when confronting offenders. But it also had its successes, boys whose lives were turned around by the Wiltwyck experience. However, the school soon became more than the Mission Society could support and would have closed had Mrs. Roosevelt not intervened.

Beyond addressing the school's funding issues, Roosevelt also gave her time. She strolled the campus wearing a fox stole, pausing to engage the boys in conversation. Her Independence Day picnic at Val-Kill was the highlight of each school year. "We would hop, skip, and jump for lollipops and hotdogs and ice cream," Cliff Arnesen, a Wiltwyck alumnus, said. "Then she would read Winnie-the-Pooh stories to us. It was really nice. All the kids would gather around after the hotdogs and ice cream and she would read those stories in that high-pitched voice."[10] She also read from Rudyard Kipling's *Just So Stories.* And, when it was time to serve the holiday meal, she made a point of personally taking part in buttering the rolls served to the boys. When Wiltwyck's director told her she didn't need to go to such lengths, she said, "When the King and Queen were here we had buttered rolls for them. Why should the children of Wiltwyck be given anything less?"[11] Floyd caught Roosevelt's eye, and he was among the students invited to spend two Christmases at the Roosevelt Hyde Park estate. Those visits began a friendship that lasted until her death in 1962.

The Wiltwyck experience eroded Patterson's cynicism and transformed him into something of a juvenile egalitarian. It also taught him that he was a natural when it came to smashing his fist into another kid's face.

Three or four times a year, Walter Johnson, Wiltwyck's executive director, staged boxing bouts for the boys, coaching them himself beforehand. With prodding from his mother during one of her Wiltwyck visits, Patterson agreed to give ring fighting a try. The first kid he boxed was bigger and had boxing experience, so Patterson doubted he could beat him — until the first round was under way. Floyd discovered that he could easily dominate his foe. He flattened the other kid's nose, and with that, Floyd had his first boxing victory. He showed little style in winning. In fact, he looked flat-out clumsy, leaping into the air to launch punches, throwing haymakers that missed the mark by feet, not inches. The boys in the audience howled at his missteps, but at the same time, they rooted for him and gave him a rousing ovation when he won. It was the first time he had ever heard a crowd cheer for him, and he loved it. He fought two more bouts while at Wiltwyck and, as the audience favorite, won them both.

Patterson left Wiltwyck at age twelve feeling like a winner for the first time in his life. During his two years at the school, he'd learned to read and write. He'd overcome his paralyzing shyness. He could look people in the eye and hold a conversation. The fits of screaming at night had

disappeared. He never again sleepwalked. He would come to understand his experience at the school as fostering in him the belief that
ghetto-formed nihilism can be overcome, that hope exists for even the
most downtrodden, that black people and white people can live and
work together. Now, he was ready to go back to New York City to finish
his public school education. More important, he wanted to get back
into the ring. "My mind," he would later recall, "was already taken up
with boxing."[12]

2

Taken Up with Boxing

IN THE MID-1940s many young black men and boys found their minds taken up with boxing. It was the one major sport that was integrated to any significant degree. Big-league baseball boasted not a single black player. Top-flight college football programs were almost without exception white. Black players turned up in the National Football League only sporadically — a situation that would not change until 1946, when the Los Angeles Rams signed African Americans Woody Strode and Kenny Washington, a move that prompted other teams to add black players to their rosters as well. Professional basketball would not integrate until 1950.

But blacks had been making their mark on boxing for decades. The most lauded athlete in the world immediately after World War II was heavyweight champ Joe Louis, from Detroit. Louis was the first African American to become a national hero, a status he acquired by hammering the German Max Schmeling in 1938's "Battle of the Century" fight. His private life was one thing, but his public persona was that of a clean-living, hard-working, respectable black man, and he inspired countless other young black men to pursue success inside the ring, not the least of whom were Frank, Billy, and Floyd Patterson. They started at the most basic of makeshift boxing gyms. Brooklyn's Carlton Avenue

YMCA had virtually no training equipment except sparring gloves and a solitary speedbag hanging in a corner.

It was all asses and elbows out there on the basketball court of the Carlton Avenue Y, where pairs of kids faced off and threw punches at each other, all of them going at it simultaneously. The boxing matches Floyd participated in at Wiltwyck had been wild exhibitions between untrained boys. But here he began to learn how to keep his hands up, how to feint jabs, and how to slip punches thrown at him as he sparred round after round. It was akin to figuring out how to swim by being thrown into a deep lake, but it worked for Floyd and his brothers. Frank Lavelle, the trainer in charge of Carlton Avenue's boxing program, took notice of the Patterson boys. They seemed to have potential.

Lavelle, whose day job was at the US Custom House at the port of New York, was not unlike other white trainers in big cities across the country. Boxing had been integrated as far back as the late 1800s, except for championship bouts — white promoters ensured that only white boxers competed in those. But that changed in 1902 when Joe Gans won the world lightweight title. While Gans's victory did not immediately create complete integration of championship-level boxing, it opened the door. More and more blacks appeared in the prizefighting ring as the twentieth century progressed, most taking up the sport as a way to escape poverty. After the war, as African American fighters were becoming more and more dominant in the professional fight ranks, men like Lavelle prospected for future pro talent in gyms catering to blacks in poor neighborhoods. If he could find a fighter capable of eventually winning some pro fights, Lavelle stood to make some money. As much as a third of a fighter's purse went to his manager and trainer. Lavelle didn't necessarily have to find a potential champion. In those days before television became pervasive, pro boxing matches took place in auditoriums around the city every week, so there was plenty of demand for boxers, a few of whom earned a living from the ring without ever contending for a championship. Their managers and trainers made out well enough too. After a couple of years of working with the Pattersons at the Y, Lavelle decided it was time to take Frank and Billy to the next step. Floyd tagged along.

• • •

That next step was the Gramercy Gym, which was situated across the river in Manhattan. It occupied a rundown space upstairs at 116 East Fourteenth Street. The neighborhood was familiar to Floyd. After leaving Wiltwyck, he began attending classes at the Cyrus W. Field School, a vocational elementary/junior high school better known as PS 614. It was one of two "600 schools" for "maladjusted" students that had recently opened in New York, and it was located on East Fourth Avenue, not too far from the Gramercy. With their emphasis on teaching trades, the schools catered to students who stood little chance for academic advancement. Floyd excelled at PS 614, just as he had at Wiltwyck. But the Gramercy offered him the chance to learn skills that would prove far more valuable than any training he received at school. The boxing gym was also far more demanding.

Just getting from the street to the gym involved a test of will. The street entrance was a heavy, zinc-plated door on which had been painted "Gramacy Gym," owing to a sign painter's careless ways. Before boys could get to the sparring ring and heavy bags upstairs, they had to open that big door. Some never could screw up enough courage to do so, fleeing instead to the candy stand next door, never to consider boxing again. But some did continue. On the other side, past some garbage cans, were two flights of dimly lighted rickety wooden stairs that disappeared into darkness. Who knew what really waited at the top? Climbing the stairs took even more courage — it was almost as if you were climbing the steps of a gallows — and many boys made it no farther than halfway up before they turned tail and hustled back to the candy stand. The boys who did make it all the way to the top encountered another door in the shadows. This last barricade dissuaded a few more. A square had been cut in the door and covered with chicken wire, and behind that square was a snarling German shepherd. That was enough to scare away even some tough kids. But those who braved the dog and pushed the door open entered a kind of dingy wonderland of sights, smells, and sounds guaranteed to entice most boys, a wonderland lorded over by a stocky, middle-aged man named Cus D'Amato. Floyd passed these tests of courage and entered the Gramercy Gym for the first time, trailing Frank Lavelle and his brothers.

The gym's size impressed Floyd. He thought it looked like the inside of a big barn. The odor of stale sweat clung to the walls — hardly pleasant, but oddly inviting, evidence of serious work getting done. The windows were closed tight — they were never opened — and the air felt hot against Floyd's skin. He let his eyes travel around the enormous room. Men sparred in the ring. A couple of boxers slugged away at the two heavy bags. The hypnotic *rat-tat-tat* of speedbags drowned out conversations. Across the way, fighters shadowboxed in front of cracked mirrors. Someone who'd finished his workout lay face-down on a table for a rubdown. There were some steel lockers, a few showers. Floyd took all this in and knew he belonged here, though he wasn't quite ready to tell that to the odd white-haired proprietor. "My old-time embarrassment kept me from it for a while," Patterson said. "It wasn't the fear of getting hurt. It was the fear of starting something new."[1] So he just watched his brothers go through their drills.[2]

Patterson was now fourteen, already closing in on six feet tall but weighing just 147 pounds, with rounded shoulders and long, straw-thin arms. But he had learned, at the Carlton branch YMCA and during scuffles at school, that he could hit. After watching his older brothers work out a few times, he approached D'Amato and said he wanted to fight. D'Amato was definitely interested; Lavelle had already told Cus that Floyd might have the right stuff to become a pro. Cus asked him how old he was. Fearing he might be turned away for being too young, Floyd fibbed, telling Cus he was fifteen. D'Amato agreed to give him a shot at boxing and explained what the deal would be: he would allow Patterson to train at the Gramercy; provide him socks, trunks, T-shirts, a no-foul protector, and the other equipment he would need; and permit him to spar with the other Gramercy boys — all at no charge, with the understanding that D'Amato would be Patterson's manager, guide his career, and, if he turned pro, claim a percentage of his purses. None of this was written down, but Floyd accepted the offer, and the spindly Bed-Stuy kid became one of D'Amato's protégés. No relationship was more important in shaping Floyd's life.

During his heyday, in the 1950s and '60s, Constantine "Cus" D'Amato was a mysterious figure to sportswriters and boxing fans alike. No one doubted that he was a veteran of the rough-and-tumble boxing scene in New York, though he never fought professionally himself. But whence he came and why he wound up doing what he did seemed to be anyone's guess. Newspaper accounts of the time sometimes mentioned that he had no family and suggested his age was unknown. In fact, he did have family, and his birth date was available. He was born on January 17, 1908, to Italian immigrants living in a tenement in the Bronx's Clason Point section. His father was Damiano D'Amato, a one-time Italian folk wrestler who loved boxing. Damiano was a strong-willed man who had taught himself to read and write as an adult.[3] He passed on that willpower to his sons.

Cus's mother, Elizabeth, died of pneumonia not long after his fifth birthday. "I don't remember my mother," he once said, "and I was fortunate, because I was self-reliant at a very early age. I was not confused by the ideas, the thoughts of mothers and fathers who, well-meaning though they may be, mess up the minds of their children."[4] The world he encountered outside the D'Amato home was difficult, too. Their Clason Point neighborhood wasn't an easy place, and the five D'Amato brothers discovered they'd have to get tough — and tough in a hurry — if they were to survive. Cus's brother Tony developed a fearsome reputation as a street brawler. Family legend had it that Tony could take on four or five police officers single-handedly and walk away from the fracas when it was over, leaving the cops stretched out cold in the street.

Cus's brother Gerry proved to be the most talented with boxing gloves.[5] An attractive, strong man, Gerry soon developed into a promising up-and-comer in New York's featherweight ranks. Outside the ring, he dazzled friends and family with his creative gifts. He drew cartoons, painted everything from miniatures to murals, and designed logos for boats. The New York Public Library once exhibited his art at its main building. But a drunken altercation with a New York City cop ended Gerry's life when Cus was sixteen.

Hardened by the violent demise of the beloved Gerry, Cus tried to adopt his brother Tony's credo — never let anyone step on you — as he made his way through life in the Bronx. Cus was much like any other street tough except that he became something of a philosopher. He paid close attention to what went on around him and pondered the meanings of cowardice, strength, courage, and survival. Cus flirted with politics, served in the Army during World War II (perhaps the happiest time of his life; he loved military asceticism),[6] then became a boxing manager. Through it all, he learned that taking charge of fear was key to success in the world as he knew it.

"The first thing I do with a young fighter," D'Amato said, "is explain fear. Most people don't know much about fear. They think it's a sign of being yellow. But fear is normal. It's like fire. If you let it get out of control, it will destroy you and everything around you. If you can learn how to control it, you can make it work for you. Fear is just nature's way of preparing you to fight."[7]

D'Amato soon had the opportunity to teach Patterson his first lesson in confronting fear.

Floyd trained at Gramercy Gym for a couple of weeks, awkwardly trying to mimic the things he'd seen his brother Frank do in the ring. When D'Amato decided it was time for Floyd to attempt some serious sparring, he paired Patterson with an experienced boxer — Frank. For his part, Frank Patterson believed Floyd had no business trying to box. Frank knew his little brother would cry if you hit him too hard. So Frank was not shy about taking young Floyd to school in the ring. At one point, Floyd stepped in the pocket to fire some close-range punches at Frank,[8] but he made the novice mistake of failing to hold his right hand high enough to protect his head. Frank uncorked a hard left hook to Floyd's temple that sent the younger Patterson staggering.

After taking the blow, Floyd wanted nothing more than to escape the ring as fast as he could. His head spinning, he fled to the locker room and began to cry. Presently, D'Amato was standing over him. Typically the no-nonsense tough guy, D'Amato had a gentle, nurturing side, and at that moment he revealed it to Floyd, assuring Patterson that getting tagged with a hook happened to many kids attempting to box for the first time. D'Amato did not dismiss Floyd as a crybaby not man enough for boxing, as many managers would have done. Instead he encouraged Floyd to keep trying. He knew what Floyd was up against. "Boxing," he once said, "is seventy-five percent psychological and only twenty-five percent physical."[9]

Patterson responded to D'Amato's psychological ministrations in the same way he had to Vivian Costen's at Wiltwyck. He determined to prove that D'Amato's faith in him was not misplaced. The bond between manager and fighter was set.

Patterson's confidence increased as, under D'Amato's tutelage, he picked up the rudiments of boxing. Just six months after Patterson began training under him, Cus decided it was time for Floyd's first amateur bout. Patterson would fight under the auspices of D'Amato's Empire Sports Club, which was an accredited member of the New York Metropolitan Amateur Athletic Union. At his stated age of fifteen years old and weighing 147 pounds, Patterson would compete in the subnovice class of a city AAU tournament for his first fight. It occurred at an old boxing club in Queens, and Floyd won without breaking a sweat — his opponent failed to show. Still, it was a victory. He now had an amateur record of 1-0.

This "win" advanced him to the tournament's second round, held at the Downtown Athletic Club. There, with Cus and his brother Nick D'Amato working his corner along with Frank Lavelle, Floyd faced a full-grown Navy man. Patterson made a typical novice mistake when he gave in to the adrenaline rush prompted by the bell and began throwing punches wildly through the first round. Sensing he had a chance to defeat an inexperienced kid, the Navy man came at Floyd fast and hard in the second round. But somehow Patterson landed a punch on his opponent's jaw, and the sailor went down. Floyd didn't think he'd hit him all that hard. He'd seen cowboys in the movies take what appeared to be much harder punches, and they were able to pop back up and continue slugging. So he expected the sailor to do the same. But Floyd learned that real fights were different. In real fights, you could clip your opponent in just the right place with a relatively short punch, and that would be enough to knock him out. The sailor failed to make it back to his feet before the referee's count ended. Patterson had his first real victory: a knockout at thirty-four seconds into the second round.

Patterson enjoyed a few days of exuberance before his third tournament fight. On that day, egged on by his brother Billy, he went for a run in Brooklyn's Prospect Park. That night, he felt drained. His opponent had enough ring savvy to understand that Patterson was fatigued, and beat Floyd handily. Up to that time Floyd and Billy had had an uneasy relationship, at best. Floyd decided that Billy, who was more knowledgeable about training, had encouraged him to run that day to ensure he lost the contest. Floyd held it against him for years.

Floyd lost his next two fights as well, but he could not blame his brother for those. Floyd's amateur record stood at two wins — and one of those was by way of forfeit — against three losses. That record would be enough to discourage many kids from continuing, but not Floyd — boxing was the only thing providing him with direction in life. He wasn't about to turn his back on it. D'Amato and Lavelle saw the problem with Patterson's ring performances so far: simply put, he was getting hit too much. So they began schooling Floyd in protecting himself, emphasizing an unconventional boxing stance that became known as the peek-a-boo.

Conventional strategy called for a right-handed boxer like Patterson to stand more or less sideways, left shoulder aimed at his opponent, knees bent slightly, feet spread shoulder-width apart to provide good balance, right hand high and close to the chin, left hand also high but a bit lower than the right, left elbow in tight to protect the midsection, chin tucked into the hollow of the left shoulder. "That's a good place to keep it, too," observed the great prizefighter Barney Ross, who won world titles in three weight divisions. "You'll avoid a lot of trouble."[10]

In the peek-a-boo, however, a boxer stood with his gloves cupped around his face, his arms so close that his elbows were nearly touching. This created a kind of shield that the boxer could use to block punches. "I call it a tight defense," D'Amato said. "It enables you to move in aggressively without leaving any vulnerable openings."[11] But for the stance to be effective, the peek-a-boo fighter stood squared up to his opponent, and even D'Amato admitted that throwing blows with power from this position was a challenge. He also recognized that a peek-a-boo fighter always faced risks when battling a boxer with a good uppercut.

Whatever the peek-a-boo's drawbacks, D'Amato and Lavelle began training Patterson to use the stance to protect himself in the ring. It proved effective, enough so that they planned to enter Floyd, who in recent months had filled out to become a 160-pound middleweight, in the premier East Coast amateur boxing competition, the 1951 New York Golden Gloves championships, his losing amateur record be damned.

The Gloves tournament was the brainchild of *New York Daily News* sports editor Paul Gallico, and had been around for nearly twenty-five years. It proved popular, and other cities began sponsoring their own Gloves competitions. These amateur showcases had become spawning grounds for future professional world champions like Barney Ross, Leo Rodak, Ezzard Charles, Joey Maxim, Harold Dade, and Wallace "Bud" Smith. In 1951 sixteen-year-old Floyd dreamed that his name might be added to the list. The New York tournament's finals occurred at the nation's top boxing venue: Madison Square Garden. This third incarnation of the Garden stood at Fiftieth Street and Eighth Avenue, and fighting there was every up-and-coming New York boxer's dream. Two of Patterson's boxing heroes, Joe Louis and Sugar Ray Robinson, each fought more than ten pro bouts there. When Patterson walked under the Garden's famous marquee and saw "Golden Gloves" spelled out on it, he must have known he was entering boxing's big time.

But just how well he might do was in question, given his poor amateur record. As it turned out, Lavelle and D'Amato's peek-a-boo strategy worked. It was in the 1951 New York Golden Gloves that Patterson first proved himself to be a boxer likely to have a gilded future. He won his first four fights with surprising ease. "I was credited with two third-round technical knockouts when the referee stopped my first two bouts of the tournament to save my opponents from further punishment," Floyd said.[12] The next two fights ended even faster. Then, on February 19, 1951, he faced Richie Hill, a Police Athletic League fighter, for the New York middleweight championship. A crowd of 12,233 gathered in the Garden to watch, including the mayor, the police commissioner, the district attorney, and former world heavyweight champ Gene Tunney. The bout went the distance. After the final bell, the decision was announced and Floyd Patterson was New York's middleweight Golden Gloves champion.

Patterson scarcely had time to celebrate. As the city's middleweight champ, he qualified to take part in the Eastern Golden Gloves cham-

pionships. On February 28, winners of elimination fights held earlier in various cities in the East and Puerto Rico battled at Madison
Square Garden. Patterson displayed ever-growing confidence and boxing skills in the Eastern Golden Gloves, even winning one fight with
just three punches thrown during the first twenty-two seconds. In the
three-round Garden final, he decisioned John Gibson from Syracuse
to claim his second amateur title. This win set him up to compete for
what was essentially the national amateur crown.

The Intercity Golden Gloves Tournament pitted winners from the
Eastern tournament (the New York team) against the winners from
the Western tournament (the Chicago team). By 1951, a bitter rivalry
existed between the two squads. That year, they clashed in New York,
with the finals at Madison Square Garden scheduled for March 19.
Patterson and the other New York winners traveled upstate to train
at Bear Mountain Inn on the Hudson River before returning home to
fight their rivals.

Floyd went into the tournament with good press behind him. Writers were impressed by his speed, power, and toughness — and especially by his left hook, a power shot he threw while lunging. The *Lowell
(MA) Sun* called Patterson "one of the best men on the East's team."[13]
He was favored to win, but he faced one of the best boxers ever to compete in the Golden Gloves, Richard Guerrero. About five years older
than Patterson, Guerrero was a local legend in Chicago. He had already claimed two lightweight championships in 1948 and '49 in the
New York–Chicago rivalry, and after skipping the 1950 Golden Gloves
he had moved up to middleweight, hoping to become the first fighter
in Gloves history to win three titles. Guerrero fought as a southpaw,
which was always a challenge for a right-hander like Patterson.

Guerrero's left-hand tactics did frustrate Patterson. The older
fighter moved with lightning speed as he delivered smashing blows to
Patterson's body, then effectively blocked Patterson's attempts at counterpunching. Halfway through the fight, Guerrero shifted into a right-
handed stance, adding to Patterson's mounting frustration. Floyd was
the favorite to win, but Guerrero wound up with an easy victory, leaving Patterson confused as he tried to understand how things went so
wrong.

More success followed by disappointment lay ahead. In the spring Floyd made it to the semifinal round of the Amateur Athletic Union national boxing championships in Boston. But he fell to defeat in the semis. Still, at age sixteen, Patterson had proved that D'Amato and Lavelle's faith in him as a prospect was not misplaced. As a newcomer to New York's fiercely competitive amateur boxing scene, he'd made his mark. His premiere in the Golden Gloves competitions was just one victory shy of spectacular.

Patterson and his handlers knew he had a ways to go to succeed against boxers of Dick Guerrero's caliber. Floyd had looked exhausted at the end of the Guerrero fight, so improving his stamina through roadwork became his highest priority. Running took on a new purpose for him, and he remained, until his final days, a dedicated runner.

Lavelle oversaw some of Patterson's most challenging roadwork, picking him up early on Saturday mornings and taking him to Coney Island. There the trainer instructed him to run on the sandy beach to strengthen his ankles, calves, and thighs. It wasn't easy, but the older man convinced Patterson it was necessary to develop the leg power he needed in the ring. On other mornings, Patterson ran closer to home. He did his roadwork before dawn, often accompanied by his uncle Charley Johnson, in Prospect Park. He chugged along in Army shoes, long underwear, overalls, and a hooded sweatshirt. With each step, he reminded himself that boxing could be the financial salvation for him and his family.

Patterson's dedication to training was unmatched. He trained everywhere, even when he wasn't at the Gramercy Gym or clicking away the miles in Prospect Park. At home, he locked himself in the bathroom and shadowboxed in front of the mirror, occasionally throwing jabs at the string hanging from the old-fashioned light fixture. He even employed paper bags and pillows as makeshift punching bags.

Though he claimed boxing was his only concern, Floyd was still a teenager and found some time to hang out with other neighborhood kids. Through one of his buddies, he met a girl who had a pretty smile and who seemed to be about as shy as he was. Sandra Elizabeth Hicks was

her name, and Floyd guessed she was about his age. The Hicks family
lived on Bainbridge Street, not far from his maternal grandmother's
house. With Sandra so close by, Floyd suddenly found a reason to visit
his grandmother much more often. He started running into Sandra on
his way to his grandmother's, just as he hoped he would. It didn't take
long before his visits to Bainbridge Street were directed toward visiting
Sandra and Sandra alone.

It took a while, but Patterson shared snippets of his past life with
his new friend, if not the whole story. He feared she might think he
was stupid. He also hid details about his family, such as just how many
brothers and sisters he had and even the address of the apartment the
Pattersons called home. The Hicks family was not affluent, but they
were better off than the Pattersons, and Floyd thought she might break
things off with him if she found out. But when she learned about all
these things, and also about his time at Wiltwyck and his experiences
at PS 614, none of it seemed to bother Sandra. She introduced Patterson to her parents, who were impressed by his polite demeanor.
Eventually, Floyd worked up enough nerve to ask Mrs. Hicks if Sandra
could be his guest at one of his fights. Mrs. Hicks responded by saying,
over Sandra's protests, "Do you have any idea how old Sandra is?"

"No, Mrs. Hicks," Patterson said, "Sandra and I have never discussed
that."

"Floyd, Sandra's only thirteen." He left the Hicks household that
night knowing that if he were to have a relationship with Sandra, it
would have to develop more slowly than he'd first thought. The good
news was that Mrs. Hicks had not prohibited Patterson from seeing
Sandra. "You're a gentlemanly young man," she told him.[14]

The exposure to the Hicks family affected Patterson in a way beyond the potential for romance with Sandra. They were devout Roman
Catholics, and Sandra attended parochial school. At the time, Floyd
was not particularly religious, and the Baptist Patterson family seldom attended church. But his involvement with the pretty girl with
the straight white teeth stirred a spiritual awakening in Floyd. After
witnessing her displays of sweetness and decency time and again, he
began to wonder if her faith made her who she was. He and Sandra
began to discuss religion frequently. Eventually, she took him to her

church's parish house and introduced Floyd to the priest. Floyd said he wanted to start catechism classes.

As Patterson studied the teachings of Roman Catholicism, he continued Cus D'Amato's ring catechism to prepare for whatever boxing offered him next. No one could have been more surprised than Floyd at what that turned out to be.

3

Floyd Patterson Is Out of This World

P S 614 PRINCIPAL Alex Miller called Floyd aside and asked what he wanted to do with his life. "I want to fight," Patterson said. "I mean, I want to be a professional boxer."

"Why would you want to do that, Floyd?" Miller asked.

"It's the quickest way I know to start earning some money to help out my family."[1]

Patterson was about to turn seventeen. PS 614 was in essence a vocational grammar school for troubled students. After graduating, he would have nothing more than an eighth-grade education. Two options lay ahead of him: go to work or continue his education at a vocational high school. The prospect of high school could not have been very appealing to Floyd, given his age; he would have been about twenty-one before he finished. More than anything, he wanted money, and he wanted it now — money for himself, money for his family, money to spend on Sandra Hicks. He juggled the options: backbreaking work at some dead-end job for low pay, further education that *might* lead to something financially rewarding years down the line, and prizefighting. It wasn't a hard decision.

During the 1951 holiday season, Floyd approached D'Amato about turning pro; he wanted to start bringing some money home from the

ring. Cus listened patiently, then advised Patterson not to give up amateur competition just yet. Floyd was surprised. Didn't D'Amato think
he was good enough to fight pro? Of course he was good enough,
D'Amato said with conviction. But if he turned pro, he wouldn't be
able to qualify for the 1952 American Olympics boxing team.

The Olympics? It was the first time anyone had mentioned the
games to Floyd. He didn't understand how competing in the Olympics
could benefit him. Jesse Owens had become a hero for black Americans after his remarkable four-gold-medal performance in Berlin in
1936. But Owens's background wasn't quite like Floyd's. Owens and his
family had struggled to get by in one of Cleveland's poor black neighborhoods until Owens's track skills opened the door for him to attend
Ohio State University, and that changed everything. He became a college man, and American Olympic teams of the day were dominated by
college men. Amateur athletes by and large still looked down on the
scruffy sorts who took money to participate in sports.

Floyd was perplexed by D'Amato's thinking. His goal was to make
money, and he couldn't see how the Olympics would lead to dollars
in his pocket. But he had put his trust in this enigma of a manager. If
D'Amato's plans included an Olympic tryout, Patterson would follow
them. He decided to extend his amateur career into 1952, while taking
classes at a vocational high school.

Floyd began his Olympic quest in February 1952. A return to the New
York Golden Gloves competition at Madison Square Garden was his
first stop. Patterson had grown taller and filled out some since his
previous Gloves appearance, so D'Amato determined he should fight
in the light-heavyweight (175 pounds) class. Patterson liked battling
the heavier boxers, who fought more slowly than he. He sliced his way
through his three opponents in the Gloves with first-round knockouts.
His championship bout lasted just forty seconds. In March came the
Eastern Golden Gloves championships, again at the Garden. Patterson
easily defeated his first opponent, and then, using what was becoming his trademark looping left hook — because he often leaped while
throwing it, both feet off the mat, it became known as Patterson's
"gazelle punch"[2] — Floyd TKO'd Newark's Harold Carter to claim the

Eastern title. During the third week of March 1952, Patterson competed in the Intercity Golden Gloves tournament, winning the light-heavyweight title.

D'Amato had designs on Patterson's winning the national Amateur Athletic Union championship that spring in Boston as well. But he determined that Patterson's approach to this year's tournament should be different from the previous one. He and Patterson agreed that Floyd should go to Boston without the distraction of schoolwork. So Patterson, who'd graduated from PS 614 a month earlier, decided to stop attending the metalworking classes he was taking at Alexander Hamilton Vocational High School. In Floyd's mind, there was a right way and a wrong way to take that step. Because of his past reputation as a truant, he did not want to simply drop out. He wanted to secure working papers first. Hotelier Charles Schwefel, an acquaintance of D'Amato's and a supporter of PS 614, gave Floyd a job at the Gramercy Park Hotel, and that allowed Patterson to get the documents he desired. Floyd put in time at the hotel, but it was always clear to Schwefel and everyone else involved that his real job was training to box. Schwefel freed him from his hotel responsibilities for fights — including his travel to Boston to train for the national AAUs.

Floyd went down in weight for the AAUs, fighting as a middleweight — a bold move, given that middleweight was a much more hotly contested class than light-heavyweight. It was all part of D'Amato's plan to mold Floyd into a versatile boxer, one who could bang with heavier boxers but also match the speed of lighter ones. The middleweight competition caused Floyd no problems. He hammered his way to the finals. On April 9 at the Boston Garden, he won the AAU championship with a knockout. Of his four matches in the tournament, three had ended with his opponents on the mat, and Floyd was named outstanding boxer in the AAU tournament. With the Golden Gloves titles and now the win at the AAUs, he moved into the ranks of American amateur boxing's elite, poised to claim a spot on the Olympic team bound for Helsinki, Finland.

Patterson competed as a heavy-middleweight in the Olympic qualifying tournament.[3] The winners of eight sectional qualification competitions for AAU boxers were to receive an invitation to compete in the

Kansas City finals in late May. (The boxing champions of the National Collegiate Athletic Association, or NCAA, as well as the Army and Navy champions were also invited to Kansas City.) Patterson fought in the sectional tournament held in Albany, where he "stole the show" at Hawkins Stadium, according to the *Berkshire (MA) Evening Eagle*. The paper's reporter noted that Patterson "stalks like Joe Louis" and came to the New York state capital "with a reputation of a future champion."[4] Floyd proved that reputation was warranted as he scored consecutive technical knockouts — amazingly, both TKOs occurred precisely at one minute, thirty-eight seconds of the opening rounds.

At the finals in Kansas City, Patterson continued his string of impressive wins, racking up more knockouts on his way to the title match. On June 18 he stopped NCAA boxing champion Gordon Gladson with a hard left hook. Awarded a technical knockout, Patterson became an Olympian: "I beat a college guy — me who had trouble getting through grammar school."[5]

The 1952 squad was by far the best Olympic boxing team the United States had ever dispatched to the international sports festival. Dr. Barry Barrodale of Houma, Louisiana, managed the boxing Olympians, and he boldly predicted that the Americans would win four gold medals. The team's two coaches, Pete Mello, who mentored New York Catholic Youth Organization boxers, and J. T. Owen, who headed the boxing program at Louisiana State University, agreed. But all three knew their charges would have to take a different approach from previous American Olympic teams if the team were to harvest that many medals.

Past American teams in Olympic competition faced an unfamiliarity with international boxing rules. Barrodale said, "We've lost many a chance at titles in the last two games because of minor infractions. The referee warns you once for something like not taking a full step back on the break. Then if you hit and hold, or push off on the break, or bob and weave below the waist, then they can disqualify you and do — for the second violation. In the '48 games, [Washington] Jones knocked a guy cold and then was disqualified for hitting with an open glove."[6] Barrodale's fighters, while supremely talented, would have to be disciplined enough to avoid tripping over the rules if they were to win medals. That became the focus of their training.

As for the potential gold medalists Barrodale saw coming out of the games, he included Floyd. "Floyd Patterson is out of this world," Barrodale said. "He knocked out all eight of his opponents in the 165-pound trials. Brother, if he doesn't win, the guy who beats him will have to be somewhat super-special."[7] Floyd joined three hundred other American Olympians for a grand departure celebration in New York, which included a lower Manhattan ticker-tape parade, a reception at City Hall, and a luncheon at the Waldorf-Astoria — events all new and wonderful for the kid from Brooklyn.

The Pan Am plane began its descent. From his seat, seventeen-year-old Floyd could see evergreen forests extending to the horizon. There was one clearing and the plane was slowly flying into it. The plane touched down around sunset, and Floyd joined the other American Olympians in exiting the aircraft. It was an extraordinary experience for him. While other American teenagers were engaged in summer vacations and thoughts of the upcoming school year, Floyd was preparing to represent his country while battling the best amateur boxers from around the globe. On the drive into Helsinki from the airport, he sensed he was entering a place far different from anything he'd known, a city that looked ancient and yet seemed almost like a frontier community. He'd later say it was an experience he could never forget. When he arrived at the camp, he received his Olympic uniform. His was like everyone else's on the American team, all red, white, and blue.

Barrodale assigned Mello to be Patterson's Olympic trainer, and Mello filled the role more than adequately as Patterson attempted to digest the odd rules the Olympics imposed on boxers. Patterson also made a friend of fellow New Yorker Tony Anthony, a member of the American boxing team. Once in Helsinki, the two fighters spent their free time exploring the Olympic Village and beyond. One day they passed the Soviet team as it worked out, and Floyd saw firsthand just how different an approach the Eastern Europeans took toward boxing compared with the Americans. The Soviets stood in a line, wearing matching blue sweatshirts. Their trainer shouted a command, and the boxers responded in unison, throwing jabs. Another command, and the Soviets all threw rights. Patterson was surprised by how mechanical — and ineffective — it all seemed. He dismissed the Soviets as not being much of a threat to the Americans.

But he did worry about the Finns — not the Finnish athletes, but the people who called Finland home. When Patterson and Anthony roamed the Helsinki streets, they saw that many residents lived in poverty as dire as that of Bed-Stuy. By contrast, the athletes in the Olympic Village were treated to spreads of food the likes of which Floyd had never witnessed in his life. The discrepancy between the hungry Finnish hosts and the pampered visiting athletes troubled him as he recalled the many nights he himself went to bed hungry as a child. He decided to do something about it. He began helping himself to extra food from the Olympic Village cafeteria lines, sometimes taking as many as three or four steaks. He then made up little packages containing the extra food, which he'd pass on to Finns he'd meet on the street. Mello saw him doing this and was dumbfounded. "I'm in this business forty-one years," he said, "and this is the nicest kid I ever handled."[8]

In the Olympic boxing ring at the arena called Messuhalli, however, Patterson was anything but nice. Red Smith saw him in action there and was mightily impressed by the young fighter with "paws faster than a subway pickpocket."[9] Writing at the time for the *New York Herald Tribune*, Smith had a reputation as America's most literary daily-newspaper sports columnist. Receiving favorable notice from Smith boosted the career of any athlete. But Smith went beyond merely mentioning Patterson. He devoted a whole column to the young boxer, the first lengthy piece of journalism about Floyd. The *Herald Tribune* had a national readership itself, but Smith's column was also syndicated to dozens of other papers around the country. His piece on Patterson helped make Floyd's name familiar to sports fans nationwide.

It was clear to Smith and other reporters in Helsinki that Patterson was far more talented than the international boxers he faced. Floyd did, however, struggle against the rules, which favored European-style orthodox boxing (standing straight up with the arms precisely positioned) over the looser, more improvisational American-style boxing. In one fight, Floyd drew a warning for simply throwing a left hook, then crouching — a standard tactic in American boxing. The European referee could have disqualified him for two more such infractions, but Patterson safely finished the fight, scoring a win.

Floyd defeated fighters from France, the Netherlands, and Sweden to advance to the gold-medal round. The other finalist was a Romanian named Vasile Tita. Given the tenor of the cold war era, Patterson guessed he would have a difficult time defeating a Soviet-bloc fighter with a Soviet-bloc referee making rules decisions, and a large pro-Soviet contingency in the audience shouting its approval. So he was determined to knock out Tita, removing any possibility of hanky-panky in the judging. And Patterson did just that — easily, as it turned out. Just twenty seconds after the opening bell, Floyd landed a crisp right uppercut on Tita's chin, knocking out the Romanian fighter and securing the gold medal for himself.[10]

After a blur of congratulations and impromptu celebration, he found himself on the Olympic platform with a gold medal around his neck and a bouquet of flowers in his arms. After the conclusion of "The Star-Spangled Banner," he bowed to the cheering crowd, the first time he'd ever bowed to anyone, he would later claim. Overwrought with emotion, he bowed and bowed and bowed again, until someone told him enough was enough.

Floyd was part of a spectacular showing for the 1952 American boxing team. For the first time in nearly a half century, five American boxers made it to the Olympic finals, and all five claimed gold medals. No other country came close to claiming that much boxing gold that year. And all five of these men were African Americans, hailing from all across the country — Brooklyn, Cleveland, Washington, DC, Gary, Indiana, and the Watts neighborhood of Los Angeles. It was a significant event in African American history, though hardly recognized as such at the time or since. Had it happened a few years later, it would no doubt be compared to Texas Western's defeating Kentucky for the 1966 NCAA basketball championship. (In that game, the Texas Western Miners played five black starters against the Wildcats' five white starters — and won, 72–65. The Miners' victory has been celebrated as a milestone in the fight to integrate college sports ever since.) In 1952 five black Americans entered the ring on the world stage, and all five emerged as champions — winning for their country its greatest Olympic boxing triumph.[11] But the champions' race went largely unremarked upon in an America in the grips of a Red scare, an America where most schools were segregated and blacks were expected to know their place.

Arriving back at New York International Airport at Idlewild, the five champions lined up with Barrodale and Mello for a photograph. In it, most of the fighters are beaming, but Patterson has a stare of determination locked on his face. After the picture taking, reporters approached him and asked if his next step was to turn pro. Patterson had forty-five amateur fights under his belt now, Golden Gloves and AAU titles, and an Olympic gold medal. If he never fought another bout, he would go down in history as one of the dozen or so best amateur boxers America had ever produced. He knew he wasn't ready to stop now. He knew he wanted to fight for money, but he didn't share that. He looked over at the barrel-chested, white-haired man who, along with his former teacher Vivian Costen, had come to greet him at the airport.

"Cus answers the questions," he told the reporters.[12]

4

❖

Cus Answers the Questions

THE TEENAGE FLOYD PATTERSON returned home to Brooklyn as a history maker. But the home he went back to was a rundown, crowded (Thomas and Annabelle's family eventually numbered eleven children) apartment in a crime-ridden ghetto. Even though newspapers carried accounts of his amateur boxing heroics during the previous two years, he had earned no money whatsoever from sports. Except for the pittance Charles Schwefel paid him for part-time work at the Gramercy Park Hotel, plus some cash from manual-labor jobs here and there, he had nothing to contribute to the family coffers, and the Pattersons seemed as financially desperate as ever. He seldom had dollars for dates or to purchase small holiday presents for his girlfriend, Sandra. The situation was frustrating for him, and he was ready to turn pro as soon as possible to do something about it.

D'Amato agreed it was time. Cus had directed Floyd's amateur career masterfully to ready him for a professional career. Patterson had fought in four different weight classes, giving him experience against opponents ranging from fleet-footed lightweights to hard-slugging light-heavyweights. He'd also squared off against boxers from different parts of the United States and from Europe, all employing different stances and styles. All of which had seasoned Floyd for what he would face in New York's bloody prizefighting halls. Not long after Patterson returned from Finland, D'Amato took the steps necessary for Floyd to turn pro.

First on D'Amato's agenda was drawing up a formal, written contract under which Cus would manage Floyd's career as it moved forward. "With character that ran so deep," D'Amato said publicly, "it was plain that Floyd's word and faith were more important than a contract."[1] That was fine as far as an amateur career went. But bitter experience had taught D'Amato that when money is involved, agreements should be in writing and signed.

Early in his career at the Gramercy Gym, D'Amato had schooled a talented middleweight named Rocky Graziano, but Cus failed to sign Graziano to a contract, and lost his boxer to different management — management with deep mob ties. D'Amato sourly watched as Graziano won the world middleweight title in 1947, and never missed an opportunity to dismiss him thereafter as a gutless bum who couldn't fight.[2] D'Amato was not about to let that happen again with one of his fighters.

So he insisted Floyd sign a contract.[3] The contract essentially gave D'Amato complete control and, significantly, excluded the man who had "discovered" Floyd, Frank Lavelle. For the time being, it appeared things would continue as they had been for Lavelle. He would still participate in training Patterson and would work his corner during fights, only now he'd get paid for his efforts. But he was, in fact, a marked man in terms of Floyd's long-term future.

D'Amato was under no illusion about just where the Gramercy stood in the hierarchy of New York boxing gyms. He knew it was second tier and lacked the quality of sparring partners Floyd needed to develop into a first-rate pro. He also knew that Patterson needed better training than either he or Lavelle or anyone else at the Gramercy could provide. So shortly after he signed Floyd, Cus took his young fighter to Stillman's Gym, which occupied a soot-covered three-story building just a short walk from Madison Square Garden. The most successful prizefighters worked out here under the stern gaze of the very best trainers in the world. It was here that D'Amato hired the man who would mold Floyd into a contender.

Dan Florio seemed to have been around the New York fight scene forever. As early as the 1920s, he was refereeing fights on the East Coast, after which he turned his focus to training. He worked with the best. With his brother Nick, he coached Tony Canzoneri, Battling Battalino, Petey Scalzo, and Freddie Miller to world titles. He also had been responsible for resurrecting the career of Jersey Joe Walcott, working the corner in the infamous 1947 title fight in which Walcott floored Joe Louis in the fourth round and seemed to completely dominate the rest of the fight, but lost the decision to Louis. Florio was verbose, so, naturally, the hands hanging around Stillman's called him "Silent." His brother, who almost never talked, became known as "Gabby." For the next dozen years, Silent and, sometimes, Gabby seconded Patterson in key fights. But at first, Silent took one look at Patterson and, discounting Floyd's stellar amateur career and Olympic gold medal, said to D'Amato, "He has to learn everything. His stance. He fights with his legs too far apart. He hops around all the time. He jumps like a kangaroo and throws a right. He don't keep his hands up."[4] D'Amato charged Florio, not Lavelle, with fixing all that.

From the beginning, Floyd wanted to look good at Stillman's. The important managers, matchmakers, and promoters in the gallery eyed all the fighters, trying to determine who had heart, who didn't, who was being brought along by their trainers at just the right pace, and who was being pushed too fast. The impressions a boxer made on these men, leaning forward in their filthy folding chairs, overcoats securely tucked under their arms, could affect the whole course of a career. A bad showing would stay burned in their memories for years, preventing a fighter from getting plum spots on lucrative fight cards.

One day at Stillman's, Charley Goldman, who trained Rocky Marciano (shortly to become world heavyweight champion), approached Floyd and asked if he could go a few rounds with a new fighter Goldman was working with, Tommy Harrison. Patterson wasn't so sure he was ready for that. Harrison was one of Marciano's regular sparring partners, and he was taller and heavier than Patterson. And he was fast, nearly as fast as Floyd himself. Patterson told Goldman to ask D'Amato, who was cautiously bringing Floyd along, not rushing him to spar fighters substantially better than he. D'Amato, to Patterson's surprise, gave the OK.

Early in the first round, Harrison unloaded twelve unanswered jabs, most landing in spite of Patterson's bobbing and weaving. Those blows hurt Floyd, even though Harrison wore padded sparring gloves. In all his amateur career, even fighting for the championships of the AAU and the Olympics, Floyd never encountered punches as hard as these. It was a brutal introduction to just what Floyd could expect as a pro. The eyes of the Stillman's cognoscenti locked onto Patterson as he took those heavy shots — *Would the kid collapse?* Patterson knew he had to do something. He timed Harrison's next big jab. When it arrived, Patterson threw a stiff right cross above it, tagging Harrison in the face. The experienced pro staggered. After that, Floyd pursued Harrison, firing combinations that Harrison struggled to ward off. The men in the folding chairs nodded their approval, happy with how Floyd had overcome adversity, transforming it into an advantage. A buzz began to spread around New York about D'Amato's up-and-comer, a kid who someday soon just might be good enough to put in the ring with the likes of Sugar Ray Robinson.

There was some question, however, about whether a bigtime matchup for Floyd would be made. No one inside boxing doubted the talent that the Bed-Stuy kid had shown so far. There were plenty of questions about his manager, however, the most eccentric man in the New York fight community. He was a weirdo, someone who read too many books, someone who believed in flying saucers and welcomed visitors from another planet, someone who never smoked or drank — the latter all but unheard of in the world of professional boxing. And there was more. For reasons no one could quite understand, D'Amato refused to play ball with the men who ran professional boxing. It seemed as if he bore a vendetta against something, but just what that something was left boxing insiders scratching their heads. It also seemed as if he were preparing for a war of some kind. He lived in his gym, sleeping in a small room to the left of the boxing ring, a baseball bat within easy reach, a gun or two hidden away, his fierce dog curled up on the floor next to him. He never rode subways, fearing enemies could push him onto the tracks as he waited for a train. What was this all about?

It was simple, actually. D'Amato was plotting to become the most powerful force in professional boxing. This was his raison d'être, and it was no small ambition. Nor was it a safe one. For boxing, from the smallest club venues in out-of-the-way places like Houston or New Orleans to the big action at Madison Square Garden or Yankee Stadium, was controlled by men who responded to challenges to their authority with lead pipes, stilettos, and snub-nosed thirty-eights. Organized crime had exerted sway over professional boxing for generations, but in the early 1950s its hold was complete.

The mob used a front organization, the International Boxing Club of New York, to ensure prizefighting functioned according to the wiseguys' whims. A promotional organization on paper, the IBC did far more than promote fights. It essentially determined which boxers would be allowed to fight for which titles, who their managers and trainers would be, which matchmakers would be allowed to set the fight cards. The IBC also decided where and when fights would occur and who would be paid how much — and occasionally who would win fights and who would lose. Its influence extended to the new broadcast medium of television as well as to tried-and-true radio. It accomplished all this through strong-arm tactics combined with what boiled down to bribes and kickbacks.

The face of the IBC was a Chicago swell named James Norris. On the surface, Norris appeared to be about as white-bread as anyone could possibly be. His father was one of America's best-known businessmen, with holdings in grain mills, transport ships, and cattle operations. The elder Norris was also an important early team owner in the National Hockey League. Once his son became involved in the family business, it moved more heavily into sports, buying Detroit's Olympia Arena and the Chicago Stadium and acquiring majority interest in the Madison Square Garden Corporation. But there was a side to Jim Norris that the sports, society, and business pages overlooked. Since at least 1930, he associated himself with the Al Capone faction of the Chicago Outfit. Norris's IBC functioned at the bidding of a Mafia figure known in crime circles as "Mr. Gray."

His real name was Paolo Giovanni Carbo, but he was better known as Frankie Carbo. Born on New York's Lower East Side, Carbo became a soldier in the Lucchese crime family. Eventually he was recognized by crime bosses across America as the underworld's unofficial commissioner of boxing. Carbo's police record showed seventeen arrests for vagrancy, suspicious behavior, felonious assault, grand larceny, robbery, and violation of New York boxing laws. But worse than that, he had been a gunman for Murder Inc. in his younger days, and it was widely believed that he had killed, either directly or indirectly, no fewer than eight men. "There wasn't anyone over him," New York District Attorney's Office detective Frank Marrone said.[5] Certainly Jim Norris answered to Mr. Gray when it came to matters of the IBC. If a manager, trainer, promoter, matchmaker, or boxer balked at the IBC, Carbo simply dispatched pipe-carrying thugs to convince the offender of the error of his ways.[6] No one understood this better than Cus D'Amato.

D'Amato knew how the IBC worked from firsthand, inside experience. The International Boxing Guild was an organization of boxing managers, and it had fallen slave to the IBC, even though the IBC's interests usually ran counter to those of the managers. In order for a manager to get a fighter on TV, he knew he'd pay a tribute to the IBC, which would be collected by the guild. For a time, D'Amato was the guild's bagman, picking up those payments. But at some point, for reasons he didn't discuss publicly, Cus washed his hands of the whole matter, retreated, and began to formulate plans to move to the top of the boxing power structure on his own terms. To do this, he'd need a fighter of such public acclaim that the IBC could not shut him out. D'Amato believed Floyd Patterson could be that fighter.

After his first pro fight at St. Nick's, Floyd walked around with the three crisp hundred-dollar bills he'd won in his pants pocket for a day or two, feeling like a millionaire. He figured that only millionaires could afford to carry that much cash around with them. Then he handed most of the money over to his mother for household expenses, keeping only a small part of it for himself. He used those dollars to indulge himself on clothes, oversized hand-me-downs being an all-too-haunting memory. More money was coming. Within the next thirty days, Patterson easily won two more fights, each with a significantly larger purse. Combining his winnings from those fights, he took home $1,100 for what he calculated to be twenty-two minutes of work. It would take an unskilled laborer like his father months to earn that kind of money in the early 1950s; Thomas Patterson took home $73 a week at the time. Mindful of how they struggled with the bills, Floyd gave half of his boxing earnings to his parents for the next few years.

Patterson rose in the boxing ranks remarkably fast, enough so that by the end of 1952, he starred in the main event of a fight card. The venue was Brooklyn's Eastern Parkway Arena, and it was in this converted skating rink that Floyd developed the core of the fan base that would follow him through the peak of his pro career. At the time, Eastern Parkway was the home base of Teddy Brenner, the best matchmaker in the business. He was able to match Floyd with boxers who'd give action-packed shows. Eastern Parkway didn't seat many people, but its audience extended well beyond the arena itself because owner Emil Lence had cut a pioneering sports broadcasting agreement with the DuMont Television Network. The Eastern Parkway fights ran for 156 straight weeks on dozens of TV stations affiliated with DuMont. Those fights were popular because of the number of upsets that occurred in the arena — fans and sportswriters called it the House of Upsets — and, with the TV revenue flowing in, the small arena was making more money than most larger facilities. And the hometown hero Patterson, with his flashy ring speed, soon became the most popular boxer on Eastern Parkway cards as he recorded win after win.

The arrangement worked out well for everyone involved. Brenner had declared his independence from the IBC by walking away from an earlier job at Madison Square Garden, so D'Amato was able to enter his fighter into bouts without dealing with the enemy. But Cus no doubt was aware that Eastern Parkway was not as clean an operation as it might have seemed from the outside. Owner Lence had a silent partner in the business who ran mob rackets in the garment district. No doubt this individual kept the IBC at bay.

D'Amato and Brenner were able to handpick Patterson's opponents without interference from Mr. Gray's minions. D'Amato did so following boxing tradition. He selected progressively more difficult opponents, but none who had a real chance to beat Patterson. "You don't take a young fighter and throw him in over his head," Patterson said later, defending D'Amato's choices.[7] A fight against Lalu Sabotin of Warren, Ohio, marked a professional first for Floyd: he entered the ring as a light-heavyweight this time out, though he weighed only 167 ½pounds, some 8 pounds lighter than Sabotin. Sabotin was a solid opponent, if not a contender, who'd begun his pro career with fifteen straight wins. He was now approaching the end of his career though,

and losses appeared on his record more often than wins. Still, the selection of Sabotin was D'Amato's way of serving notice to Floyd that
he was not content with Patterson's fighting as a middleweight, that
D'Amato had something more in mind for his charge. As it turned
out, Patterson had no trouble defeating the heavier Sabotin by technical knockout. Boxing veterans like Ray Arcel — the venerable trainer
known as the dean of Stillman's Gym — were saying that Patterson
might just be the best young boxer at any weight in the world.

Patterson was skilled, yes — no one had ever seen faster hands. But
some insiders were beginning to whisper to each other about whether
Floyd had the mental toughness to go far in the sport. Was he just
too nice a guy for boxing? His first out-of-town pro fight pitted him
against Chicago's Chester Mieszala in Mieszala's hometown. Patterson
arrived in Chicago a week early, planning to train at the famous Midtown Gym. But when Floyd discovered it was Mieszala's home gym, he
refused to work out there. Floyd feared he might inadvertently pick up
some tips by watching Mieszala that would give him an unfair advantage in the fight. That sort of attitude was unheard of in the cutthroat
world of boxing.

The fight itself stirred up doubt about Floyd's toughness. Toward
the end, he hit Mieszala in the face, dislodging the Chicago fighter's
mouthpiece. Unbelievably, Mieszala stopped fighting, bent over, and
tried to retrieve his mouthpiece from the canvas. It would have been
completely within the rules for Patterson to go into full attack mode
at that point, scoring an easy knockout. Instead, to the shock of everyone who saw it, Patterson joined Mieszala in his attempt to retrieve
the piece of gear. Finally the referee called a time-out and reinserted
Mieszala's mouthpiece himself. Floyd won the match by technical
knockout. Though Patterson was certain the people watching on TV
must have thought it odd to see him trying to help an opponent, he
stood by his actions. It doesn't make you any bigger, stronger, or more
important to take advantage of another person, he insisted afterward.
But the boxing old-timers weren't so sure.

D'Amato believed it was time for Patterson's "ceiling of resistance"
to be tested, so Cus scheduled him for eight rounds against light-
heavyweight Dick Wagner from Toppenish, Washington. Wagner, ten

years Patterson's senior, was a journeyman boxer at best, closing out an up-and-down career. But he had fought professionally more than fifty times, knew the tricks of the ring, and was an expert at delivering body punches. The fight was, in a sense, choreographed. D'Amato told Patterson he did not want him to attempt a knockout. Instead, Patterson was to stretch the contest out for the full eight rounds. D'Amato was concerned that Floyd had yet to box an entire fight, and he knew that Patterson had yet to learn how to pace himself, how to endure taking hard blows over a prolonged period of time, how to score sufficiently with the judges to win a decision. Patterson complied. And Wagner tortured him severely. In the middle rounds, Floyd came close to folding under the onslaught of body shot after body shot. The crowd sensed at one point that he was out on his feet and called for the referee to declare a knockout. But Patterson recovered, finished the fight, and won a close split decision, though he had sore ribs to nurse for the next few days. At least when it came to absorbing punishment, Patterson proved he was tough enough.

Patterson's impressive ring wins caught the attention of a sports columnist who would come to play an important role in his career. On the eve of Rocky Marciano's title fight with Roland LaStarza, Milton Gross of the *New York Post* devoted his column to Patterson, "a kid everybody says should displace tomorrow's winner within two years." Gross put the emphasis on the word *should*, explaining that Patterson was being shut out of competition because D'Amato refused to connect himself to the IBC. Patterson clearly was the best talent among young boxers, Gross believed, but that alone did not ensure he would someday compete for coveted titles. "It isn't the survival of the fittest," Gross said, "but the survival of those who can finagle the best."[8] Gross had yet to see evidence that D'Amato could successfully finagle. D'Amato would soon get a chance to do some finagling, though — over, of all things, Floyd's age.

Under the rules of the New York State Athletic Commission — the most important boxing sanctioning board of the day, with influence reaching far beyond New York — Floyd could start fighting ten-round bouts once he turned twenty. A year after that, he would be able to compete in fifteen-round championship bouts. In the 1950s pro boxers began their careers fighting four-round bouts. As they gained more experience, they fought longer fights of six and eight rounds. To be considered "contenders" for a world title — one of the ten top boxers in their weight categories — they had to battle in ten-round fights. New York rules prohibited fast advancement of boxers, to prevent putting them in dangerous fights before they were sufficiently experienced, and, perhaps in vain, to encourage boxers to finish their education before devoting their attention to the ring full-time. Throughout Floyd's amateur and early pro careers, D'Amato had reported Patterson's age based on the fib Floyd told him back in 1949: that Floyd was born in 1934. But at some point, D'Amato discovered the truth. He certainly must have known by 1952, when he helped Floyd prepare for his trip to Helsinki, which included applying for a passport. Floyd was a year younger than advertised.

In late 1953, when a reporter commented that Patterson would be turning twenty in January 1954 and thus eligible for ten-round fights, D'Amato responded peculiarly, muttering something about not being sure if Floyd would or wouldn't be. This certainly raised the reporter's eyebrows. Now that Cus knew the truth, he wasn't forthcoming with it. Cus's evasiveness sent reporters scurrying to find some record, any record, that would establish Floyd's actual age. They found it when they turned up his original passport application — the date listed on it was January 4, 1935.

A small ruckus ensued, and the New York State Athletic Commission suspended Patterson until he could provide documentation showing his true age. He didn't have a birth certificate — poor black kids of his generation from places like Waco, North Carolina, typically did not. But he was able to get a sworn statement from county officials that fixed his birth date at January 4, 1935. Now that the issue of his age was resolved, the impatient Patterson accepted the reality that another year would pass before he could become a true contender, and two years under the rules of the time before he could challenge for a title.

Some consolation arrived in January 1954 when the New York Boxing Writers Association named Patterson the Ring Rookie of the Year. Receiving the award at a banquet at the Hotel Astor in front of hundreds of people, Floyd was scarcely able to mumble his thanks, mostly because the presenter of the trophy was Joe Louis, the greatest fighter America had ever produced. Born in Alabama as the grandchild of former slaves, Louis had spent much of his youth in Detroit. He rose out of poverty to become heavyweight champion, which made him a hero to African Americans across the country. But Louis won over white Americans as well, especially after he destroyed German Nazi Party favorite Max Schmeling in a 1938 fight that lasted just two minutes, four seconds. Before the fight, Louis had been invited to the White House, where President Franklin Roosevelt told him that America needed muscle like his to defeat Nazi Germany. The victorious Louis was the very embodiment of American might as he stood over the fallen Schmeling. No African American in history had ever held such important symbolic value to the nation. Floyd stood in awe of the man who was now honoring him.

Patterson had little time to relish the moment, however. That February, the nineteen-year-old Floyd began battling some of the best boxers in the world, starting with a fighting fisherman from Canada.

Yvon Durelle was the first contender-quality boxer Floyd faced as a professional. Durelle hailed from the tiny village of Baie-Sainte-Anne in New Brunswick, Canada, and had worked in the brutally tough commercial fishing trade while training as a boxer. He took a never-say-die attitude with him into the ring. And he went into the ring often. Sometimes, Durelle fought with no more than five days of rest between bouts when even the busiest contenders of the time typically entered the ring no more than once a month. The twenty-four-year-old Durelle was a mystery to American fight fans. He'd already fought more than four dozen fights of record, but most were club bouts in small Canadian towns unfamiliar to many New Yorkers. His light-heavyweight fight with Patterson marked his first outing in America. Just two weeks had passed since his last matchup, and Durelle arrived at Eastern Parkway tired. He was also hungry. His manager had dumped the small-town boy in New York, and Durelle was so overwhelmed by the city that he skipped meals. He was so green he didn't know how to find restaurants or corner groceries. At the weigh-in, he tipped the scales at just 158 pounds, 13 pounds under what was announced at the weigh-in and subsequently reported in the sports pages.[9] Patterson outweighed him by 9 pounds, but fight promoters were not wont to announce that kind of weight difference, fearing a mismatch of that many pounds might drive away ticket buyers.

Given all that, it should have been an easy fight for Floyd, and indeed, he cruised through the early rounds. But as the fight progressed, Patterson sank deeper and deeper into trouble as the bobbing-and-weaving Durelle delivered uppercut after uppercut while managing to avoid Patterson's retaliatory strikes. In the eighth and final round, Durelle floored Patterson, and the oddsmakers who had made the fighting fisherman a four-to-one underdog seemed foolish. Floyd unsteadily rose to his feet before the referee's count ended. Then Durelle went to work on him, pounding the groggy Patterson unmercifully with body shots. Somehow, though stunned, Floyd made it to the final bell. Durelle went to his corner, certain he'd won the fight. But the Floyd-friendly judges at Eastern Parkway stunned Durelle and the fans by awarding a unanimous decision to Patterson.

The newspapermen at ringside didn't buy it. The consensus among them was that Patterson had just proved himself clearly unready to battle in prizefighting's upper ranks: "That was plastered on the records last night at Eastern Parkway," Caswell Adams of the *New York Journal-American* said, "where one Yvon Durelle, fighting as if in one of his beloved lobster pots off his native Canadian shores, showed Patterson still to be a confused novice as a fighter."[10] A bitter Durelle, who later became the stuff of legend for his hard-fought contests with Archie Moore, left the arena telling anyone who would listen that Patterson was overrated. Any good boxer could defeat Floyd, he believed. He wanted another chance to prove that. For his part, Patterson could only say that Durelle was the most complicated boxer he'd ever faced.

Six weeks later, Floyd made his first trip below the Mason-Dixon Line as a pro boxer. He and his traveling companions stopped at a Baltimore rest stop to eat, but the waitress refused to allow him to sit at the dine-in counter because he was black. She shoved a bag of burgers at him and told him to eat outside. Floyd turned and walked out without the bag. As a professional boxer, he would be traveling around the nation to fight, and this experience reminded him that racial prejudice was something he was going to have to face. With his actions in Baltimore, he served notice to those around him that he was not going to accept it.

There was time for more lighthearted matters than boxing or the prejudice he encountered on the road. Now nineteen and sixteen, respectively, Floyd and Sandra spent many blithe hours together. They especially loved to go on dates to Coney Island, where Floyd proved his strength to her at the ring-the-bell concession. He consistently was able to hit the hammer hard enough to make the bell sound. The carny working the game pronounced Floyd to be strong as a boilermaker. Floyd once slipped into a tattoo parlor off the Coney Island boardwalk and had "Sandra — 1954" inked on the inside of his left forearm. Sometimes they took Floyd's car to Manhattan to take in a show at the Apollo Theater. Other times they went roller-skating.

Sandra was outgoing and full of laughter, in many ways Floyd's opposite. Floyd, a self-admitted sad sack, credited her with bringing him out of his shell and teaching him how to feel comfortable around other people. She helped him with his catechism classes, worked with him on improving his vocabulary, and recommended books for him to read.

For several months, IBC representatives had been hinting that the organization would like to stage a match at Madison Square Garden between Patterson and former world lightweight champion Joey Maxim, a boxer the IBC controlled completely. The IBC's interest in such a fight had made some of the boxing columns in the New York newspapers, which Patterson read. (The IBC had every reason to believe it might be able to stage such a fight. Earlier, D'Amato had allowed Floyd to fight at the Garden one time before whisking him back to Eastern Parkway.) Though Floyd had beaten Durelle only through the charity of the hometown judges, he believed he was ready to fight Maxim. But D'Amato rebuffed the Maxim bout overtures and instead booked Floyd to fight three unknowns over the next three months. Meanwhile, Cus and Teddy Brenner negotiated a Maxim fight behind the scenes, ensuring it would occur at Floyd's home court, Eastern Parkway, not at the IBC-controlled Madison Square Garden. It was a victory — a small one, but a victory nonetheless — for D'Amato in his war against the IBC. He'd elevated Floyd's reputation to such a point that the IBC could not ignore him. In the contract, Maxim received a $10,000 guarantee from the IBC, plus a kickback of $1,500 for his manager to use as "walking around money," as Brenner put it.[11] For his part, Patterson was guaranteed $5,000 — easily the most he'd made so far for a fight.

Maxim's real name was Giuseppe Antonio Berardinelli. His ring moniker, derived from the Maxim machine gun, was applied to the boxer because of his ability to throw left jabs repeatedly. Maxim held the world light-heavyweight title for three years, although he was not the best light-heavyweight during those years. (Archie Moore was the best, but he was denied a shot at the light-heavyweight crown until he signed with a manager aligned with the IBC.) Maxim's willingness to play ball with assorted mob types put his career under suspicion, but one thing could not be denied him: in 1952 he'd beaten the great Sugar Ray Robinson.

With dozens of fights behind him, Maxim knew the tricks necessary to survive in the ring. By matching Patterson with Maxim, D'Amato would be moving his fighter into the big time, no doubt about it. Cus wanted to emphasize to Patterson that this was a big step up in his career, so he told Floyd that they would leave New York and conduct a training camp away from the city's distractions. Cus and Floyd were driving around upstate, sniffing out possible sites, when Floyd realized they were near Esopus. They decided to stop at Wiltwyck.

Vivian Costen had retired by this time, but Patterson found plenty of other friends there, including Ernst Papanek, who was now the school's director. Walter Johnson, who had been executive director when Patterson attended Wiltwyck and who had first encouraged Floyd to box, still worked there. When Johnson learned why Patterson and D'Amato were in the area, he offered them the use of Wiltwyck as a training facility. They also discovered that they could lodge at a nearby farm owned by relatives of Sandra, whose romance with Patterson was growing ever deeper. So it was set: Patterson would conduct his first full-fledged training camp at Wiltwyck.

It was a productive camp and Floyd stepped into the ring feeling optimistic about the eight-round bout. He opened aggressively, attacking the one-time light-heavyweight champ with a series of left hooks and right crosses. Maxim came back in the second round, but Floyd hit

him with a straight right that cut Maxim above the right eye. The next
two rounds were dominated by Maxim, although Floyd came back to
win the fifth. It seemed to most of the crowd and to the sportswriters
at ringside that Floyd won the next three rounds as well. After the final
bell, it looked as if Floyd had scored a lopsided victory. But Maxim
was announced the winner, eliciting boos from the crowd. The eleven
sportswriters who had covered the fight all had Floyd winning and
were perplexed by the judges' decision. Floyd was stunned. D'Amato
quickly announced that he planned to protest the decision with the
New York State Athletic Commission. (The commission ruled to let
the decision stand.) Patterson's first professional defeat went into the
record books.

Patterson tried to put on a good face for the press in the dressing
room and did not criticize the judges. But he was sorely disappointed
by losing on his home turf, Eastern Parkway, and proving its nickname, the House of Upsets, true yet again. The refrain *you lost, you
lost* echoed through his thoughts. In a pattern that would replay itself
in more extreme ways in years to come, he retreated into himself. He
spent the better part of a week hidden away in the Brooklyn apartment
he'd rented for himself, until some neighborhood friends stopped by
and brought him out of his funk.

Over the next year, D'Amato matched Patterson with boxers who
wouldn't come close to winding up on anyone's all-time-great list, perhaps to build up Floyd's confidence. Mostly Floyd threw his punches at
Eastern Parkway, but sometimes D'Amato worked out deals with the
IBC that allowed Floyd to fight at Madison Square Garden or St. Nick's.
Boxing-beat writers who covered these fights were not sure what to
make of this up-and-coming pugilist from Brooklyn — a fighter who'd
try to help a fallen opponent rise from the canvas, a fighter who'd try
to signal the referee to end the bout whenever he thought his adversary had endured too much punishment, a fighter capable of slicing up
an opponent's face with lightning jabs and delivering knockout blows
with a left hook as powerful as any ever seen in boxing.

Columnists after the quick, colorful one-liner weren't likely to get it
from Floyd. They were more likely to encounter silence. If they asked

questions, a good deal of the time Floyd referred them to D'Amato. When Patterson did answer, however, he sometimes delved so deeply into his inner motivations that it left many writers perplexed and uneasy. Soon enough, some of the boxing writers began to joke that a better name for him might be Freud Patterson. Eventually, some writers would call him the first Beatnik boxer, and his appearance reinforced that notion. He wore his hair in a style known as the "front," unprocessed, trimmed with a rise over the forehead and short the rest of the way around, usually with fairly long sideburns. It was a hip new look, which, combined with Patterson's growing taste for sharp clothes and big cars, gave him some flair. Yet it was a flair that came with a curious reserve.

Although Patterson shared few values with Beat Generation writers and their adherents, he was in his own way emblematic of a significant cultural shift taking shape in America. Just as pop culture icons Elvis Presley (also born in early January 1935) and Marlon Brando represented a break from what went before them in music and acting, so too would Patterson represent a break from what preceded him in boxing. Boxing writers who covered him as he came into his own in his early pro fights in New York were observing the dawn of a new age in boxing. In his quiet way, Patterson was setting the stage for one of the most exhilarating periods in boxing history.

The new era being ushered in was, among other things, obsessed with speed: fast new car models like the Corvette and the Thunderbird, jet airliners, rock 'n' roll, frenetic Neal Cassady raps captured in the novels of Jack Kerouac. Patterson was the perfect championship material for this speed-obsessed age. No one had ever seen a boxer of his size who had the hand speed he did. Remarkably, as he grew heavier, his hands didn't slow down one bit.

Yet Floyd, ever the walking contradiction, adhered to tradition as well. He began training in Summit, New Jersey, at a facility that was hallowed in boxing lore. Founded by a Turkish-born diplomat's wife, Hranoush Agaganian Bey, the camp had been known as Madame Bey's during its early years, and its list of star clients included Battling Siki, Gene Tunney, Max Schmeling, Primo Carnera, Max Baer, Henry Armstrong, and Tony Canzoneri. The facilities were anything but stellar: a large yellow farmhouse, a barn, and a barracks-like structure on a hillside that functioned as both a gym and a dormitory. Following Madame Bey's death, the camp came under the control of Ehsan Karadag, who earlier had been a partner with her in an unsuccessful rug-import business. The parade of champions who trained there didn't stop with the change of ownership. Jersey Joe Walcott, Rocky Graziano, Kid Gavilán, Ike Williams, Kid Chocolate, Jake LaMotta, and Sandy Saddler all became associated with Karadag's place.

At Karadag's camp, D'Amato began to reveal his long-term goal for Patterson. He had Floyd work with the toughest light-heavyweight and, significantly, heavyweight sparring partners he could find. The sessions became intense, much more so than any sparring Patterson had engaged in previously. D'Amato didn't tell Floyd that he was paying these sparring partners as much as $100 a round—absolutely top dollar for the 1950s. Each of them received the same instructions from the mystifying white-haired man: *Do your best to knock out Patterson. Go all out, no pulling punches, bang away as hard as you can.* D'Amato preferred that his fighters spar without headgear. "It gives the fighter a false sense of security," he explained. "It cuts down his vision, forces him to keep his chin up, and, in the end, causes him to get hit more often."[12] But D'Amato knew that the ferocity of what was to come was going to be out of the ordinary. So this time, the sparring partners and Floyd donned head protection along with the thickly padded sparring gloves. Patterson proved up to the test, knocking down twenty-two of the twenty-five men who entered the ring against him. Only one fighter, Tommy "Hurricane" Jackson, was able to stay on his feet for more than one round.

It was an impressive display. Sportswriters visiting the camp left Jersey thinking about the heavyweights Patterson had sparred. Could it be Cus's intention to have Floyd eventually challenge the undefeated Rocky Marciano for the world heavyweight championship? If so, D'Amato didn't admit it. The man who answered the questions said at the end of 1954 that Floyd's long-term goal was to fight Archie Moore for the world light-heavyweight title. More than a year would have to pass before Floyd would be eligible to fight Moore, though. Much could change in a year's time. Moore might not be champion by the time Floyd was eligible to fight him.

Frank Lavelle still numbered among Patterson's seconds when Floyd signed to fight Don Grant in January 1955. In the weeks leading up to the contest, things were tense in the Patterson camp, and most of that tension involved Lavelle. His importance as a trainer had eroded ever since Patterson signed his pro contract with D'Amato. Dan Florio had clearly established himself as the principal trainer. A neighborhood buddy of Floyd's, Buster Watson, had entered the entourage at Patterson's invitation as an unpaid trainer. Lighthearted, gregarious, up on all the latest music, Watson was almost Floyd's alter ego. He was the lone black among Patterson's seconds, and he was also young, close to Floyd's age. So he and Floyd established a natural bond. With D'Amato in charge and Florio and Watson carrying out their roles, Lavelle had become the odd man out. As a result, hard feelings reigned. D'Amato certainly did nothing to improve the situation. Lavelle was the only one of Floyd's handlers whose relationship with the fighter extended back further than Cus's. Complete-control Cus undoubtedly thought Lavelle was the sole person on Patterson's team who might in some way challenge his authority. If anything, Cus seemed as if he'd just as soon be shed of Lavelle.

The breaking point came when Floyd insisted that Sandra be allowed to visit him at Karadag's. Lavelle was dead set against it, believing Sandra would be a distraction. Floyd didn't see the problem. Sandra planned to stay just long enough for dinner and a movie, then take the train back to Brooklyn. But Lavelle refused to budge. Floyd held his ground too. Finally, Lavelle said he would quit as a member of Patterson's team if Floyd went ahead with his plans to see Sandra. Again Floyd didn't blink. And D'Amato was mute on the situation — Lavelle had to understand that he definitely did not have Cus's back. Sandra came to New Jersey, and she and Floyd went out on their date. Then she returned home, just as they'd planned. For Lavelle, this answered any questions he had about where he stood in the Patterson camp.

On January 17, 1955, Floyd TKO'd Don Grant at Eastern Parkway, with Lavelle as one of the trainers working the corner. When it was over, Lavelle changed his clothes, then said to Floyd, "Well, kid, I'll be seeing you."[13] He walked out the door. For good. He left behind the talent he'd first spotted in a Brooklyn YMCA. And D'Amato was rid of the man who'd first discovered Floyd's boxing potential. Cus was now completely in charge and ready to move his fighter on to bigger and better things. Lavelle slid into boxing's most woeful shadows, complaining to whoever would listen about how Patterson was taken from him.

5

Do I Have to Fight Floyd?

D'AMATO WANTED TO build up a national reputation for Patterson, because if he became well enough known around the country, fans and sports columnists would demand that Floyd be given a title fight. And if those demands grew loud enough, the IBC would have to accede eventually. Besides that, good money could be made out in boxing's hinterlands. Six of Patterson's next seven fights took place outside New York in venues removed from the IBC's immediate clutches.

One was Patterson's first professional bout outside the United States. His opponent: the ever-dangerous Yvon Durelle. Durelle had fought thirteen times in the sixteen months that had passed since his first matchup with Patterson. He lost five of those, and had grown somewhat disenchanted with his boxing career and his manager. But he still ached for a grudge match with Patterson, and he was delighted when it was arranged. This time, the fight was to occur on Durelle's home turf of Newcastle, New Brunswick, where he was confident he would not be robbed of a decision by the judges. "I beat Patterson in New York," a defiant Durelle said, "and I wanted to show the people I could beat him here, and this time get credit for the win. He was ranked number one light-heavyweight [contender] in the world by now, and it would be a big break for me. I wanted that fight so bad I said I'd fight him winner-take-all, or even for nothing."[1]

But Durelle's manager had also signed him to fight in Moncton, New Brunswick, just a week before the Patterson bout. In that fight, Durelle felt a bone snap in his right hand as he landed a punch. So now he faced the prospect of battling Patterson with a broken hand. The fight should have been canceled, but Durelle, fearing he wouldn't get another chance to fight Patterson, would have none of that; Patterson-Durelle went on as scheduled in Newcastle. Exhausted and injured, Durelle looked bad from the first. Fighting off nausea from the pain shooting up his right arm, he made an unsuccessful attempt to knock Floyd out in the fourth round. After that, Durelle was completely spent. He managed to stay on his feet, but once he hit his stool after the fifth round, he was done. He couldn't answer the bell for the sixth round. Patterson had bested the tough fighting fisherman.

Floyd went back to New York with a nice paycheck. When all was said and done, it cost the Newcastle promoters close to $6,000 to get Patterson to fight there. By now Patterson was receiving for one fight what some big-league baseball players earned for an entire season. Still, that was chump change compared to what the top heavyweight contender could demand for a fight.

An enduring irony in the world of boxing was that the lighter weight classes boasted of more-skilled fighters than the heavyweight division, and title fights involving smaller men almost always produced superior contests compared to those staged by the heavyweights. Yet heavyweight battles always drew more fans to the box office — fans who were willing to pay premium prices for their tickets. As a result, the manager of the heavyweight champion of the world held incredible power, the very power Cus D'Amato so desired. After the second Durelle fight, D'Amato posed a question to Floyd: Can you see yourself beating Rocky Marciano?

Patterson had been thinking about the thirty-two-year-old heavyweight champ. Rocky seemed to lack good boxing technique, yet he had a way of winning — and winning, and winning. Marciano had never lost a prizefight, besting forty-seven opponents, all but six of them by knockout. Still, Floyd came around to believing that he could possibly beat the Brockton Blockbuster. But he also wondered how realistic his chances were of getting a shot at the champion, who was in the pocket of the IBC. Could D'Amato, with his vehement opposition to the IBC, ever line up the great Marciano? One thing was clear: Floyd needed to put on weight to survive in heavyweight fights. For the second Durelle fight he weighed just 170 pounds, small for even a light-heavyweight. Patterson also had to get some experience absorbing the hard blows that heavyweights delivered before he'd be ready to battle the toughest of them all. D'Amato wasted no time. He booked Floyd to fight his first heavyweight match in July 1955, and found an opponent who ensured he would brush up against literary history, if nothing else.

Budd Schulberg was among the top American authors to write about boxing since Jack London had first taken up pen in 1910 to despair of Jack Johnson's winning the heavyweight championship. Schulberg had been introduced to the sport by his father, Paramount Pictures head B. P. Schulberg, and grew up idolizing Benny Leonard, the superb lightweight champion of the 1920s. Schulberg wrote the first major American boxing novel, *The Harder They Fall*, in 1947. He also wrote the screenplay for the 1954 classic boxing film *On the Waterfront*, with the unforgettable "I coulda been a contender" line.

Schulberg went beyond just writing about boxing. He became an actual part of the sport when he opened a fight gym in an old barn on his Pennsylvania farm. Soon local Golden Gloves competitors were working out there. Eventually an aspiring pro heavyweight named Archie McBride showed up at the barn, and in short order Schulberg became his manager. After scoring a series of early-round knockouts, McBride emerged as a rising star in New Jersey and Pennsylvania. Decisioning the tough Cuban heavyweight Nino Valdes earned him enough respect to start fighting in New York.

To get McBride matches at Madison Square Garden, Schulberg had to do business with the IBC and its behind-the-scenes overseer, the infamous Mr. Gray. He took on a comanager with Frankie Carbo ties and stepped into a world populated by characters even a gifted novelist would find hard to dream up. In 1955 Schulberg received a call from a matchmaker wanting to know if McBride was available for a fight in the Garden. The opponent? Floyd Patterson. "The name stuck in my throat," Schulberg said. "Patterson was the current sensation. He had knocked out everybody he faced that year, including the tough Canadian Yvon Durelle. The maestro Cus D'Amato was crafting his masterpiece. When Archie came in from his workout in the barn, I told him who he'd be meeting. He said quietly, 'Do I have to fight Floyd?' This wasn't fear. Archie had pride and heart. Just realism setting in."[2] Schulberg set aside his writing work and invested all his energy into prepping McBride.

Floyd was happy to be back in New York for the McBride bout because it allowed him to spend time with Sandra. The absences caused by out-of-town fights had been difficult for him, making him realize just how much he needed her company. By this point, Floyd and Sandra had reached an agreement to marry at some point in the near future. Sandra seemed to understand just how much boxing meant to Floyd. She also could salve his anxieties. She seemed to understand that Floyd's career would demand that he be away from home a great deal. Sandra showed no signs of resentment in those early days. But they were still young and callow — neither had experienced anything approaching a serious romance with anyone else.

Floyd went into the Madison Square Garden ring for his first heavyweight fight at a significant weight disadvantage, giving up sixteen pounds to McBride. In the early rounds, he struggled to take charge of the bigger man. After the fifth round, Floyd's cornermen implored him to get busy, fearing he could be slipping behind on the judges' scorecards. He went out for the sixth round punching, and one hard counterpunch dropped McBride. A right-left combination to the jaw knocked McBride down again early in the seventh. McBride answered the count but remained shaken. Patterson was able to batter him at will before knocking him out with a body shot a little more than halfway through the seventh round. McBride was no Marciano, but he was a solid heavyweight. Floyd had just demonstrated that he could go toe-to-toe with a bigger man and come out the winner.

After watching McBride hit the mat, Schulberg was hurrying from ringside to the dressing room when he was collared by the most influential figure in sports journalism at the time. Jimmy Cannon wrote the daily sports column for the *New York Post,* a column that was nationally syndicated. He received handsome compensation, rumored to top $100,000 annually, and with good reason. His byline alone could sell newspapers by the thousands, and his influence over other sports-writers was immense because of his success. Cannon was a reformed alcoholic and a bit of an egotist who believed he knew more about boxing than any other writer. Guzzling coffee instead of gin, he made the rounds of the Stork Club, P. J. Clarke's, and Toots Shor's. He palled around with the likes of Ernest Hemingway and Frank Sinatra. The opinion of this man about town counted, and he now proclaimed to Schulberg that he'd just watched a fixed fight — McBride had, in Cannon's eyes, taken a fall to give Floyd a victory.

Schulberg was stunned and insulted. Patterson-McBride was not the sort of fight that lent itself to fixing, given that Patterson was the favorite and won it handily. What was the point of fixing it? It was not a fight to stir particularly much interest among gamblers. No one stood to profit greatly from the outcome except for the fighters themselves. In that instant, Schulberg decided Cannon was a fraud, at least when it came to boxing. Cannon repeated his accusation in his column the next day, but it didn't seem to hurt Patterson's standing as a prizefighter. Floyd would have good reason to regard Cannon warily from this point onward. For now, though, he packed his bags and set out on the road again.

Floyd fought in Canada and in California, winning all his contests by knockout, which only increased the buzz surrounding him. While he was in Los Angeles, he allowed himself to enjoy some time off to take in the sights. He was given a Hollywood studio tour, which included a visit to the set of *The Man with the Golden Arm,* where he met Frank Sinatra. Sinatra, a boxing enthusiast, and Floyd hit it off. From then on, the Chairman of the Board became a big Patterson fan.

While in LA he also befriended Billy Eckstine. The smooth big-band baritone was one of Patterson's favorite singers as well as a man Floyd admired on several levels. Eckstine was an artist who managed to be both a traditionalist and an innovator, much as Patterson was as a boxer. As a biracial American, Eckstine had run head-on into racism as he built his career yet emerged victorious. Eckstine predicted that Floyd would become a world champion, which left Patterson beaming. Floyd was now rubbing shoulders with the very people he used to see projected bigger than life on the Banco Theatre's movie screen back in Bed-Stuy. Patterson was becoming ever more prominent in the sports pages, he was filling big arenas like LA's Olympic Auditorium, his fights were broadcast on radio and, sometimes, television, and he was earning a lot of money. Since the loss to Maxim, he had put together a string of fourteen straight wins, twelve of them by knockout. No doubt about it, Floyd Patterson was a star.

Floyd had been looking the part for a while. He dressed stylishly when in the public eye. He drove a Cadillac, the ultimate status symbol for the newly affluent in the 1950s, not to mention the automobile famously associated with Sugar Ray Robinson. Floyd indulged himself with hi-fi equipment and TVs, and he and Sandra attended movies obsessively whenever he was in New York. But he was no spendthrift. He saved money and made regular contributions to his parents to help support the children still at home. Floyd made a pledge to himself that he would buy a house so his family could escape Bed-Stuy. And he did just that when he bought a ten-room, shingled dwelling on a large corner lot in Mount Vernon, New York. The house was bright, airy, and roomy — a dream home for any ghetto kid. For Floyd, liberating his family from poverty was the American dream come true.

Floyd and Sandra planned to start calling the Mount Vernon house home after their February 1956 wedding — at least until they could buy their own house. They planned a Niagara Falls honeymoon but never made it farther than their first stop, Schenectady. They were two innocents, not entirely sure just who they were. Floyd had just turned twenty-one; Sandra was eighteen. Floyd had been a teenage world traveler himself, but Sandra had never been away from home. The stay in Schenectady was her first night in a hotel, and she was fascinated by such luxuries as room service. They decided to forgo Niagara Falls and stay a week in the hotel, but after a few days, Floyd became restless. Sandra sensed what was calling him.

The next fight, then maybe another, and then — would that be the title shot against Rocky Marciano?

Marciano had won a remarkable forty-nine straight fights by early 1956. Not only had he never lost as a pro, he'd been knocked down just twice, the most recent coming in his latest fight. The wily light-heavyweight champ, Archie Moore, moving up in weight to attempt to capture the heavyweight crown, struck Marciano on the chin in the second round, sending the heavyweight champ to the floor. But Marciano made it back to his feet and went on to dominate the rest of the fight. He was well ahead on the judges' scorecards when he knocked out Moore in the ninth round. But Marciano found the fight taxing and said afterward that he was glad it was over. He also told reporters he was contemplating retirement.

At first, it appeared Rocky might fight on. At least one more time. That would give him the opportunity to claim his fiftieth victory in fifty fights. Talk floated around that the fight could occur during the summer of 1956. But after a long South American vacation, Marciano decided he'd had enough of the rigors of the ring. In April he announced his retirement, with Jim Norris of the IBC standing at his side, which was appropriate, for no boxer was more associated with the mobbed-up organization than Marciano.

Rocky's stated reason for his decision involved his wife and young daughter and his admission that he'd been a poor father because of the time he had devoted to his career. Certainly Marciano's celebrity status was such that he stood to make a lot of money in business and public relations — more money than he could make boxing and with no risk of injury. But the real reason he quit was the one significant fighter in the heavyweight division he'd yet to defeat: Floyd Patterson. Though Patterson had fought just one heavyweight, considerable attention had been paid to his prospects of becoming heavyweight champ. He and Marciano were approximately the same size, and both could deliver hard punches. But there was one big difference between them. No one had ever seen a heavyweight with the speed, in particular the hand speed, that Patterson had shown in dispatching opponent after opponent since the Maxim loss. No one knew how — or even *if* — Rocky would be able to cope with hands that fast. It was a very real possibility that Marciano could suffer a humiliating defeat to the boxer eleven years his junior, especially given Rocky's tendency to leave himself unprotected as he fought close to his opponents. Word spread that some people close to the champ feared Marciano risked getting killed in the ring with Floyd. Likewise, the Patterson camp was confident its man would win easily. "It'd be no contest," Floyd's trainer Dan Florio said.

"Patterson is just too fast. I've trained a lot of old guys. I trained Joe Walcott. They get tired, and if you get tired in there against Patterson, then God help you. I'd hate to be the guy."[3]

Rocky opted not to be that guy, so sports' most coveted throne was made vacant. And Cus D'Amato had played his chess game perfectly. The prize he sought was available for the taking, and he'd maneuvered Patterson into a position where he had to be considered in whatever plans the IBC had for determining a new champion. The outcry would be too great if Patterson were slighted. All Floyd had to do now was get bigger.

At the time, the best training minds in boxing believed that 185 pounds was the ideal weight for a heavyweight.[4] Rocky Marciano, for instance, fought at between 184 and 188 ¼ pounds for his title bouts; Jack Dempsey, at between 185 and 192 ½ pounds; Ezzard Charles, at between 180¾ and 186 pounds. Joe Louis won the championship from Jim Braddock in 1937 at 197 ¼ pounds and subsequently fought most of his title defenses weighing just above 200 pounds, but he was something of an exception.[5] Most trainers dismissed boxers weighing that much as muscle-bound, so bogged down by their body mass that they were unable to make speedy athletic moves. But Patterson presented a different problem. He weighed in the 170s, which meant he did not have enough mass to put enough power into his punches to knock out bigger men. Nor was he likely to be able to withstand repeated blows from a bigger man without crumpling. So Floyd needed to bulk up. And he did just that in time for his first fight of 1956. Topping the scales at 183, he defeated a boxer ten pounds larger with a second-round knockout. The extra weight did not slow Floyd down one iota. He looked strong enough to withstand a hurricane.

In May 1956 the IBC announced its plans to fill the vacant heavyweight throne. Floyd would fight the number one heavyweight contender, Tommy Jackson[6] — better known as Hurricane Jackson — in June at Madison Square Garden, with the winner to take on Archie Moore for the world heavyweight title.[7] Both Floyd and the Hurricane were guaranteed $40,000. The Friday-night fight would be broadcast nationwide on TV.

In 1956 Archie Moore, Hurricane Jackson, and Floyd Patterson were black men on the verge of history. It was still rare for such an important competition in the United States not to include whites, and any event that guaranteed a new champion would be black was significant in terms of race relations in America. African American athletes were breaking down color lines in baseball, football, and basketball in the 1950s, and their presence in the upper rungs of prizefighting was growing as well. Likewise landmark events in the civil rights movement were rattling America beyond the realm of sports. Three weeks before Patterson fought Joey Maxim, the US Supreme Court handed down its unanimous ruling in *Brown v. Board of Education of Topeka,* which declared segregated public schools unconstitutional. In August 1955, a month after Floyd fought Archie McBride, a fourteen-year-old black youth named Emmett Till was tortured and killed by white men in rural Mississippi for either whistling at or speaking to — accounts vary — a white woman. Till's murder became a civil rights cause célèbre. In December 1955, a month before D'Amato announced his intention that Floyd contend for the heavyweight title, a black woman named Rosa Parks refused to surrender her seat in the white section of a Montgomery, Alabama, city bus, thus setting off the boycott of city transportation there — a boycott led by a then largely unknown black Baptist preacher named Martin Luther King Jr. Sports and political activism did not mix in the '50s, but black athletes like Floyd were well aware of these developments.

Hurricane Jackson was not unknown to Patterson. In fact, Floyd once considered Jackson a friend, and the two boxers had sparred together on a number of occasions at Stillman's. Not quite four years Patterson's senior, the Hurricane had much in common with Patterson. Born in Sparta, Georgia, he grew up in Far Rockaway, Queens. Far Rockaway, like Bedford-Stuyvesant in Brooklyn, had once been a Jewish enclave and in midcentury had become home to more and more African Americans. Its streets could prove hard, especially for a strange boy like Jackson, who never fit in. Jackson was a monster of a kid, towering over other students at school, and slow-witted, unable to learn to read and write. The boys in his class taunted him mercilessly, sometimes bombarding him with sticks and rocks as they chased him down Far Rockaway streets after class. He became a boxer in order to survive. "He was disturbed, lonely, unhappy," a sympathetic Floyd once said.[8] In the New York boxing world, the Hurricane became known as a fighter with unsteady, if undeniable, talent — and a definite head case.

After the two boxers became acquainted with each other at Stillman's, Jackson developed a kind of fixation on Patterson — much like Lennie's fixation on George in *Of Mice and Men* — which lasted until one of their sparring sessions turned into a brawl, going beyond just a practice session to an out-and-out fight. Jackson left the ring at Stillman's injured, blaming Floyd. After that, their relationship turned sour.

Jackson roared through the heavyweight ranks, winning eleven fights against a single loss, even beating former champion Ezzard Charles twice. His victories piled up until he became the top heavyweight contender. And yet, most observers on the boxing scene were not convinced he was truly of championship caliber. He could unleash stinging flurries of punches, never seemed to run out of gas, and could take hard shots to the chin. But he was also undisciplined, sometimes leading with his right hand, swinging off balance, and clumsily attempting double uppercuts. Worse was his wandering mind. He once lost a bout to a lesser boxer because he "clean forgot" about it, spent the evening before the match partying, and arrived at the arena on fight night hung over. He became something of a laughingstock, even among his own supporters.

Jackson was bigger than Floyd, had more experience in the heavyweight ranks, and had defeated a former champion, but bettors believed his liabilities outweighed his advantages. They made Patterson a two-to-one favorite. They might not have done so, however, if they knew about Floyd's secret. During a prefight sparring session, Patterson broke his hand. But he kept the pain to himself. A prudent person might have postponed the fight so a doctor could treat the injury. But Floyd wasn't about to delay the most important fight of his career. He dealt with his pain in silence.

On June 8, 1956, Patterson and Jackson fought at Madison Square Garden. Floyd pummeled Jackson hard early on, as if he wanted to end the bout quickly — not surprising, given his broken hand. Jackson endured a great deal of punishment in those early rounds, but his iron chin held up and he remained on his feet. As the fight progressed,

Patterson seemed to be on the verge of scoring a knockout on several occasions, but Jackson was able to stage surprising rallies, which brought the crowd to its feet in support of the underdog. Patterson grew more and more perplexed by Jackson's unorthodox fighting style as the Hurricane crouched at odd moments, threw strange combinations of punches, and sometimes even slapped Floyd. Jackson used his size advantage to bully Patterson around the ring, tying him up, and leaning on him. By the seventh round, the well-conditioned Patterson was panting while his right hand throbbed painfully. Jackson battered Floyd at will through the next three rounds. Patterson might well have thought he was far enough ahead on the judges' scorecards to be able to surrender those rounds. In fact, he had fallen behind in the estimation of at least one judge. Patterson needed a strong tenth round to ensure a win, and he produced one. But the outcome was not at all clear when the final bell rang. After collecting the judges' tallies, the referee announced a split decision: One judge declared Jackson the winner, but two favored Patterson; Floyd would thus move on to fight Archie Moore. Some columnists, not knowing about the broken hand, questioned if Patterson could hit hard enough to defeat the Old Mongoose, Moore, a fighter who was already a legend for his knockout skills, when the two boxers met in Chicago that November.

6

Youngest King of the Mountain

I N SEPTEMBER 1956, at Chicago's Bismarck Hotel, in a room crowded with boxing dignitaries along with a throng of newspaper reporters and broadcast journalists, Floyd Patterson and Archie Moore signed a contract to fight for the heavyweight championship of the world. The fight was set for November 30 of that year at the Chicago Stadium. The Old Mongoose was a press favorite because he always made for good copy.[1] He understood how to sell an upcoming match, just as he understood how to conduct psychological warfare against an upcoming opponent. A later master of self-promotion and psyching out the competition, Muhammad Ali, would learn a great deal from Moore. After the contracts were signed, one of the broadcast journalists asked Moore to predict the outcome. Moore said he'd probably knock Patterson out. Asked to respond, Floyd said, "If Moore can knock me out, more power to him."[2]

This was Moore's cue. He rose to his feet and began a blistering verbal attack on Patterson as the cameras rolled and the sportswriters scribbled notes. Patterson was completely taken aback. He believed in treating the opposition with dignity. There was nothing dignified about the words spewing from Moore's mouth. Finally, Patterson could stand it no longer. He fled the room and hurried through the lobby and out onto the street, where he sucked in some deep breaths of fresh air.

He found a pay phone, called Sandra, and poured his heart out. She was always effective in those days at calming him down. But now he had even more reason to check in with her. Sandra was pregnant and their baby was due to arrive about the same time as the heavyweight title fight. Sandra directed the conversation to the soon-to-arrive baby and how she herself was feeling. She soothed his anger over Moore's tirade. Patterson returned to the hotel and completed the interview, although he was irked by later questions about how he planned to stand up against a fighter with Moore's decades of experience. Floyd believed that he'd learned as much in a short time as Moore had learned over many years, but no boxing prognosticators seemed to consider that possibility.

As his nickname suggested, the Old Mongoose had been at it a long time. He'd begun fighting professionally before Patterson was born; Moore's own birth year was anyone's guess. It seemed likely to be either 1913 or 1916, but who could say for sure? Moore himself may not have known. Without question, though, he was a living, breathing link to an earlier era.

Born in Benoit, Mississippi, Moore grew up in St. Louis. As a poor teenager, he became involved in petty crime with a group of street-toughened kids. A botched attempt at stealing the change box from a streetcar landed Moore in a juvenile reformatory. There he established a reputation as a fearsome slugger after he coldcocked an older, much larger inmate who'd made sexual advances toward him. He participated in the reformatory's boxing program, fighting and winning sixteen times, fifteen by knockout. Paroled, he pursued boxing whenever he could, idolizing the fabulous Cuban-born junior lightweight champion known as Kid Chocolate. Eventually Moore wound up at a Civilian Conservation Corps camp in Poplar Bluff, Missouri, where he competed on an amateur boxing team.

Moore began training for the amateur Golden Gloves competition while at the same time secretly fighting for cash, sometimes using the ring name "Fourth of July Kid." His early pro fights of record pitted him against largely forgotten men like Piano Man Jones, Kid Pocahontas, Dynamite Payne, and Ham Pounder. His fights often occurred in out-of-the-way towns like Hot Springs, Arkansas; Quincy, Illinois; Keokuk, Iowa; and Ponca City, Oklahoma. Over the years that followed, Moore fought often, usually at least a dozen times a year, taking fights wherever he could and racking up an extraordinary number of knock-outs. Eventually he established San Diego as his home base. But as a West Coast fighter independent of the New York boxing establishment, he was not allowed to compete in the richest boxing venues until he was well into his thirties. He made do with tours of Australia and South America, sometimes fighting with no more than three days' rest, until he finally emerged into boxing's highest ranks.

The Old Mongoose fought in a style that made the peek-a-boo look absolutely orthodox. Moore would ball himself up behind the shield of his arms like a crab and absorb blow after blow in this protective stance before shooting out a scoring right. He loved to eat, and his walking-around weight typically was more than 200 pounds. When fighting as a light-heavyweight, he went on diets that became the stuff of leg-end; the most famous was his practice of chewing a piece of steak for what seemed to be an endless amount of time, swallowing the juices as he masticated, and then spitting out the pulp. Moore claimed to learn this weight-loss secret from an Aborigine during a trip to Australia. "I never saw a fat Aborigine," he said.[3]

Moore was never shy. After he'd won his light-heavyweight title, he designed customized stationery, which included his image, select newspaper clippings, and the wording "Office of the Light-Heavy-weight Champion." There was barely enough room left at the bottom of the paper for Moore to write a brief message. Moore also cut quite a figure whenever he visited New York, sometimes strolling the crowded streets wearing a shirt, tie, and suit jacket with Bermuda shorts while carrying an elegant walking stick.

Although not formally educated, Moore had somehow managed to pick up a remarkable command of English, which he enjoyed demonstrating at every public opportunity. Sometimes his choice of words befuddled those who heard him. He once said that the best way to dispatch an opponent was with a blow to the "goozle pipe," which caused observers to ask each other just what part of the anatomy he was referring to. Moore came close to knocking out Rocky Marciano in the second round of their 1955 heavyweight title fight but wound up falling far behind the champ as the fight progressed. At one point the ring physician examined the battered Moore between rounds to determine if the Old Mongoose's injuries were serious enough to end the fight. "Don't stop it, Doc," Moore said. "Let me try once more with a desperado." The doctor allowed the fight to continue. After losing, Moore addressed the press in his dressing room: "Welcome, gentlemen. I found this evening most enjoyable. I trust you did likewise. Now if you have any questions, I shall be happy to answer them."[4] None of the reporters present had ever heard anything like it. Archie Moore was no ignorant palooka, to say the least.

The gregarious, verbose, weathered Moore presented a stark contrast to the retiring, quiet, young Patterson. Oddsmakers made Moore a six-to-five favorite, mostly because Floyd had failed to knock out Hurricane Jackson, but also because they believed Moore's experience would trump Patterson's youth. Moore, advertised to be thirty-nine at the time though probably as much as four years older, would become the oldest heavyweight champ of the modern era if he won. At twenty-one, Patterson stood to become the youngest.

Patterson, D'Amato, and company set up camp at a Chicago horseracing track closed for the season, Sportsman's Park. It was a bizarre experience for Floyd. He did his roadwork on a course designed for racehorses and sparred in a makeshift ring erected in the grandstand penthouse. He shivered through the nights with his friend and unpaid trainer Buster Watson on cots in the jockeys' quarters. D'Amato was consumed by fear that one of his enemies would attempt to poison Patterson, so he slept on a cot positioned so that it barred the door to Patterson's room.

D'Amato's peculiar behavior did not go unnoticed by sportswriters. At other training camps, they'd seen D'Amato actually sleep in the same bed with Floyd. Whatever his explanations, D'Amato's actions seemed to go beyond propriety. He seemed obsessed with his fighter, but what was the source of his obsession? Was the guy a genius or was he half-mad? Or was there something else?

"I remember a story that Patterson told me," author Gay Talese, who knew both Patterson and D'Amato well, once said. "I got the impression that D'Amato had a sexual thing for Patterson — not that Patterson reciprocated. Patterson told me he was lying in bed and D'Amato was lying next to him, slipped perhaps into bed, I don't know. It was a training camp, you know. Prizefighters in training camp are intimately open, not sexually, but you are naked, you are free, there is a lot of openness. But this one time in bed, D'Amato had his foot on Patterson's foot, sort of playing with his toes." Perhaps it was totally innocent, an involuntary action by a man deep in slumber. But Talese was not alone in speculating about D'Amato's feelings toward Patterson. It was hard to tell the truth of the matter, for D'Amato was such an off-center man. "D'Amato was an eccentric," Talese said, "amusing, but I think probably borderline psychotic or paranoid."[5] But Floyd himself once gave a curious answer to a question about his relationship with D'Amato, one bound to raise eyebrows in the 1950s: "He makes mistakes, but the more they try to turn me against him, the more his quality comes out. Lucky he isn't a woman. I might have married him."[6]

Sleeping arrangements, worries about his pregnant wife, and the frigid weather aside, Floyd went through what he considered a successful camp at Sportsman's Park, particularly in developing a game plan for the fight. In addition to running and sparring, Floyd spent hours with Dan Florio watching again and again the films of the Marciano-Moore championship bout. During each viewing, Florio noticed that Patterson would tense up at one particular point in the fight. He ran and reran the film until Floyd pointed out that Moore responded to right-hand leads with a right of his own. Floyd decided he should avoid right leads.

Of course, Florio had seen the same thing, but he wanted Patterson to detect it on his own, believing the lesson would be more effective if Floyd figured it out for himself. In the makeshift ring, Patterson worked on options to a right-hand lead with his sparring partners as he and Florio devised a strategy designed to keep constant pressure on the older, heavier Moore. They wanted to wear the Old Mongoose down, then put him away once he was fatigued.

At noon on November 30, Patterson and his entourage arrived via station wagon at the Chicago Stadium for the weigh-in before that night's championship fight. Patterson registered at 182¼ pounds; Moore, at 187¾. Patterson retired to his dressing room and, as was his custom, went to sleep. But not all was calm in the hours before the opening bell.

That morning's issue of the *Chicago Tribune* carried a story suggesting the IBC was up to its old tricks. Charley Johnston, Moore's manager of record at the time, had inadvertently disclosed that Moore had been given an under-the-table $200,000 guarantee. This was at odds with contracts on file at the Illinois Athletic Commission, which called for each fighter to receive 30 percent of the combined gate receipts and TV and radio broadcast revenue. Promoters estimated that, based on this formula, each fighter should receive about $150,000. But the *Tribune* article suggested another agreement was in place, one kept hidden from D'Amato and Floyd. If Moore was guaranteed $200,000, regardless of the gate, that meant Floyd would be receiving less than D'Amato expected. In exchange for the $200,000 guarantee, Moore agreed to give the IBC exclusive ownership of his services as heavyweight champ. D'Amato was livid.[7]

Besides that morning's *Tribune* story, there was an even bigger reason for turmoil in the Patterson camp. When Floyd tried to telephone Sandra after the weigh-in, there was no answer. He was sure that could mean only one thing — she had gone into labor earlier than expected. He hurriedly placed other calls until he was able to confirm that she was indeed at the hospital. He dialed Queens Memorial, and his brother-in-law came on the line to assure Floyd that she was fine and that nothing was happening yet. He promised to give Floyd a call when Sandra went into delivery. Later that afternoon, Patterson became the father of a six-pound, two-ounce daughter. But Floyd's handlers did not let him know, fearing it might distract him from the business at hand. Four hours after Seneca Patterson drew her first breath, Patterson stepped into the ring in the Chicago Stadium to fight Moore.

There was all the usual pomp and circumstance associated with a heavyweight title bout at the Chicago Stadium that night. Photographers, cameramen, newspaper reporters, and broadcasters competed for space along all four sides of the ring. Past champions were introduced and waved at the crowd. Every two-bit politician worth his salt had nabbed a ticket in the front rows and showed up well preened, hoping to be seen, as did all manner of national and regional celebrities.

After the referee's traditional midring delivery of instructions, the bell rang and Floyd took command, driving long jabs into Moore's face, first from outside and then up close, scoring on the Old Mongoose seemingly at will in spite of Moore's vaunted protective shell. The first round ended with a hard Patterson right smashing into Moore's head. In the next round, the boxers exchanged blows fairly evenly, although Patterson clearly was the sharper, faster fighter. The third round was pivotal as Floyd opened a deep cut in Moore's left eyebrow. Patterson thereafter beat Moore to the punch time after time, making the Old Mongoose look his age. At the close of the fourth round, Patterson drove Moore to the ropes with a flurry of lefts and rights, finishing with a hard right-hand body punch as the bell rang. A stunned Moore wobbled to his corner. Just past the two-minute mark of round five, Patterson floored Moore with a left hook. Moore made it back to his feet before the referee's count ended, but seemed confused. When the fight resumed, Patterson hit him with a crisp combination of punches and Moore fell again. He struggled to a kneeling position, but this time could rise no farther. The heavyweight championship belonged to Floyd Patterson. Even so, Floyd found himself feeling sorry for Moore.

Patterson went through the celebratory motions, allowing himself to be hoisted to the shoulders of D'Amato and Florio. On the way from the ring to the dressing room, a reporter stopped Floyd to show him a wire service photo from New York of Sandra holding Seneca. And that's how Patterson learned he was a father. After that, much of the fight melted into a blur for him as he thought about his new daughter. He was "the happiest ever."[8] With his purse of $114,257, it seemed nothing but good times lay ahead of him.

Though a victory party was planned at a Chicago restaurant, Floyd, ecstatic though he was about his win, ditched it. He and two friends climbed into an automobile and hit the road for New York. He had no time to celebrate the magnitude of what he had just accomplished, fighting the best fight of his career, humiliating Moore, who was widely considered to be among the twenty or so best boxers to ever tie on the gloves.[9] But for now Floyd and his friends focused on the white lines of the two-lane highways of the upper Midwest as they roared through the crisp November night. Floyd ached to see his wife and Seneca.

Meanwhile, as a huffing Moore sat sweating in his dressing room, fight reporters swarmed in to get his postbout comments. Moore hoisted himself onto a bench and said, "It seems that even I must bow to the thing called youth. Youth and those fast legs. I came to the end of a very hard road, and when I got there I found the gate closed."[10] Moore's manager, Charley Johnston, listened, but didn't believe him. Once the reporters had cleared out of the dressing room, Johnston lit into his fighter: "I don't know what was going on out there but it didn't look good to me. As a matter of fact, it looked goddamned funny."[11] Moore protested that he'd fought as well as he could. Johnston refused to believe it. Later, Moore said that he was under undue stress in Chicago because a former lover was attempting to blackmail him by claiming, among other allegations, that Moore had raped her twelve-year-old daughter. Moore said that because of the blackmail ruckus, his head just wasn't into fighting Patterson. The bout was like something he watched as a spectator, not participated in. But allegations that Moore had taken a dive in a fixed fight began to spread. Eventually, Moore felt obliged to respond by releasing a statement:

> I must protest strongly when it is hinted that I dumped the fight. To do so I would have had to have a reason, and the only reason would be that I had bet money on Floyd. It takes a minimum of two to make a bet, and if the man I bet with will come forward I'll be glad to meet him for the first time. If I had won the fight, I would have been the holder of the heavy and light-heavyweight titles. I think it would have meant quite a few dollars in the Moore bank account. The odds were favorable for a "killing," because I was a 6-to-5 favorite, and when you rule out money there isn't another reason for me to go into the tank . . . I openly admit I was beaten fairly by a good fighter. I've lost many fights but never did I lose one in such a sorry fashion as the night I fought Floyd Patterson.[12]

Moore's statement, however, only fueled fixed-fight speculation.

Naysayers aside, plenty of writers were impressed by Patterson's victory, none more so than Arthur Daley of the *New York Times*. "Patterson appears to have the brightest of fistic futures," he said. "Being the youngest man ever to hold the richest prize in sports, he faces the opportunity of becoming the greatest of heavyweight champions.

In many respects he's better equipped than Joe Louis was when the Brown Bomber ascended to the throne at the age of twenty-three."[13]

Others agreed with Daley. Less than two weeks after the Moore fight, Patterson was voted the unanimous winner of the Edward J. Neil Memorial Plaque, an award given to the fighter of the year by the New York Boxing Writers Association. This put him in the company of such luminaries as Joe Louis, Henry Armstrong, Rocky Marciano, Sugar Ray Robinson, Benny Leonard, and Jack Dempsey. Chicago boxing writers and broadcasters chimed in as well, giving Floyd their boxer of the year award. Even more significant, *The Ring* magazine, "the Bible of Boxing," named him its fighter of the year.[14]

The hubbub surrounding him was not something Patterson relished. He discovered he could not step into a restaurant or stroll among the rides at Coney Island without people stopping to stare at him. He rode in a victory parade and felt awkward: parades were for kings or presidents. He retreated to the comfortable house he'd recently purchased in Rockville Centre, a well-scrubbed suburb populated by families of professional men who took the train to and from their day jobs in Manhattan, traded their Brooks Brothers suits for chinos or Bermuda shorts once they returned home, and sipped highballs as they congratulated themselves for living out the American dream. Floyd, too, could congratulate himself, his uneasiness aside. As a twenty-one-year-old black man, he'd accomplished what the middle-aged white men living in Rockville Centre had spent decades trying to achieve. He was wealthy enough to liberate not only himself and Sandra from the ghetto, but also his parents and her parents. He was famous, respected, and stood at the peak of the boxing world as the youngest man ever to do so. How could he top all of this?

7

A Black Champion in America

B Y JANUARY 1957 Patterson was back at training camp, this time at Greenwood Lake in New York, though his next opponent had yet to be announced. Floyd thrived psychologically and physically in a rural training-camp setting, removed from the distractions of family and fans, surrounded only by trainers and sparring partners. This set him apart from other champions who dreaded the Spartan regimen of camp. Floyd rationalized away any concerns he may have had about being absent from his new daughter and wife, saying that once he retired from boxing, he would have much more time on his hands to devote to them than the average breadwinner. So he was back into training — but for whom?

Plenty of fighters wanted a shot at the new king of the mountain. But D'Amato asserted his power as Floyd's manager, letting it be known that the IBC would have nothing to do with determining who challenged his fighter. In May D'Amato indicated that he had received five offers from promoters not affiliated with the IBC, including one possibility in the United Kingdom. He chose to cut a deal with his old associate from the Eastern Parkway Arena, Emil Lence, to promote Patterson's first defense at the Polo Grounds. D'Amato was so confident of the outcome, he announced that Floyd's *second* title defense would take place somewhere in the Pacific Northwest. As for whom

Patterson would fight, D'Amato said he planned to start at the top of the rankings of contenders. At the time, Tommy "Hurricane" Jackson stood as the number one contender, so he was the first choice. But in order to get the fight, Jackson had to accept Lence as the promoter and agree to his terms. If not, Jackson would be out and D'Amato would move on to the number two contender. Jackson's handlers were willing to make the deal — albeit only after a good deal of haggling — and the Polo Grounds fight was set for July 29, 1957.

Jackson was the ideal choice to be the first challenger for Floyd's title. Their closely fought encounter the previous summer had ended in a split decision, which left unfinished business for Patterson, who, up until his bout with Jackson, had been demolishing the opposition. If Patterson could win convincingly over Jackson in their rematch, it would clear up any nagging questions about whether he truly was Jackson's ring superior. Floyd looked forward to the summer matchup.

In the meantime, Patterson went on a five-city American tour fighting exhibition matches. Such tours were common for champions at the time. The matches were essentially sparring bouts conducted in front of paying audiences to earn the champ some extra cash while keeping his boxing skills sharp and his name in the paper. But Floyd's tour also gave him an opportunity to take in what he saw around him and to reflect on what it meant for him to be a black champion in mid-twentieth-century America. While champion from the late 1930s into the 1940s, Joe Louis had never decried racial prejudice in the United States. Patterson would break with the Louis tradition. As he made his exhibition tour, he decided that the time was right to begin speaking out. "Segregation and discrimination were not anything new to me," he said. "I had lived with them all my life, and like a good many Negroes, I was powerless to do anything about them until I gained a distinctive position."[1]

There was plenty of prejudice to confront, as stops on his exhibition tour proved. In Kansas City, Floyd, Dan Florio, Buster Watson, and two sparring partners were refused service at one downtown restaurant after another. Finally, the group stopped at a grocery store and bought cheese, crackers, and milk. Then they retreated to their hotel. A seething Patterson told his friends that if he hadn't been contractually committed to the exhibition that night, he would have left town. When Floyd learned that Jersey Joe Walcott was staying at the same hotel, he and Florio decided to visit the one-time champ in his room. Walcott greeted his old trainer and the new world champion enthusiastically. Patterson noticed a bottle of milk and a bag of cookies on the bedside table. It was clear that Walcott, too, had been unable to eat in the downtown restaurants.

After other stops on the exhibition tour, Patterson and his entourage boarded a train for Fort Smith, Arkansas, where the tour would wrap up. At the time, the state was the center of the conflict over integration. Its demagogic governor, Orval Faubus, had rebuffed the Supreme Court ruling in *Brown v. Board of Education*. In just a few months, federal troops would be deployed to ensure that black students were enrolled at Little Rock's Central High School. With racial tensions already inflamed, Floyd arrived at the Fort Smith station to find an all-white "reception committee" waiting for him. They glared as he stepped onto the platform, then formed a semicircle to block his path. No one spoke a word, but Patterson understood their message. A short standoff ensued as Patterson glanced around for the exhibition's promoter, who, as it turned out, was nowhere to be found.

A few anxious moments later, a priest appeared on the platform, waded through the crowd, and introduced himself to Patterson. Samuel J. Delaney, who pastored the St. John the Baptist Catholic Church in town, offered to transport Floyd and those traveling with him into town. Floyd gladly accepted the ride, as well as Father Delaney's proposal that Floyd and company stay at the St. John the Baptist rectory that night rather than lodge at one of Fort Smith's "colored" hotels. As it turned out, Father Delaney numbered among the soldiers in the integration movement in the South. For eight years he'd been working to persuade his white parishioners to welcome African Americans to the church. Delaney was also involved in the movement to integrate the public schools.

That night, Patterson showed up at the arena for his exhibition match — again, only to fulfill his contract. Not until he climbed through the ropes, tested the tautness of the canvas a couple of times, and then looked around did he realize that he was performing before a segregated audience. Every face he saw was white. The crowd was

well-enough mannered, though subdued, offering up only polite applause. Once the fight began, though, Patterson heard blasts of enthusiastic cheers coming from somewhere in the distant shadows of the
big room. It was only after the match that he discovered where those
ovations came from — a single, remote section of seats where black
fans were allowed to sit. In that instant, Patterson resolved he would
never again fight at a venue that was not fully integrated.

While changing into his street clothes, Floyd received a surprise
invitation to dinner that night at a downtown Fort Smith restaurant,
where he would be the guest of honor. But there was a catch: the black
men traveling with him would have to enter through the back door.
Infuriated, Patterson refused. The whole Patterson crew fled the arena
to eat with Father Delaney at a restaurant on the outskirts of town.
Floyd then spent a restless night at the rectory, impatient for the early-
morning train that would take him away from the South. Back in New
York, Patterson sent Father Delaney a check for $3,000 for improve-
ments to the St. John the Baptist building in hopes that it would help
the priest's integration efforts. After his experiences in Arkansas, Patterson also became a lifetime member of the NAACP, the nation's oldest civil rights organization, which was then battling in the courts to
systematically desegregate America.

The exhibition tour behind him, Floyd ensconced himself at the Long
Pond Inn in Greenwood Lake, New York, to train for his first title defense. He believed he still had to show the boxing world he was a legitimate champion, one with a real knockout punch, and Hurricane
Jackson's prefight antics helped make Floyd want to put him down.
Jackson told a reporter that the heavyweight title meant nothing to
him, that the upcoming fight was just another fight. Patterson was flabbergasted. How could Jackson discount everything Floyd had worked
for? Jackson also announced that he regarded Patterson as an enemy.
When pressed about why that was the case, Jackson maintained that
the two boxers had once made a pact never to fight each other, and that
Patterson violated it when he fought Jackson a year earlier. Of course,
if such a pact existed, Jackson had also violated it when he stepped into
the ring to fight Floyd, but that fact didn't seem to register with the
Hurricane. All this caused Floyd to fume in anticipation of the fight,

but he knew that knocking out Jackson would be difficult. Jackson was the most durable fighter he'd met in the ring.

In late July, as the fight date grew close, Gay Talese, on assignment for the *New York Times,* joined the group of reporters at the Long Pond Inn. Talese was different from the other sportswriters Patterson had encountered. For one thing, he was very neatly attired. In the shirt-and-tie-required 1950s, most sportswriters dressed as shabbily as they could, the cigarette burns in their lapels and the egg stains on their ties worn almost as badges of honor. But Talese, who came from a family of Italian American tailors, gave his appearance a lot of attention. His reporting style was different as well. Talese seemed to prefer overhearing conversations to scribbling down answers to interview questions. When he did conduct an interview, he liked to probe his subjects about what was going on inside their heads. He took as much time and care as deadlines allowed to get everything just right.

"You know I did try to bring the sense of a short story writer to my sports pieces," Talese explained. He found he could take chances with stories in the *Times*'s sports section that would not be allowed in other parts of the paper. "There is a general acceptance of people in sports as being fair game for scrutiny, held to account in a way that people not in sports are not held to account. For instance, in the 1950s, you couldn't write about — or shouldn't write about — the adulteries of a person in business or politics, but you certainly could about anyone having to do with sports. I am just showing why I could write about sports with the freedoms that I had in the 1950s. I wasn't interested in putting people down. I was trying to understand them. I never had a person that I wrote about that I couldn't call up again. In the case of Patterson, I called up fifty times and I did fifty pieces."[2]

Talese was just three years older than Patterson, who was used to dealing with much older sportswriters. Their youth created a bond between them, but they also connected in other ways. Talese had grown up in the island community of Ocean City, New Jersey, as the Roman Catholic son of Italian immigrants surrounded by middle-class Protestants. As a consequence, he had a sense that he was a marginal American, "an outsider, an alien in my native nation."[3] He could appreciate Patterson's own feelings of being an outsider. Patterson found in Talese someone who listened carefully and did not interrupt. Talese began penning pieces about Floyd that were different from the Gray Lady prose typical of the *Times,* and the two forged a lifelong friendship. Neither man's career would have gone the way it did without the other.

The young *Times* reporter filed a characteristic dispatch from the Long Pond Inn, detailing how much money the camp was spending on food, including $9,000 on steaks, most of which seemed to be winding up in the belly of Floyd's brother Sherman. Some of Floyd's siblings participated in his career, most particularly his kid brother Raymond, who would become a regular member of Patterson's entourage when Floyd was at the peak of his career, and who was a Golden Gloves champion before becoming a professional boxer himself. But as for Sherman, his purpose at Long Pond, other than consuming groceries, was never quite clear to Talese.

Hurricane Jackson may have been the top contender, but Patterson entered the fight as a five-to-one favorite. As the fight at the Polo Grounds played out on July 29, Floyd proved the oddsmakers were right. Floyd knocked Jackson down in the first round. In the next round, the Hurricane stayed on his feet, but Floyd seemed to score at will. In his corner between rounds, Jackson performed a set of jumping jacks, astounding the Polo Grounds audience. Perhaps he was attempting to show that Patterson's punches weren't hurting him. Before the fifth round, Jackson stomped out a sort of war dance in his corner. But for all of Jackson's show, Floyd's punches were taking a toll. Floyd scored another knockdown, and then, in the tenth round, referee Ruby Goldstein declared a TKO after the Hurricane fell for a third time. The Polo Grounds crowd jeered the decision — perhaps they wanted more jumping jacks. And Jackson made a show of protesting the call, but it was the right decision, for Jackson was clearly out of the match by that point.

Any doubts about whether Patterson was the better fighter were erased, although some fans grumbled about why Patterson had not been able to put Jackson down for the count, given how poorly the all-but-defenseless Hurricane had battled. And there was bad news in terms of money. Patterson had been guaranteed $175,000, but the gate receipts fell short of expectations. D'Amato agreed to waive the guarantee in exchange for 40 percent of the gate. Lence handed over only $123,859 to Patterson's manager.[4]

There was more bad news. Within hours of the bout's finale, Jackson began urinating blood. His mother took him to a Long Island hospital, where he was admitted with what was reported as kidney contusions, the result of the many body shots he'd taken from Patterson during the fight. The doctor who examined him diagnosed him as "fairly sick, but not dangerously so. He needs rest." The doctor advised Jackson to remain in the hospital for a few days. The hospital staff admitted only one set of visitors — Floyd and Sandra Patterson, who arrived with Cus D'Amato. Jackson was shocked that the Pattersons came to see him. The mercurial Hurricane shook hands with the champ and wished him luck in his upcoming fights.[5] Patterson left knowing that the tragic man-child Jackson was likely finished as a boxer of any significance.[6]

If Cus D'Amato proved masterful in his triumphant campaign to gain control of the heavyweight championship, his management of it turned out to be a whole other matter. His announcement that he planned to have Patterson fight the best contenders one by one was admirable. To have done so would have placed his fighter in league with the great Joe Louis, who did just that in his day. If D'Amato had stuck to his guns, Patterson's next challenge would have come from Eddie Machen, who, prior to Jackson's loss to Patterson, had been the number two contender. But Cus nixed him, claiming that Machen's managers were tied to the IBC. Number three was Harold Carter, who was then in the Army and thus unavailable. Willie Pastrano? He turned down D'Amato's overtures. Nor would it be Bob Baker, Zora Folley, Ingemar Johansson, Johnny Summerlin, Johnny Holman, or Wayne Bethea — the boxers who rounded out the rest of the list of the top ten contenders. D'Amato deemed all to be unacceptable for one reason or another, most for IBC ties.

In the end, D'Amato signed . . . Pete Rademacher?

Rademacher was not unknown to American boxing fans. In fact, he was something of a sports hero. Just the previous year, he had won the heavyweight gold medal at the 1956 Olympic games in Melbourne, Australia, where he scored a first-round knockout of his Soviet opponent. The fight came during the cold war, and like all American-Soviet Olympic battles of the time, it was a politically charged contest. After Rademacher put down the USSR's Lev Mukhin, members of the Hungarian boxing team rushed the ring and carried the American champion around on their shoulders. At the time, Hungary was set to explode in revolt against the Russians, an uprising that infamously was crushed by Soviet tanks. Against this backdrop, Rademacher's victory ensured his heroic status back home in the United States. "Just the same," said *Newsweek*'s influential sports columnist John Lardner of the challenger, "it is hard to believe in Pete, even for those of us who saw him win the Olympic title last year."[7]

The balding twenty-nine-year-old was much bigger than Floyd, and he had a lengthy amateur career that went back years. A Washington State native, he had tried his luck in the boxing ring as early as the eighth grade, and he continued fighting while a student at a military academy in Tennessee. He racked up dozens of amateur victories and won a national Golden Gloves title. His Olympic championship crowned his nonprofessional career.

He learned about Marciano's retirement after returning from Melbourne, and, pumped by his victory over the Soviet champion, decided he wanted to take a shot at the pro title, improbable as winning it may have seemed at the time. He convinced two affluent friends to put up guarantee money for a matchup with Patterson after Floyd defeated Moore. The Rademacher camp then contacted D'Amato and offered a $250,000 guarantee for a fight. At first D'Amato thought the idea was preposterous, but a quarter of a million dollars was nothing to blow off. Besides, D'Amato was having trouble lining up challengers who weren't IBC affiliated. Rademacher had no ties to Jim Norris or Frankie Carbo. Or anyone else. At the time of the offer, Patterson had yet to defend his title against Jackson. But Rademacher's backers were ready to make the deal. So D'Amato accepted, and the match was set for Sick's Stadium in Seattle, with "Deacon" Jack Hurley, who'd served as the model for the manager in W. C. Heinz's classic boxing novel, *The Professional,* acting as promoter. Its announcement spawned a chorus of hoots from the boxing fraternity. Floyd stood by his manager's decision — and the $250,000 guarantee that came with it.

Floyd was now operating as a corporation. Floyd Patterson Enterprises took in money from his ring earnings, product endorsements, and personal appearances, paid to cover Floyd's training costs, and gave him a salary.[8] Expenses for the Moore and Jackson fights had left a serious dent in the corporation's earnings for the year. Floyd needed the Rademacher payday to shore up his company's profits. Viewing the contest as something of a gimme, one step above an exhibition, and tired from the Jackson fight, he did not train in earnest.

The fighters battled each other on August 22, 1957, less than four weeks after the Jackson fight. Rademacher was the hometown favorite and had an enthusiastic crowd rooting for him. But the boxing cognoscenti at ringside agreed among themselves that the fight would last no more than a round, possibly two. As soon as Patterson had a chance to connect, they thought, it would be all over for Rademacher. But in the second round, it was Rademacher who connected with a right cross, and Patterson fell to the mat. The ringside timekeeper counted off four seconds before Floyd rose. If Patterson had been lackadaisical about Rademacher before, the knockdown changed his attitude. He was now energized and angry. As the fight proceeded, Floyd knocked Rademacher down seven times, the final one coming at two minutes, fifty-seven seconds into the sixth round. Referee Tommy Loughran, himself a 1930s boxing champion, waved his arms to end the fight. Floyd had another knockout to add to his record. But the lingering image from the Patterson-Rademacher bout was that stunning right cross that had put the champ on his butt. How could a first-time pro do something like that to the heavyweight champion of the world?

Patterson did not fight again for a year, as D'Amato went through torturous machinations to line up a challenger who met his standards. Floyd continued to retreat to remote training camps, away from his wife and daughter in Rockville Centre and away from the press. So isolated was he that some columnists began referring to him as the unknown champion. Patterson was hopeful that D'Amato could find a way to make a fight with the boxer who had had the greatest connection of all to the IBC: the retired Rocky Marciano.

Patterson enlisted Emil Lence to arrange the match, using a million-dollar guarantee to entice Rocky back into the ring. Lence was not the only one trying to make the match. Frank Sinatra, in partnership with Irving B. Kahn, the CEO of the TelePrompTer Corporation, tried as well. TelePrompTer was making a fortune, not so much from the speech-aid machines it sold to politicians as from its technology that allowed it to show lucrative closed-circuit championship fights live at movie theaters across the country. Sinatra wanted to promote the fight just for kicks, but Marciano stood to profit handsomely from Kahn's offer: $750,000 in cash and TelePrompTer stock. But the Rock wanted no more of boxing. He remained retired.

The Sinatra-Kahn offer did wind up affecting Patterson's career, though. Kahn's associate Bill Rosensohn promoted the next Patterson bout — a fifteen-round title fight against Roy Harris at Wrigley Field in Los Angeles.[9] But it wasn't quite that simple: nothing was simple when Cus D'Amato was involved.

The making of the Patterson-Harris fight is representative of the maddening way D'Amato typically did business. First, a story ran over the United Press International wire claiming that negotiations were under way to stage it at the Roosevelt Raceway on Long Island once the 1958 harness season ended. The day after the story hit the papers, D'Amato — who most likely was responsible for leaking the story to UPI in the first place — told the *New York Times* that nothing definite was in the works. He said he was in negotiations with five different fighters for a possible title defense. And, yes, Roy Harris, a recently ranked contender whose name was being bandied about as a possibility, was one of the five.

Next a Texas promoter offered a guarantee of $250,000 for Patterson to fight Harris in Houston. D'Amato spurned the proposal. Then the World Boxing Committee, which was headed by Julius Helfand, who also chaired the New York State Athletic Commission, announced it would lift its recognition of Patterson as the world heavyweight champion if he didn't defend his title against a ranked defender before September 30, 1958. A little more than two weeks later, as that deadline edged closer, the Associated Press reported that the fight would take place in Los Angeles, pending final settlement of the date and approval by the California Athletic Commission. Al Weill was listed as promoter. Weill had been Marciano's manager and had always been tight with the IBC. Why would D'Amato agree to a fight with an IBC man like Weill at the helm? Within a week, the question became moot.

The California Athletic Commission denied Weill's application for a promoter's license. So Bill Rosensohn replaced him, pending approval of *his* application. Coming in as copromoter was the Deacon, Jack Hurley, who'd staged the Rademacher fight. With all this in place, the fight was set for August 18, 1958.

California matchmaker George Parnassus howled about the decision because he'd already booked heavyweight matchups between Zora Folley and Pete Rademacher and Carmen Basilio and Art Aragon to occur within weeks of the proposed Patterson-Harris bout. The championship fight would no doubt hammer ticket sales for the two nontitle fights. But the Patterson-Harris bout was given the OK, and the fighters began preparing. Promoters expected the fight to generate around $650,000, more than $200,000 of it to come from closed-circuit TV. Fans could pay between $3 and $7.50 to watch the fight at a movie theater or on the big screen at a drive-in. Tickets at the Los Angeles Wrigley Field sold for as much as $40 each, extraordinarily expensive by 1950s standards.

And so the fight was made, the prices set. But it all took a lot of time to arrange. Patterson worked out and sparred, but that wasn't the same as actually fighting. He would enter the ring against Roy "Cut 'n Shoot" Harris with a year's worth of ring rust.

Cut and Shoot, Texas, was such an out-of-the-way place, no one knew for sure how to spell it. The *Handbook of Texas* and the United States Postal Service used "Cut and Shoot," no hyphens. But newspaper stylebooks of the 1950s preferred "Cut-and-Shoot." There were a half dozen other variations. The wide spot in the road in Montgomery County, Texas, was called Cut and Shoot on roadmaps, but its most famous son became known as "Cut 'n Shoot."

When Roy Harris was a small boy in the 1930s, Cut and Shoot was one of the most remote, most insular communities in the continental United States. Its white population drew from families whose lineage tracked back to Scotland and Ireland, and clan competition in Montgomery County could be fierce. Often law enforcement officials prudently turned their heads while disputes were settled according to ancient codes. For generations, Montgomery County men made their living cutting timber and hunting wild hogs in the region's all-but-impenetrable jungle-like forest. Things started to change with the arrival of the oil companies in the 1930s. The area became more "civilized" as outsiders moved in, and money began to trickle down to longtime residents. Yet it remained a region where violence was a constant. The measure of a man was judged by how well he could ride, shoot, use a knife, and fight with his fists. No one in Montgomery County could best Roy Harris's father and uncles at any of these tests.

It was a hard place that demanded hardness from everyone and everything living there. The streams teemed with alligators and the razor-toothed fish called gars. Wild boars in the woods were capable of killing a man with their tusks. Clouds of particularly aggressive mosquitoes attacked any exposed skin. Equally aggressive ticks awaited the opportunity to suck blood from anyone who brushed up against a bush or clump of grass. In fact, there are stories that Harris showed up for boxing events early in his career with ticks embedded on his back. No one thought anything of it.

"Big Henry" Harris, Roy's father, became known throughout East Texas and beyond for his boxing skills, both in gloved matches of record and illegal bare-knuckled brawls. Legend around Montgomery County holds that word of his fighting prowess reached Joe Louis's managers, who proposed a bout. Big Henry was amenable, as long as Louis traveled to Texas for the fight. Big Henry wasn't about to go north to Louis's home turf, suspicious that everything would be rigged against him. The matchup never occurred. Not surprisingly, Big Henry's sons wanted to emulate their father, and Roy proved to possess the mental toughness and physical coordination to be a very successful boxer. Roy signed on with a somewhat larger-than-life character named Lou Viscusi — "Viscusi could talk the eyes out of a bullfrog," claimed one rival Houston manager. Viscusi was a New York native then managing boxers in Houston while maintaining ties with mobsters on the East Coast.[10] With Big Henry working his corner, Roy began defeating all the boxers Viscusi could arrange for him to fight.

Most of Harris's bouts occurred in Houston, far removed from the boxing establishments of New York, Philadelphia, Chicago, Detroit, and Boston. At the time of the Patterson fight, the American Boxing Association had Harris ranked as the number three heavyweight contender, trailing only Zora Folley and Eddie Machen. Harris was

22-0, with quality wins over Bob Baker, Willie Pastrano, and Willi Besmanoff, and he received an award from *The Ring* magazine for the fighter who made the most progress during the previous year (1957). He also regularly appeared in the magazine's listing of top ten heavyweights for several years. Novelist Joe David Brown wrote in *Sports Illustrated* that Harris might well be the best heavyweight produced by the state of Texas since Jack Johnson emerged from Galveston some fifty years earlier.[11]

The matchup of boxing skills between Patterson and Harris was lost in the prefight publicity, which centered on Montgomery County and Harris's extended family—all of which were ideal fodder for Americans who were still caught up in the Davy Crockett craze and who giggled over the antics in Dogpatch as they read the daily comics. Patterson was OK with the publicity focus on Harris rather than himself because it kept him from getting distracted, allowed him to focus on the fight. And Patterson knew that Harris was a Montgomery County anomaly. True, he came from a family that just a generation before wore buckskin clothes with coonskin caps, but Harris was also a college graduate who had been a military officer and who taught school when he wasn't boxing. Patterson also was all too aware that a fighter with Harris's skills could be dangerous for a rusty champion such as himself.

There was another dynamic to this matchup—perhaps the most compelling one from an outside-the-ring perspective. Patterson was an urban African American hailing from New York. Harris was a rural white southerner—Harris's part of Texas is much more akin to the Deep South than it is to the West. "'Nigger' was just the common word used back then to describe black people," Harris said in describing the Big Thicket country in which he grew up. "It was the only word we knew. It wasn't said with hate. We didn't know that in other places it was considered a hateful word."[12] Nevertheless, there was plenty of hate in East Texas. Montgomery County was known as a hotbed of Ku Klux Klan activities, and lynchings were not unknown in East Texas. There was no question that Harris sprang from the same sort of social milieu as Emmett Till's murderers (agrarian, southern, white) just as Patterson sprang from the same sort of social milieu as Till himself (urban, northern, black). The conflict between what the boxers represented resonated as questions such as public school desegregation and voting rights for blacks divided the nation. Patterson read newspaper accounts saying that some Montgomery County people viewed the fight as a battle between the North and South. That was fine with him.

But neither fighter felt up to snuff as the August 18 bout approached. Patterson thought his timing was off because of ring inactivity. As for Harris, he set up camp at Arrowhead Springs in the San Bernardino Mountains above LA. He subsisted on a high-protein diet that melted too much weight off him. At one point, he was down to 174 pounds before realizing he was carbohydrate-deficient. Two weeks before the fight, he was advised to address the situation by imbibing beer. He'd gained back twenty pounds by the time of the weigh-in, but the yo-yo effect of shedding weight then putting it back on sapped Harris of his energy.

Gamblers made Harris an eight-to-one underdog early on, although that changed when Texas bettors, wagering with their hearts rather than their best judgment, began placing big-money bets on the pride of Cut and Shoot. By the day of the fight, Patterson was down to a three-and-a-half-to-one favorite. More than 21,600 spectators crowded into Wrigley Field, including 1,600 Marines from nearby Camp Pendleton, to watch the fight, setting a California live-gate record for the time of $234,183.[13] Theaters carrying the fight on closed circuit numbered 151, including the drive-in theater in Conroe, Texas, where scores of Harris fans were ready to blow horns, hoot, and launch soda water and moonshine bottles into the air whenever Cut 'n Shoot might seem to take an advantage.

As the fight unrolled in LA, it seemed that folks in Conroe might just have a lot to cheer about. Patterson struggled with lethargic feet, the result of too much time out of the ring. Good footwork was key to the success of any boxer, but it was especially true for Floyd. He depended on speed both as a weapon of attack and for defense. He relied on his ability to slip in and out of the pocket quickly to win. But without speed, he left himself open to be hit. Good footwork was also necessary for him to effectively execute his gazelle punches without being off balance. Patterson was indeed off balance in the second round when Harris launched a right uppercut–straight left combination that knocked Floyd down. "I saw punches coming and didn't get out of the way," Patterson said. "I thought he sort of pushed me down, but if it will settle matters, let's call it a knockdown."[14]

Harris had planned to attack Floyd early, and it seemed with the knockdown that his strategy was paying off. "I noticed something about Floyd before we fought," Harris said. "You had to make him mad before he started fighting his best. So I tried to take him down early in the fight, before he got worked up."[15] Unfortunately for Harris, Floyd didn't stay down. And he was a different fighter once he was back on his feet. He began to take Harris apart in round after round. By the seventh round, Harris seemed exhausted and was bleeding profusely. Floyd was enough in command of the fight that he was able to pick an opening. When one presented itself, he threw a left hook–right cross combination that felled Harris. Harris was able to rise to one knee as the referee counted, and the round ended before Patterson could levy further damage. A left hook dropped Cut 'n Shoot to the canvas for a count of seven in the eighth round. Just before the bell, Patterson knocked him down yet again. Patterson continued to rack up points over the next three rounds as a battered, hemorrhaging Harris could do little to stave off Floyd's attack. In the twelfth round, Patterson sent Cut 'n Shoot tumbling one more time. Blood cascaded down Harris, and observers at ringside speculated among themselves that if the referee didn't stop the fight soon, one of Cut 'n Shoot's eyes might fall from the socket. Big Henry, seconding his son, had seen enough. He told referee Mushy Callahan that the Harris corner was throwing in the towel. Cut 'n Shoot pleaded to go on, but Patterson heard Big Henry tell Roy that continuing was futile.

Fifty years later, Harris still wished his father had not stopped the fight. He believed he could have found a way to win it. "This is someone I should have beaten with ease," he said. "I think about the fight all the time. I have never stopped thinking about it."[16]

Patterson's share of the Wrigley Field ticket sales totaled $101,000, and his payday from closed-circuit TV was $210,000. Floyd Patterson Enterprises made a lot of money from the fight. But Patterson himself was not happy with his performance, believing he'd been stale and slow. Fans and sports columnists were critical of how he boxed, as well, supplying new timbre for the chorus of nonbelievers in the legitimacy of his heavyweight championship. "Falling Floyd," as Patterson detractor Jimmy Cannon sometimes called him, had allowed yet another boxer to drop him to the canvas. If he had been a true champion in the tradition of Joe Louis, he would have floored Harris, the reasoning went. "You should have knocked Harris out before his corner stopped it," Cannon said to Patterson afterward. Patterson explained that he believed he could have dispatched Harris earlier, but the sight of Cut 'n Shoot's hideously bloodied face caused him to back off. "Compassion is a defect in a fighter," Cannon said.[17] That Harris had gone into the fight as one of the top contenders in the heavyweight class seemed to be immediately forgotten as soon as Big Henry threw in the towel. Harris became another nobody, "the hitless wonder of Cut and Shoot," as Red Smith described him.[18]

The criticism stung Floyd, and he wanted change. He thought the best plan was to start with the top contender and work his way down the rankings. In order, the first three would have been Eddie Machen, Zora Folley, and Willie Pastrano. Pastrano had earlier turned the Patterson camp down. He, Machen, and Folley went to Europe for what they thought would be easy bouts with healthy paydays.[19]

But a remarkable six weeks of upsets occurred following Patterson-Harris. In September 1958 Machen, Folley, and Pastrano all had contractual obligations for those European fights before they could sign to meet Patterson. On September 14 Machen fell to Ingemar Johansson in Sweden. Just two weeks later Brian London, the British heavyweight champ, knocked out Pastrano. Two weeks after that, Folley lost a ten-round decision to England's hard-hitting Henry Cooper. Sweden's undefeated Johansson, on the strength of his record and his defeat of Machen, emerged as the highest-ranking contender.

There was much about a Patterson-Johansson fight that would make it a marketable show. Johansson was the European champion, and that meant that the radio broadcast and the subsequent films of the fight would play well in Europe. In the 1950s fight promoters continued to believe that America's primarily white boxing fan base still wanted "great white hopes" to root for — Joe Louis's and Sugar Ray Robinson's fights against white challengers always made more money than their fights against black boxers. And finally, Johansson was handsome and had a bit of the playboy's air about him. He was very promotable.

Immediately after his fight with Machen, Johansson signed a promotion contract with Bill Rosensohn. In it, Rosensohn agreed that within forty days he would secure a contract for Johansson to fight Patterson. If he were unable to do so, he would give Johansson $10,000 and the Swedish fighter would be freed of his contractual obligations. If the fight occurred and Johansson won, Rosensohn would have Johansson under contract for a return bout. And thus the negotiations began. On November 25 D'Amato said that he was optimistic the fight could be scheduled, once he was able to "clarify previous misunderstandings" with Johansson's manager, Edwin Ahlquist.[20] Again, the negotiations were complicated, made more so by D'Amato's distrustful nature, but in January 1959 Patterson and Johansson signed the contracts for a fight in June.

It was understood by both sides that Patterson would get one tune-up fight prior to his bout with Johansson. For this, D'Amato had lined up Henry Cooper. The balding Brit was a good choice.[21] Though notorious as a bleeder — it was said that the blood would start gushing if you did no more than spit on him — he was a game boxer, the only fighter ever to win three Lonsdale Belts outright.[22] Before his fight with Folley, Cooper had agreed in principal to fight Patterson for a guarantee of $75,000; after his upset win, Cooper raised his demand to $150,000. D'Amato would have no part of that, so he began to look elsewhere. He settled on Brian London, the rugged British fighter who had upset Willie Pastrano. Patterson would fight him May 1, 1959, less than two months before the Johansson bout.

London, known as the British Bulldog, held the title of British Commonwealth champion, though Cooper, who had beaten him twice, was clearly the superior boxer. But London's no-nonsense style won him the admiration of many British fight fans. Unfortunately for Patterson, with a tough fight against Johansson looming, the London tune-up bout provided plenty of distractions as it turned into a promotional nightmare, with no one seemingly able to agree about a site or a promoter. Finally Indianapolis was designated the location of the match, and, after several promoters had been named and dropped, Bill Rosensohn emerged as the man primarily in charge.

Patterson signed the four sets of papers presented to him by D'Amato, and everything seemed ready to go. But then, a week later, D'Amato showed up at Ehsan Karadag's New Jersey facility, where Patterson was in training camp. Instead of going into the gym, however, D'Amato sent an emissary to fetch Floyd and bring him out to his car. When Patterson climbed into the backseat, a distressed D'Amato informed him that there was trouble with the deal. Patterson would be receiving less for the London fight than D'Amato had thought — and his take in subsequent fights would be less as well. D'Amato confessed that it was all his fault. With the confusion surrounding the fight's promotion, he claimed he had failed to read the contracts carefully and had signed away some of Patterson's future earnings. But now that the ink was dry, fighter and manager had no choice but to accept them as written. Another thing Patterson learned was that there was no television-revenue guarantee for the bout. Finally, D'Amato told Floyd he feared there would not be sufficient time for an effective publicity campaign in Indianapolis, which meant that the Indianapolis gate receipts might be less than anticipated. Stunned, Patterson climbed out of the car and trudged back to the gym as D'Amato drove away. D'Amato promptly went underground, and Patterson publicly acknowledged that his manager had made some mistakes that would affect Floyd Patterson Enterprises, though no dollar amounts were ever disclosed. Floyd said he was still committed to D'Amato, even while beginning to wonder to himself about his manager's acumen. Or maybe that something else was going on with D'Amato.

Everything seemed odd about the developing title fight. Just two weeks before the contest, London, typically a publicity seeker, was still hidden away in New York. Normally, a boxer would have been in the city of the fight by this time. He was registered under an assumed name at a hotel. Why? No one would say. But the mystery surrounding London seemed to bear D'Amato's stamp, especially after London, his father, his brother, and his local boxing manager were spotted leaving the East Side's Gramercy Gym. When word spread that Patterson's foe was training at his home gym, working out with Patterson's regular sparring partners, and no one outside the D'Amato clique was being allowed up the stairs, observers wondered if Floyd's manager had taken charge of his challenger as well. That seemed weird — as did D'Amato's complete absence from the scene.[23] Only later did it become clear that D'Amato did indeed have a role in London's New York management, but the details were not disclosed. Floyd remained silent about the matter.

"Those men in white coats at the Patterson-London fight won't be there to sell peanuts," said *Sports Illustrated*'s Martin Kane. "They will be psychiatrists, assembled for the clinical study of one of the more lunatic sporting promotions of our century, surpassing in some aspects even such demented delights as bunion derbies and dance marathons."[24]

In late April, London finally arrived in Indianapolis, and he was his old talkative self. The $75,000 guarantee he received for the fight was the biggest of his career, and he was certainly happy about that. The opportunity to compete for the champion's belt was something he'd never come close to achieving earlier in his career. He said he would gladly fight Floyd for free, just to have a shot at the crown. He knew that his opponent regarded this as nothing more than a tune-up for his meeting with Johansson, but London predicted that Patterson just might get the surprise of his life. Floyd was no Marciano or Louis, in London's estimation, and could be defeated.[25]

Patterson may not have been a Marciano or Louis, and he may have been viewed as a flawed champion by columnists like Jimmy Cannon, but at the time of the London fight, he was held in high esteem by African Americans, who considered him a hero. While in Indianapolis in the days before the London bout, Floyd visited the all-black Crispus Attucks High School. Like southern schools, midwestern public schools of the time were typically racially segregated, and black schools wound up on the losing end of budgetary decisions. Facilities were often substandard, including playing fields and gymnasiums, and there was little money for adequate athletic gear; as a result, black public high school teams often struggled against larger white high schools with more money. But two years earlier, Crispus Attucks High School had made national history by becoming the first African American high school to win a state sports championship. Led by the legendary Oscar Robertson, Attucks had come out on top of the equally legendary Indiana state high school basketball tournament. Another Robertson-led Attucks team repeated as champions the next year, becoming the first high school basketball team in Indiana history to go undefeated for the season. Floyd received an enthusiastic welcome from the sports-crazed student body. In particular, he impressed a fifteen-year-old girl. "In 1958," said Janet Langhart, who was then living with her mother in a housing project, "on the heels of Little Rock and all the racial turbulence that had engulfed the country in the wake of Brown v. Board of Education and the Montgomery bus boycott, Floyd Patterson was one of the heroes who gave 'the Negro' a sense of power, a conviction that in spite of prejudice and hatred, we could compete and triumph."[26] Langhart later became an author, playwright, and TV personality, as well as wife of Defense Secretary William Cohen.

The visit helped energize Floyd. Sportswriters in town to cover the fight were impressed by his workouts. The consensus among them was that he looked sharper than at any time since the fight with Moore in 1956. "Patterson gave [sparring partner Ike] Thomas a hard body pumping in Sunday's workout," wrote an Associated Press reporter. "He floored him once with a quick left-right combination and then with a hard left hook to the jaw."[27] It seemed likely that London would be in for a hard night. In spite of D'Amato's fears about the lack of publicity, ticket sales turned out to be brisk. About ten thousand fans filed into Indianapolis's Fairgrounds Coliseum, expecting to see Floyd knock out London in his warm-up for the *real* fight with Johansson to take place six weeks later. Johansson himself was among the VIPs seated at ringside.

But Floyd wound up fighting methodically at best against London, showing little inspiration through the first ten rounds. It was just enough to keep him ahead on the judges' scorecards. Finally, early in the eleventh, Patterson went into full attack mode, delivering a flurry of hard punches topped by a devastating left hook. London went down with a thud, quivered on his back, and then rolled over to kiss the canvas, as an old trainer might say. London remained motionless for more than thirty seconds after the referee signaled him out.

Once London's handlers were finally able to get him back on his feet, Patterson raced across the ring and hugged his vanquished foe. *Time* magazine dismissed the fight as comic opera, "a tea-and-cakes farce from the beginning."[28] At ringside, Johansson was baffled by what he'd just witnessed. Why had Floyd taken so long to end the fight? Why did he hug London afterward? What was up with this guy? He shrugged it off and traveled back to Sweden, never guessing that he was about to enter one of the most celebrated rivalries boxing has known.

8

◆

Lightning and Toonder

A T EHSAN KARADAG'S TRAINING facilities in Summit, New Jersey, Floyd felt confident that he would perform better against Johansson than he had against London. In fact, he even quantified it: he'd be 50 percent better at their Yankee Stadium title fight on June 26, 1959. What that meant was anyone's guess. Did he expect to knock out Johansson in five rounds instead of the eleven it had taken him to floor London? Patterson had less than two months to prepare, but he had never been in better physical condition, so that wasn't too much of a worry. To ensure that Floyd had the mental toughness he needed, D'Amato put him through more than five hundred sparring rounds, forcing Floyd to keep battling after he felt spent, no pulling punches. Partners left the ring with bloodied noses, blackened eyes, and sore torsos. The undefeated Johansson was a bruiser, and Floyd would have to hurt him to win. And so the sparring-ring carnage mounted.

When it was finished each day, Floyd retired to the most austere of accommodations. "The single room in which I slept," he said, "was only a couple of nails above a squatter's shack . . . It is a hard business."[1] But Johansson didn't see much that was hard about it. Not in the way he approached it, at any rate. While Floyd practiced self-denial in New Jersey, Johansson lived the high life at a resort hotel in the

Catskills known as Grossinger's. It was a training camp the likes of which no one had ever seen. Johansson had hired Whitey Bimstein to act as his American trainer. Bimstein's cornerman pedigree went back to Gene Tunney and beyond, but Bimstein was unable to impose any old-school discipline on Ingo, as Johansson was popularly called, an imperious man, not one to forgo life's pleasures. Johansson's notion of training was playing golf, riding horses, and swimming. He made frequent trips to New York for entertainment, taking in the comedians appearing at the Terrace Room and going dancing. He imported a chef from a world-class ski lodge to prepare his meals. His parents, his sister, his brother, and his brother's fiancée were enjoying the good life with him in the United States. As was one Birgit Lundgren, a Swedish beauty who captivated the press covering Johansson's camp. About to make the transition from his "secretary" to his fiancée, she appeared everywhere with him, nuzzling his ear, fondling his arm, staring into his deep blue eyes. It was clear to everyone who witnessed it that much more than ear nuzzling occurred when the couple were alone in Johansson's room.[2] Rocky Marciano was among the many appalled by the spectacle.

Could any two boxers be more different? It hardly seemed so. And yet the two men shared one thing: neither had ever wanted to be anything but a successful prizefighter.

Johansson believed he was born to be a boxer. He had watched prizefighting for the first time at age twelve. Standing at the top of a Swedish *Masshäll,* looking down at the spectacle, he was immediately taken by it all — the whole atmosphere of the thing, from the boxers themselves to the colorful characters outside the ring. After that, boxing was all the Swedish working-class kid could think about. He was a big, strong boy, with a physique that set him apart from his classmates. At age thirteen, he already weighed 141 pounds. A little more than two years later, he was fighting as a heavyweight. He looked to a fellow Swede named Olle Bengtsson — the first boxer he knew by name — as a role model. Bengtsson was a crowd favorite in the small Swedish venues where he boxed, fair-haired, wearing a gold vest and black trunks. And, more important: Bengtsson seemed to always knock out his opponent. Inspired by Bengtsson, Johansson began training in earnest.

Eventually he sparred with Bengtsson and discovered that he could supply the older, more experienced fighter with all he could handle.

After finishing school, Johansson knocked around, working various odd jobs at the Gotëborg harbor, portering bananas, wrestling sacks, sweeping snow. Then he went to work for Edwin Ahlquist's dockside company. That changed Ingo's life. Ahlquist was a familiar face in Swedish boxing circles, such as they were. Because of its violence, pro boxing was controversial in Sweden, and politicians debated outlawing it. But Ahlquist loved prizefighting, and, like Cus D'Amato, dreamed of taking a heavyweight prospect all the way to a championship title. His attempts at developing a contender had been disappointing.

Ahlquist knew about Johansson's fighting ability before Ingo came to work for him. He saw Ingo in action during amateur fights at Gotëborg's Lorensbergs Circus, where he witnessed for the first time Ingo's powerful right-hand punches. He saw one such blow connect with the chin of an older boxer. Abruptly the other man was out. Not staggered, but completely knocked out. Impressed, Ahlquist introduced himself to the fourteen-year-old Ingo. A few years later, after Johansson began working for Ahlquist on the docks, he began managing Ingo's boxing career. Time after time, Ahlquist witnessed Ingo's dispatching other boxers with that nearly mystical right, and he began to think that he might have found a ticket to the heavyweight title.

As an amateur, Ingo became a phenomenon in Sweden and, to a lesser extent, internationally. He awed Chicago fight fans in 1951 when he visited with a troupe of European amateurs to battle the city's Golden Gloves champs, and he enjoyed positive write-ups in the Chicago papers. Yet, on the same tour, he left an entirely different impression on fans in Washington, DC. Claiming his hand hurt, he refused to take part in the amateur bouts scheduled for the Swedish boxers in the nation's capital. An American official said that Ingo had to fight, at least make a show of it for one round before withdrawing. Ingo refused. Swedish boxing writers were outraged as well. They accused Ingo of faking his injury because he was afraid to box the American scheduled for him, Norvel Lee. Johansson stood his ground. In boxing, he said later, you have to learn "to stand up against a campaign of backbiting, threats, and slanders."[3] He didn't care if he developed a reputation as a fistic prima donna for doing so.

Regardless of what happened in Washington, Johansson seemed likely to be a serious contender for the 1952 Olympic gold medal as a heavyweight. He qualified to be a member of Sweden's team. Reluctantly. He viewed the Olympics as something he had to endure before he could begin fighting for money, which was his ultimate goal. But he felt pressured by Ahlquist and others to take part in the Helsinki games. He went into camp out of shape and feuded with trainers who attempted to remedy that. "I was regarded by people who never boxed and don't understand boxing as lazy and unwilling to train," he said. "I never do well if I'm messed about in this way — it has never suited me."[4]

As Floyd spent his free time in Helsinki smuggling food to the city's impoverished, Johansson spent his at a Finnish golf course. Meanwhile the luck of the draw worked to Ingo's advantage in the heavyweight boxing brackets. He made it to the medal round, hardly working up a sweat against the less-than-stellar Olympians he met in the ring. But in the finals, he had to box the counterpunching American Ed Sanders, a talented amateur who seemed to have a future as a pro fighter.[5] Patterson sat at ringside to cheer on his fellow American Olympian. He watched as Johansson rather shamelessly ran from Sanders in the ring. The crowd hooted its disapproval, and the referee warned Johansson for failing to fight. But Ingo continued to try to evade Sanders. Finally, the referee ended the match and disqualified Johansson. Under normal circumstances, the loser of the championship round would have received the silver medal. But because of the disqualification, the Olympic committee declined to give it to Johansson. The other Swedish boxers did nothing to disguise their disgust at their teammate. Floyd, the patriotic American boxer, could not fathom what he'd just witnessed. To his mind, an Olympic boxer was a representative of his nation. How could Johansson have let down his country this way? Floyd was certain that Johansson had performed the way he did because he was scared of Sanders.

But once he became a pro immediately after the Helsinki games, Johansson redeemed himself somewhat to European boxing fans as he notched win after win. His strong right hand grew even more effective, becoming one of the most devastating right-hand punches heavyweight boxing has ever known. Most of his ring opponents never saw it coming and never had a chance to react. Except for that one lightning-fast punch, he had no ring speed. In fact, he looked rather awkward when he fought. His jab was substandard, but Johansson felt no need to improve it, since all his moves were subservient to his nearly supernatural — at least in Ingo's mind — right hand. Johansson just let it fly, investing full faith in the punch to the exclusion of almost everything else in terms of technique. Eventually it even gained a name. It flew with the power of lightning and thunder, which came out as *toonder* when Johansson pronounced it with his Swedish accent.

Floyd discounted the mystique that Ahlquist and Johansson built up around the toonder. What kind of malarkey was that? A punch so fast it couldn't be seen? A punch that supposedly acted on its own, striking without Johansson even knowing he was throwing it? Ridiculous. "I don't want to hear about Johansson's right hand," Patterson told Al Buck of the *New York Post*. "I wouldn't want to be watching the right and get knocked out by a left hook."[6] The more Patterson thought about the fear he'd seen in Johansson's eyes in Helsinki and the absurd legend that had been built up around his right hand, the less respect he felt for the Swedish challenger. As the bout approached, Patterson felt himself getting bored and losing enthusiasm for the fight.

The people surrounding Floyd had no idea what was going through his mind; as often was the case, he kept his thoughts buried within himself. To boxing writers he looked sharp and seemed to have an appropriate mental edge. But deep down, Patterson just wanted to get the fight over and move on to the next one. He and his entourage motored from his camp in New Jersey to Manhattan, where he put up at the Edison Hotel. The weigh-in for the fight occurred on a rainy June 25 across town at the Commodore Hotel. With dozens of sportswriters looking on, Patterson tipped the scales at 182 pounds; Johansson, at 196 pounds. Patterson didn't dawdle afterward to talk to the press. He changed into his street clothes and hurried out to a waiting car, Cus D'Amato, Dan Florio, and the other members of his party trailing him. "Drive downtown on Third Avenue," Patterson said, "and then go east on Fourth Street."

"What's this?" D'Amato said.

"I'm late now."

"Late for what?"

"The graduation."[7]

Patterson had made it a point to return to the PS 614 graduation ever since he had received his own diploma from the school for troubled kids. He hadn't missed a single ceremony, and he wasn't going to miss that day's, never mind that he was scheduled that night to face the toughest opponent yet to challenge him for his heavyweight crown. The ceremony had already begun by the time Patterson rushed into the school. But he was able to present the Floyd Patterson Trophy for sportsmanship, and he went through the lunch line with the other boys — the principal ensured he received an extra carton of milk.

After that, the entourage returned to the Edison, where word awaited them that the rain had forced the promoters to delay the outdoor fight at Yankee Stadium by a day. Patterson, more anxious than ever to get the fight into the record book, felt deflated. It rained the next day as well, letting up just an hour before the evening of fights was set to begin. Everything was drenched in the famed stadium, and the air was muggy, but the promoters decided not to delay again. Promoter Bill Rosensohn had Yankee Stadium set up to accommodate 80,000 spectators. Seats were expensive, too, with ringside going for $100 a pop. But just 21,961 people braved the humid night. After arriving in the Bronx and getting to his dressing room in the soggy House That Ruth Built, Patterson still felt bored, missing his usual prefight edge.

Johansson was in an entirely different state of mind.

He had little respect for Patterson as a champion, outside of the difficulty Patterson presented with his unorthodox peek-a-boo style and his hand speed. Johansson believed that Patterson was no more than an overachieving light-heavyweight. Ingo disdained Patterson for so seldom defending his crown and for the quality of his challengers, and he could not fathom that the heavyweight champion of the world allowed himself to be knocked down as much as Patterson did. If other fighters could floor Floyd, so could Johansson. And his toonder was much more powerful than any weapon Patterson's other challengers possessed. After watching Patterson fight London in Indianapolis, Johansson told Ahlquist in private that he could knock out the champion of the world. Ahlquist thought the same thing but told Johansson not to mention a word of it to anyone. It was their little secret to keep.

And the secret remained a secret. Certainly no one in the press picked up on it. Jimmy Cannon suggested that the United Nations should step in to prevent Patterson from slaughtering Johansson, a fighter he considered no better than Brian London, Pete Rademacher, or Roy Harris. Johansson discounted whatever Cannon and the rest of the American press had to say about him. He believed the writers were unfriendly to him because he refused to bow down to Americans and their belief that he didn't train with the seriousness the writers thought worthy of a world champion. Johansson would read accounts of his frolicking with Birgit Lundgren in a pool or dancing in New York City nightclubs and shake his head. The American press simply didn't understand him or his ways. He had been confident at the weigh-in, and he was confident, relaxed, and cheerful on the night of the fight.

In the makeshift canvas-walled dressing room set up for Johansson beneath the boxing stage,[8] he put on his trunks and listened while Dan Florio's brother, Nick, representing the Patterson camp, complained that Johansson's beltline was too high. Whitey Bimstein dismissed the complaint and sent Floyd's man packing. It was the typical sort of sniping that went on before boxing matches. When the time came, Johansson climbed into the ring to enthusiastic applause, which surprised him, given what he'd read about himself in the papers. When Patterson, as champion, entered the ring, Johansson noticed that the applause was scarcely, if any, greater than he himself had received. Perhaps it was an omen.

Referee Ruby Goldstein called the two fighters to the center of the ring and recited the rules of the fight. Johansson didn't listen. He was too busy testing his footing on the ring's odd canvas-covered foam rubber mat. Patterson stood head bowed, looking at Johansson's shuffling feet. By this point in his career, Floyd avoided stare-downs with his adversaries. In fact, he could not even bring himself to look them in the eye in the moments leading up to the first round. How could he be expected to demolish another fighter after he'd seen the light in his eyes?

Watching from the press seats was a toupeed attorney from Brooklyn who'd given up practicing law in order to forge a most unlikely career as a sports broadcaster. Howard Cosell was making his debut anchoring an ABC Radio Network broadcast of a heavyweight championship fight to a national audience. Five years earlier, Cosell had been a complete boxing novice. But then he'd been introduced to Cus D'Amato through W. C. Heinz, whom Cosell regarded as the best boxing writer he'd ever read. Thus began Cosell's association with prizefighting. By 1959, Cosell counted D'Amato and Patterson among his friends: "I became absorbed with Floyd — with his personal life, his softness, both of manner and voice, the way he would express interest in a variety of things — religion, family, hobbies. He converted to Catholicism and seemed utterly at peace with himself. He was that way then as a fighter. 'If Cus says I can win, then I can win,' he would say."[9] Cosell spent hours with D'Amato and Patterson at their training camps and at the Gramercy Gym, and though he had yet to broadcast a fight live, he covered many of Patterson's bouts as an ABC sports reporter, including Floyd's triumph over Archie Moore in Chicago.

Though he liked both fighter and manager, Cosell found himself mystified by their ways, including the crude conditions under which Patterson trained. The Gramercy was always rundown, but when he saw the primitive, frigid jockey room in which D'Amato had set up Floyd for training at Sportsman's Park in Chicago for the Moore fight, Cosell thought to himself that enough was enough: Cus should have provided Floyd better facilities for a championship bout. But he knew D'Amato would always keep things primal, at least as far as training was concerned. At other times, Cus could be very generous. After Patterson won the heavyweight title, D'Amato showed up at Cosell's apartment to present Cosell with a hundred-year-old bottle of Armagnac, to thank the sportscaster for his support. The gesture indicated just how tight the three men had become.

United Artists and the Mirisch Company sponsored the ABC radio broadcast to promote the movie *The Horse Soldiers*, which starred William Holden and John Wayne. The Duke was Patterson's favorite actor: "Every picture I've ever seen him in I've liked him, because he's always the good guy, cleaning up the town or something."[10] As part of the promotion, Wayne and Holden were positioned at ringside to work the broadcast with Cosell and ABC announcer Les Keiter. Holden confidently told Cosell that Johansson would beat Patterson. Cosell laughed at him.

The moment finally arrived. Patterson raised his gaze from Johansson's feet after Goldstein finished his instructions. He stepped back to his corner, accepting the advice D'Amato and Florio had to offer, uncertain as to how this drama would play out. In his corner, Johansson felt more self-assured than ever, anxious to end the fight as soon as possible. The bell rang, and the two fighters moved forward to begin their battle.

Early on, Johansson found Patterson to be vulnerable, particularly to both straight lefts and left hooks. Nothing impressed him about the vaunted Patterson speed when the champ fought from the outside. But when Patterson stepped into the pocket to fight up close, it was a different story. Then Patterson proved elusive. "You got a smell of him but no more," Johansson said. Still, Johansson was able to score, and Johansson became convinced that Patterson couldn't punch — "he was of too frail a caliber." When he went to his corner at the end of the first round, Ingo told his cornermen, "The whole thing is shaping out."[11]

Floyd saw things differently. He felt no intimidation at all from Johansson during the first round. He was particularly surprised by Johansson's anemic jabs, all ninety-six of them. Ingo flicked them as if he were attempting to ward off mosquitoes. They inflicted no real damage on the rare occasion they connected. But Floyd was even more surprised by Johansson's strange defensive tactics, in particular how he jumped backward to avoid punches. For a heavyweight, Ingo seemed light on his feet.

The flickering jabs and rapid retreats were actually part of Johansson's fight strategy. His goal was to confuse Patterson, and by the third round Ingo believed he was doing just that. As Patterson struggled to adjust to his opponent's odd boxing style, Ingo threw a sharp, short left hook, tagging Patterson, then followed it with a hard, straight right. Toonder caught Patterson smack in the face, and he was suddenly on the mat, what Floyd described to W. C. Heinz as being in the "black spot."[12] Patterson was stunned, both physically and mentally. After Floyd regained his footing, he decided he had to get aggressive to compensate for the knockdown. It was a mistake. Johansson dispatched Floyd into the black spot once again.

And then it happened once more. Then again. And again. It was a shocking spectacle: the heavyweight champion of the world went down over and over in just two minutes. Floyd was completely discombobulated, so much so that at one point he believed that *he* had knocked down Johansson when it was Floyd himself on the mat. In the swirl of confusion that followed, Patterson arose and attempted to find a neutral corner while starting to take out his mouthpiece, never realizing that referee Ruby Goldstein had signaled for the fight to resume. Ingo clobbered him with a right to the back of the head that sent Floyd sprawling one more time.

Floyd just couldn't believe it. He was being pummeled, bulled around the ring, and he couldn't seem to do anything about it. After the fourth knockdown, he looked directly into the eyes of John Wayne. Embarrassment washed over him. The most famous movie star in the world had come all this way to watch him fight, and Floyd was letting him down. The characters Wayne played always seemed to find a way to overcome adversity and win. But Floyd was being humiliated, losing in front of hometown fans. John Wayne would never allow something like that to happen. That the eyes of the Duke were on him made the thrashing sting all the worse.

With a minute left in the third round and after Patterson suffered a jaw-dropping *seven* knockdowns, Goldstein stepped between the fighters, waved his hands, and awarded Ingo a technical knockout — and the title of heavyweight champion of the world. Johansson and his famed punch made believers of many people that night. Columnist John Lardner looked around at the thousands of fans in Yankee Stadium and surmised they'd become Ingo and toonder converts. "Never before has a prizefight been so completely identified with one symbol, a thoroughly advertised right hand," Lardner said. "Best right-hand punch I ever saw," said Rocky Marciano, who was at ringside. "Quite a sock," said former champ Jack Dempsey, also at ringside.[13] Cosell hustled into the ring. He found D'Amato and placed his microphone in front of him. D'Amato, placidly confident, said, "Floyd Patterson will become the first heavyweight champion ever to regain his title."[14]

But Floyd was hearing other things. Patterson had not even reached the dressing room yet when he found himself surrounded by hostile fans. He saw a man with a big smile who shouted to another, "See, I told you. This guy can't fight." Among the friends, family, and boxing officials waiting in the dressing room was a member of the New York State Athletic Commission, who was laughing out loud. When he spotted Dan Florio coming through the door with Patterson, he said, "So your boy finally got it!" Florio loosened his grip on Floyd's arm and started for the official, but Buster Watson interceded before blows could be exchanged.[15] Floyd's handlers quickly cleared the crowd out, and Floyd had a few moments to try to make sense of what had just happened. He felt numb. He understood that he was no longer champion of the world, but he couldn't grasp why. He didn't bother to shower. "Soap and water wouldn't wash away what had happened," he said.[16]

Had it been possible, Patterson would have kept that dressing room door closed. But he couldn't do that. He still had to admit reporters for the traditional postfight question-and-answer session. Though Patterson was not a man who favored hats, he asked to borrow Watson's — as if pulling the brim down over his eyes would prevent reporters from seeing his pain. It was a vain tactic. His sorrow was all too apparent. Once the door opened, D'Amato took charge. "We never criticize a referee," he said when asked if Goldstein had stopped the fight too soon, but he added, "I do feel, though, that when the fight was stopped, Floyd was beginning to pull out of it. But in all fairness, we could not blame the referee for ending it." He said the devastation began with a left hook followed by a looping right that came out of nowhere. "It was a bolt out of the blue," D'Amato said. "Floyd never saw it coming, so he can't describe it. But I did. It hit him flush and high on the face."[17]

Patterson, though feeling humiliated by the loss, managed some humor. When asked if the Johansson right was the hardest punch he'd ever taken, he said, "Evidently so." But the dethroned champion felt "already drowned" deep inside. He really didn't have anything else to say to the reporters. So it was back to D'Amato, who said that yes, of course Patterson would exercise the return-bout clause in the fight contract. "Where and when . . . well, we'll have to see about that."[18]

Johansson suddenly appeared in Floyd's dressing room, escorted by police officers. The new world champion shook hands with the man he had just deposed. The handshake was sincere, but not a word was spoken between the two men. Then Ingo departed to celebrate his new crown; Patterson, to mourn all that he'd lost. Floyd was twenty-four years old, and the most important thing in the world to him had just been whisked away. Was there any way that he could get it back?

9

Not the Time to Quit

ONCE HE RETURNED home, Floyd found some solitude during the dark hours after the fight. It was late at night, but he remained awake, mentally replaying everything that had happened in Yankee Stadium, chastising himself as he pondered all the people across America he'd let down. He was also thinking about his immediate family. He now had another daughter, Trina, to go along with his first daughter, Seneca, and his wife, Sandra. It was clear by now that Floyd was not a man to put his family first in terms of emotional commitment — his career took center stage — but he was not one to neglect them financially. He knew his wife and two small daughters depended on him. In addition, he knew that millions of African Americans had placed their faith in him, hoping he would have a long run as heavyweight champ, maybe even prove to be the next Joe Louis. That dream was shattered now.

After dawn, Patterson finally made it to bed. He awakened a few hours later to a blood-soaked pillow. Sandra drove him to see an ear, nose, and throat specialist, who diagnosed a punctured eardrum, a painful souvenir of Johansson's power punches. Back at home, Patterson went straight to the den and turned on the TV. He stared at it without seeing what was on the screen.

But Sandra was not content to let things lie. Striding into the room, she turned the set off and suggested that Patterson consider retiring from the ring. Floyd could not believe what he'd heard. No, he said, not after just this one defeat. But Sandra, witnessing the battering he'd taken and seeing how morose he was now, asserted that it wasn't necessary for him to continue. The family had plenty of money for the time being, she argued, and she could find a job if finances grew tight. Floyd would have none of it. "Definitely," he said, "this is not the time to quit."[1] He owed it to himself and the fans to fight again.

Their conversation ended there. But the issue was far from resolved. The endless training camps, the travel, all that time Patterson spent away from home — it had taken a toll on the Patterson family.

In the days after the Johansson fight, Floyd went free-falling into darkness. He remained holed up in his house, drapes drawn, lights off. For hours at a time, he lay on the couch and stared at the ceiling while the TV droned unheeded. He couldn't sleep — Floyd, the man who could doze off anywhere, anytime, under any circumstances. His children wondered if their daddy was sick. Maybe he was. He wallowed in despair, haunted by the memory of John Wayne's eyes.

The night of the fight, Howard Cosell had gone home to find his thirteen-year-old daughter, Jill, still up, weeping over Floyd's defeat. She ended up crying all night. Many Americans shared Jill Cosell's sentiments in the following days. But many others did not. In fact, most of the world seemed to be celebrating Patterson's dethronement. It wasn't just the big-city writers who regularly covered boxing who weighed in on what happened at Yankee Stadium that night, taking their jabs in subtle and sometimes not-so-subtle ways. In Florence, South Carolina, local columnist Ernie Prevatte hailed Johansson as a boxer who could give boxing a big boost in the United States. "He's an exciting fighter with a powerful punch and from every indication will be a fighting champion."[2] The implication was that Patterson was not a "fighting champion," that he avoided tough challengers, didn't fight often enough. Older boxers offered their opinions as well. Former heavyweight champion Gene Tunney, who had never proved to be shy when given an opportunity to criticize Patterson, said, "I always considered Patterson a built up novice, but this Johansson, he is a real fighter."[3] Tunney added that he personally was glad Johansson had won.

The first reporter to visit Patterson during these dark days was Milton Gross from the *New York Post.* "There was not a visible sign of the beating he had taken on his face," Gross said. "But there was a subdued sadness in his eyes and in his voice."[4] Patterson told Gross he felt as if he were caught up in some sort of dreadful nonreality. He wondered if he'd ever been heavyweight champion at all, or was it just something he dreamed. He then made a curious suggestion: Floyd would talk more, if that's what Gross wanted, or, if he'd rather, they could just sit quietly in the house Floyd now referred to as a funeral parlor.

Cus D'Amato, fretting about Patterson's deepening depression, asked Cosell to drive to Rockville Centre to cheer Floyd up. Cosell immediately agreed and, with a spark of inspiration, suggested taking Jackie Robinson along. D'Amato thought that was a splendid idea and called Floyd to set up the visit. At 9:00 A.M. the next day, Howard Cosell and Jackie Robinson stood at Floyd's door.

No man stood higher in Patterson's estimation than Jackie Robinson. Patterson was a lifelong Dodgers fan. Even before Robinson was called up to the team in 1947, young Patterson kept scrapbooks devoted to the Dodgers. Once Robinson broke Major League Baseball's color barrier, he stood next to Joe Louis at the very top of Patterson's pantheon of heroes. Robinson comported himself with dignity and strength, a polite man of virtue who commanded respect. There was no small amount of abuse hurled Robinson's way as the first African American to play in the big leagues since the 1800s, yet he withstood it and proved that a black man could be a standout player in Major League Baseball. Robinson's pride and poise inspired Floyd, and the ballplayer once nicknamed the Colored Comet was the perfect person to minister to him during the bleak hours that followed his defeat. But for a time after Robinson and Cosell arrived at the Patterson house, it appeared that they might not get beyond the front door.

"From the outside it looked unoccupied," Cosell said. "All the blinds were drawn. We rang, and rang again. And again. Finally Sandra appeared and let us in. Floyd . . . tried to avoid looking us in the eye . . . It was as if he were sitting in that little hole in the subway all over again."[5]

Robinson and Patterson discussed comebacks. Robinson outlined his own and suggested that Floyd had youth on his side. To Cosell, Floyd seemed to perk up. Robinson and Patterson's friendship was cemented that day. From that afternoon onward, whenever Robinson called for his help, Floyd would be there for him. "I always get sort of choked up," Robinson would say, "when I try to express how I feel about him."[6]

Although Cosell believed that Patterson felt better after the visit, Floyd's days of anguish were far from over. As each one slowly slid by, D'Amato and Dan Florio made stops at the house to assure Floyd that he'd get a rematch — negotiations already were under way — and that they believed Floyd would show the world that Ingo was no champion, that what had happened at Yankee Stadium was a fluke. But such assurances didn't make things better. What did clear the gloomy clouds away — at least for a few days — came from an unexpected source. Archie Moore sent Patterson a letter that was kind and encouraging yet blunt:

Dear Floyd,

The first bout is over. I know how you must feel. I hope you don't continue to feel bad. The same thing has happened to many great fighters. Of course, I hated to lose to you, and fate decreed it that way. Fate does strange-seeming things. If you are a believer in things that happen, happen for the best, listen to this and you can find your way out of a seeming tunnel.

First, Johansson was not so great. You fought a stupid battle. Look at the film. Evaluate it. Never once did you lead with a jab. All you did was move your feet and try to leap toward him. Now, this man was not like London. He could bang a little. You gave absolutely no respect to your opposition.

But if he had been the banger the press said he was, he would have put you away with the left hook he hit you with your back turned. Well, if you concentrate on your jab and move around this guy, you will be the first one to regain the crown. You can do it.

Your friend, Archie Moore[7]

Of course Moore was right. There was nothing mystical about Johansson and his toonder. It was just that fighter after fighter had made the same mistake with Johansson that Patterson had made: they all fought stupid fights, allowing Johansson to lure them into his style of boxing. That was how Ingo wound up undefeated and that was how he wound up with Patterson's title.

Patterson put Moore's letter down and looked up at a golden crown D'Amato had presented to him when Floyd had won the championship. Floyd lifted it from the mantel and detached it from its base. Then he hid it out of sight. He decided he was not entitled to have it on display while Johansson held the title. If Patterson could win back the championship, the crown would see the light of day once again. For the first time in weeks, Floyd believed he had a chance to reclaim it. Sportswriters speculated that a rematch could occur as early as September 1960, just three months after their first bout. Patterson's experiences with D'Amato's complicated and protracted fight negotiations had taught him it would be much later than that. But that it was being discussed already meant that an opportunity for redemption awaited him.

Many people hoped there would be no redemption for Floyd Patterson. By the millions, Americans were paying money to watch the Johansson fight at local movie houses. The showings seemed especially popular in the South, where one theater promoted the film as footage of the most exciting fight in history. The images of the Swede's humiliation of the African American champion no doubt appealed to the segregationist element in the region, as did the comments of Newspaper Enterprise Association (NEA) writer Harry Grayson, who called Patterson the "most overrated and overprotected fighter ever to wear the heavyweight crown" and "the greatest hoax since the Cardiff Giant."[8] Grayson's column, like many NEA features, appeared regularly in small-town dailies across America, including the South. Sometimes the exuberant celebration of Johansson's win had an ugly undertone. In one small southern town, the owner of a movie house exhibiting the fight footage advertised it with a sign portraying a triumphant white boxer standing over a fallen black boxer, a racial caricature featuring exaggerated white lips.[9]

The celebration of Johansson's victory in the rest of the United States seems suspect as well. He seemed to be on everyone's broadcast, from

Ed Sullivan's to Jackie Gleason's to Dinah Shore's, sometimes show-ing off his ability to sing. News magazine photographers mobbed Ingo, snapping pictures of the champ with the striking Birgit Lundgren, es-pecially relishing opportunities to shoot her poolside clad in a bikini. Ingo found himself cast with Alan Ladd, Sidney Poitier, James Darren, and Mort Sahl in a Korean War drama called *All the Young Men* — and he sang in the now largely forgotten movie.[10] Ingo was named athlete of the year in a poll conducted by the Associated Press, beating out Johnny Unitas, who had just led the Baltimore Colts to their second consecutive NFL championship. Johansson's big year was topped off when *Sports Illustrated* named him its "Sportsman of the Year."[11]

Americans love it when underdogs emerge victorious. But only a naive observer could conclude that the adoration Johansson received during the last half of 1959 was based entirely on his athletic prow-ess. When Patterson, an underdog, knocked out Archie Moore to become heavyweight champion in 1956, the parade of opportunities made available to him were slight compared to what Johansson re-ceived. Hollywood didn't come seeking Floyd to sing in the movies. Had it been a Zora Folley, an Eddie Machen, a Cleveland "Big Cat" Wil-liams, or any other African American boxer who had floored Patterson seven times in one round, he would not have been pursued by gos-sip columnists and magazine photographers the way Johansson was. It's clear that race played a large role in Johansson's celebrity. Reading between the lines, one can detect that writers of a certain age consid-ered Jack Dempsey the last great white champion. As for Gene Tunney, Max Schmeling, Jack Sharkey, Primo Carnera, Max Baer, and James J. Braddock, none of them held the title long enough to be considered great. Marciano? Well, he was Italian American and perhaps too swar-thy. But Dempsey was a solidly white American. And columnists like the NEA's Harry Grayson went out of their way to liken Johansson to Dempsey. Dempsey was the last champion to knock down a challenger seven times in a round, so it was easy for writers to rationalize a bridge between the young Viking and the Manassa Mauler, who refused to fight black contenders once he became champion in 1919.[12]

Floyd came out of what he called his black mood as he was sitting in his darkened den one night. In the late 1950s, TV stations signed off after airing a late, late movie. The signoff involved the playing of "The Star-Spangled Banner." When the national anthem ended, the TV was reduced to a slowly fading gray dot and soft hissing from the speaker. Floyd would later say that as he watched that dot, he thought about a girl he'd once met who was dying of leukemia. He reflected on how lucky he was in comparison to the stricken girl and her family. He arose from the couch and stepped over to a window, where he watched the dawn. He decided it was time to get on with his life — and win back his title.

That night he and Sandra went to a movie — not in his comfortable suburb, but in the city, the place where he'd lost his title. He'd lost track of just how many weeks had passed by since that disastrous night at Yankee Stadium. But summer had given away to the chill of autumn when he decided he was ready to begin training again. He was anxious to get started. Floyd would prepare for the Johansson rematch fired by an emotion foreign to him. He *hated* the new heavyweight champion of the world, and he planned to take that hatred into the ring with him.

It would take six days short of a full calendar year before the rematch took place — and then only after weeks of scandalous newspaper headlines about D'Amato's involvement with organized crime. At the time, Cus credited himself with breaking the back of the International Boxing Club. In fact, the IBC was dissolved in January 1959 under orders of the US Supreme Court, and its demise had little, if anything, to do with D'Amato's war against it. The IBC died under the weight of the federal Sherman Antitrust Act. Prosecutors were successful in sending the IBC's leaders to prison without D'Amato's ever once providing testimony to a grand jury or otherwise aiding the government, even though other boxing managers did so.[13] In fact, investigators discovered that D'Amato privately took loans of $15,000 and $5,000 from the IBC's Jim Norris in 1956, the year Patterson won the championship.

D'Amato's other business dealings in the mid to late 1950s turned out to be scarcely pure. D'Amato certainly knew that Bill Rosensohn had a gambling habit when Cus brought him in as a promoter. Often in debt, Rosensohn did not have the cash on hand needed for the guarantees for the first fight with Johansson. He turned to a friendly bookie for advice. The bookie referred Rosensohn to Genovese crime family leader Anthony "Fat Tony" Salerno. (Salerno, though later infamous, was virtually unknown to law enforcement at the time.)

Rosensohn managed to cut a deal for Salerno to provide the up-front money for the Johansson fight in exchange for a share of the profits. One problem existed: a friend of D'Amato's named Charley Black already was under contract to receive 50 percent of the net. Black and D'Amato's relationship went back to their boyhood days in the Bronx. Friendship aside, Black was valuable to D'Amato because Black was himself a gangster, a convicted loan shark with deep under-world connections. Black had secretly been involved in the underside of D'Amato's dealings as far back as the 1958 fight with Cut 'n Shoot Harris. For reasons never clear, Black received 50 percent of the profit from that fight. A clause in the fight contract required Harris, if he won, to take on Black as his manager. Black relinquished his claim to any percentage of the first Johansson fight in exchange for one-third ownership of Rosensohn's promotion company. Salerno himself took another third of the company for the money he gave Rosensohn.

All of this placed D'Amato in a bad light when it became public. The man who cast himself as the champion to clean up boxing was now shown to have consorted with two bigtime gamblers (Rosensohn and Black) and a shadowy Mafia figure (Fat Tony Salerno). It was this scandal of D'Amato's own making that prompted US senator Estes Kefauver, a Tennessee Democrat famous for his organized crime in-vestigations, to direct his subcommittee toward prizefighting in Sep-tember 1959. In addition, a New York State grand jury began hearing testimony about possible wrongdoing in boxing. Once the newspaper stories began to break, Johansson's team demanded a full financial ac-counting of the first fight before it agreed to move forward with ne-gotiations for the second. Finally, the New York State Athletic Com-mission admonished D'Amato for attempting to wrest control of the heavyweight division by acting as both manager and promoter. The commission also attempted to revoke D'Amato's manager's license, but D'Amato played a gambit that ultimately blocked the commission from doing so: he purposely had not renewed his license application. Subse-quent court decisions held that a license that had expired could not be revoked.

D'Amato left New York for Puerto Rico, where he stayed under an

assumed name. He refused to testify before the grand jury or the Kefauver Committee. "What did D'Amato know and when did he know
it?" asked author Montieth Illingworth. "Perhaps he didn't conspire
to drive Rosensohn to Salerno and Black. Maybe Rosensohn was just
a loose cannon moved by his own inexperience, bad judgment, and
greed. D'Amato apparently never discussed the details of what happened with anyone. It's hard to believe, however, that a man so obsessed with control would not have known about the Salerno-Black
connection."[14] José Torres, at the time making his way up the professional boxing ranks to become D'Amato's next contender, later agreed
with Illingworth's assessment.

As the legal and regulatory drama played out in the newspapers,
Patterson began to train for his rematch with Johansson, scheduled
for June 20, 1960. But he was not blind to what was being reported in
the newspapers. Patterson's distrust of D'Amato, which had its roots in
Cus's mishandling of the London fight contracts, continued to grow,
even as he prepped hard to fight Johansson again.

Floyd felt good getting back in shape after all those days on the couch.
He thrived in the outdoors and seclusion at his upstate New York camp
near Roaring Brook. Unfortunately, he couldn't train there for long.
The facility closed once the weather turned frosty. So he relocated to
a gym in Westport, Connecticut, which at first seemed to be a work-
able site. But word of his choice for a training headquarters spawned
local newspaper interest in D'Amato's behind-the-scenes shenanigans.
Patterson picked up the Westport daily paper and read the headline:
BOXING GANGSTERS INVADE WESTPORT. That was it for him. He departed the community before the day was out.

Patterson and his entourage moved thirty miles inland to Newtown
and set up shop in the out-of-business LaRonde roadhouse, owned by
the once-famous bandleader Enric Madriguera. The dance floor became the gym, furnished overnight with speedbags, heavy bags, mirrors for shadowboxing, and exercise mats. Patterson engaged himself
in a tough conditioning routine that involved chopping wood, running, and repeating heavy-bag drills. But he was not happy with his
surroundings. When Howard Cosell and his wife, Emmy, came calling,
he vented. Patterson told Cosell: "Nothing but rats. I complained to the

owner, and he said there were no rats in the house. I got a gun, shot three rats, and hung them up on the line in front of the house where he lives."[15]

Rats weren't Floyd's only worry. He was concerned about being what he called glove shy, whether fear of being knocked out again would hinder his ability to box effectively. He began sparring in the rat-infested roadhouse, and while that went well, sparring was just sparring. He needed to step up the challenge. So Floyd asked D'Amato, back from Puerto Rico and acting as an adviser, to arrange a two-week exhibition tour in Canada. Patterson fought ten times, and he felt completely satisfied that whatever glove shyness he might have had had dissipated by the time he returned to camp.

Yet one thing still troubled Floyd. He couldn't bring himself to watch the film of the Johansson fight. Whenever Dan Florio suggested the time was right to take a look at it, Patterson would say, "Next week." And when next week arrived, Floyd would postpone it again. He just couldn't confront Johansson — either as an image on film or TV or as a real person.

But Johansson seemed to be everywhere. Word arrived at Patterson's camp that Ingo would be appearing in a TV adaptation of Ernest Hemingway's "The Killers." Patterson had no interest in watching it, just as he'd eschewed watching his foe when Johansson sang with Dinah Shore on her popular TV show. Floyd assumed the other members of his camp would join him in avoiding the telecast. But then, as he and some others were playing cards, Patterson heard a Swedish voice coming from the TV set in an adjacent room. Patterson walked into the room to find his younger brother, Raymond, who had recently joined Buster Watson and Dan Florio in Patterson's training corps, taking in the made-for-TV movie.

Floyd thought about leaving, but then plopped down next to his brother. At first he kept his head bowed, staring at the floor, listening to Johansson's smooth delivery. Then, finally, he made himself look at the screen. And there Floyd saw, in stark shades of gray, the man who had taken so much from him, proving that he could be a decent-enough actor. Patterson pondered why he had avoided Johansson for so long. It wasn't fear, he determined. No, it was shame. And hate.

In fact, hatred filled his mind. "Some people think you have to hate to be a champion fighter," Patterson said later. "I have never hated an opponent except once. That was Ingemar, between the first and second fight. I hated him for a whole year, not because he beat me the first time, but because of his boasting on the Ed Sullivan program."[16] Hatred alone, however, was not going to get the job done against Johansson. Dan Florio decided it was time for Floyd to reassess his fighting style. In the makeshift gym, he told Patterson to assume his characteristic peek-a-boo stance. Patterson did as instructed, hands high on his head, body squared up to Florio's. Florio placed his hands on Patterson's shoulders and pushed. Floyd nearly fell down.

"You see?" Florio said. "You're not right. You got bad balance. Let's go back to the book. Left foot out front, angle forty-five degrees. Left hand out front, angle forty-five degrees. Right hand straight up and down. Now you got leverage. The jab got to come better. Now try it and see what you think."[17]

Patterson liked it. Fighting out of a conventional stance became the focus of the remainder of the training camp, with Florio shouting at Patterson every time Floyd strayed.

Visitors to Floyd's camp found a remade man with a remade boxing style. They liked what they saw. The license-less D'Amato was as absent as the black despair Patterson had suffered through, prevented from working either as a manager or a cornerman. Observers on the scene believed this to be a good turn of events. Floyd seemed more relaxed and confident with Cus in exile. In April, Patterson matter-of-factly told one reporter that he was his own manager now.[18] This was, within the context of the times, a shocking statement. Patterson confessed he still considered D'Amato a friend, and he said that he was now receiving some business advice from Julius November.[19] (November was a tough New York attorney who was best known publicly for his unsuccessful legal maneuvers to keep the New York Giants baseball team from moving to San Francisco.) But Patterson was also stating for the world that he was now his own man. Even greats like Joe Louis and Rocky Marciano had never boldly declared they were their own managers. Patterson's taking charge of his career was a landmark event in the evolution of black athletes. "You see," Floyd told famed New York columnist Jimmy Breslin, "I feel I'm mature now. It's like my weight.

It came naturally. I had no special program. I just grew to 190 and my neck went to size seventeen. The same with my attitude. I always used to know what I felt. I knew that, all right. But I had trouble expressing myself. Now I can do it. And I don't need anybody to do it for me . . . I'll fight anybody regardless of name or affiliations. I'm tired of arguments."[20]

It was not a clean break. Newspapers typically reported D'Amato to be Patterson's manager even after Floyd announced he was managing himself. Ever loquacious compared to the champ, D'Amato continued to be interviewed by sportswriters and seemed to speak for Patterson, even though he may not have spoken to Floyd for weeks. By this time, Julius November had more influence on Patterson than did D'Amato. It had been Cus who first brought November into Patterson's business dealings, but as time went on, November began to seem like he was D'Amato's rival. It was November who ultimately was winning Floyd's trust, not D'Amato. But November did not want anyone to assume he had become de facto manager. He told Breslin, "Don't get any incorrect ideas about the situation. Floyd Patterson is a client. And as a client he has his own mind. And let me tell you, this boy has his own mind."[21]

Patterson said, "When I talked to Cus about these terrible things which I had so much trouble understanding, as they came out one after the other, I just formed my own answer . . . 'How many agreements were there before that I didn't know about?'"[22]

D'Amato stayed away from Floyd's training camp in Newtown, but he telephoned once or twice a week. Floyd got on the phone only when he believed D'Amato had something important to tell him. Otherwise, the call was handled by Dan Florio. Shortly before the fight, D'Amato finally made an appearance at Newtown. But the relationship between mentor and protégé seemed strained. "In his early days," Red Smith said of the situation in 1960, "Patterson was brainwashed by Cus D'Amato. Today D'Amato is manager in only one sense: He still gets a cut of the purse."[23] Floyd's contractual obligations to Cus ensured that D'Amato would receive the manager's percentage of his ring earnings for the next few fights, even if D'Amato contributed little or nothing.

In addition to November, another lawyer was playing an increasingly important role in Patterson's professional life: Roy Cohn. Cohn was famous — some might say infamous — in 1960. He had become a darling of American conservatives for his work with the redbaiting US senator Joseph McCarthy, for his role in the Communist espionage convictions of Julius and Ethel Rosenberg, and for his work in bringing down Alger Hiss. He was a pugnacious foe to battle in the courtroom, yet he was a physically unimposing figure, no one you'd expect to find butting heads with promoters and matchmakers in the pro boxing demimonde.

Yet he was doing just that in 1960. He was the power behind Feature Sports Inc., which acquired Bill Rosensohn's promotion company after Rosensohn's connections with organized crime became public knowledge. With this, Cohn essentially became the promoter of the second Patterson-Johansson fight. Feature Sports turned out, like most of Cohn's business ventures, to be anything but ordinary. He installed his law partner as treasurer of the new organization and travel agent Bill Fugazy, who had known Cohn since their school days, as supervising director. But as with many Cohn-directed operations, contention soon ruled. Sometimes the principals resorted to fisticuffs to settle disputes. (From the sidelines, Cus D'Amato thought they were a terrible bunch, guilty of bringing a kind of Wall Street sleaziness to boxing, which to him was even worse than that associated with the likes of Fat Tony Salerno.)

Despite the dysfunction of his business practices, Cohn and his partners stood to make a good deal of money from Patterson-Johansson II. In addition to New York, cities desiring to host the fight included Los Angeles, Chicago, and Dallas, where American Football League founder and Dallas Texans owner Lamar Hunt wanted to stage it at the Cotton Bowl. In the end, New York won out, with the match set to take place at the Polo Grounds.

In May 1960 Feature Sports announced it had hired Joe Louis as a consultant for the Johansson rematch. One of his duties was to advise Floyd on how to avoid the mistakes he made in the first fight. The legend that Johansson was the next Dempsey still flourished, with Johansson a heavy favorite to demolish Floyd. Perhaps if Patterson received some guidance from the great Louis, fans might think the match could turn out to be closer. It seems that Feature Sports took Louis on for the Louis name more than any precise services the ex-champ could provide, and Louis, always in need of money, was more than happy with the arrangement. As a publicity stunt, it worked. Louis's visit to Newtown generated headlines. But that visit turned out to be more than just PR. "I have been studying the pictures of the first fight between Johansson and Patterson," Louis said, "and I think I have found something. I think I can show Floyd how to win."[24] Louis did, in fact, lay out a sound blueprint for Patterson: Floyd should crowd Johansson at every opportunity, never allow Ingo a chance to throw a big right-hand punch. It was the only way to beat a heavy hitter, Louis believed. Louis said Floyd should take Ingo to the ropes from the get-go and never let him escape. Louis also told Floyd not to wait any longer before he saw the film of the first Johansson fight.

Floyd took these words to heart, in spite of the fear he felt about watching it, and the two champions viewed the film together. As the projector rattled and the black-and-white images flickered on the screen, Louis told Floyd that Ingo's power was overrated. He pointed out one of the knockdowns, which occurred when Johansson tagged Floyd directly on the nose. If Ingo was a true power-puncher, Floyd would have been knocked out. But Patterson was able to get back on his feet. Also, Louis thought Johansson's ring demeanor was that of an excited amateur, not a true pro, a flaw a seasoned boxer like Patterson could exploit. Finally, Louis told Floyd that referee Ruby Goldstein had committed crucial errors. Louis recommended that Floyd demand a different ref for the next fight. Floyd agreed to insist on a change. Louis left Patterson's training camp after predicting to the press that Floyd would become the first boxer ever to regain the heavyweight championship.

If Ingemar Johansson held much concern about the outcome of the bout, he didn't show it. Not even on the night before the fight, a time when fighters typically retreat from all but necessary contact with the outside world to focus on what is to come the next day. The evening of June 19, Johansson showed up at 229 West Fifty-Third Street at ten o'clock, entered through the stage door of the CBS studio located there, and basked in the TV lights of the hugely popular quiz show *What's My Line?* He didn't make much of an attempt to fool the show's panelists about his real identity. "I'll go to bed right after this," he said afterward.

"If I go to sleep too early I can't sleep very well. Anyway, this is relaxing to me. It's fun." When asked how he felt going into the fight, he said simply, "I feel strong."

Birgit Lundgren was at Johansson's side. How did she feel? "I feel nothing," she said. With that, the glitter couple of the moment climbed into the Cadillac awaiting them and sped away into the New York night.[25]

Patterson, meanwhile, spent some of that evening with Howard Cosell, taping the prefight show. Cosell saw fury in Floyd as Patterson predicted he would beat the new champ with left hooks. Patterson had plenty to seethe about. One of the press reports out of Grossinger's, where Johansson had again been training, had quoted the new champion as saying he thought that Patterson was afraid of him. Johansson also dismissed Patterson as a mere gymnasium fighter. Patterson confronted the reporter who'd written the latter story and asked if Johansson really had said that. The reporter offered to show Patterson his notebook. Floyd demurred, but he'd been fuming since.

Floyd would need that curtness and meanness to do what had never been done. James J. Corbett, Bob Fitzsimmons, Jim Jeffries, Jack Dempsey, Max Schmeling, Joe Louis, Ezzard Charles, and Jersey Joe Walcott were all deposed or retired heavyweight champions who had attempted to reclaim their crowns. And all had failed. Would Floyd be able to accomplish what they'd been unable to do? Oddsmakers didn't think so. Bookies took bets with Patterson as an eight-to-five underdog.

As the gates opened to long lines on June 20, promoters expected around thirty thousand people to stream into the famed bathtub-shaped stadium, which was now dilapidated following years of poor maintenance. With ringside tickets going for $100 apiece, the box office take was projected to come in at around $750,000. In addition, 230 theaters were set up to carry the closed-circuit telecast of the rematch. Promoters estimated the fight could gross around $2 million and maybe as much as $3.5 million, with each fighter getting 35 percent of the gross.

Among the spectators who wormed their way up to the front was a stocky, balding, white-haired man in a black homburg who sat close to the ring apron. From Seat 1, Row 1, Section 20, Cus D'Amato would be able to clearly see as the fighters entered the ring. He had kept a low profile in the days leading up to tonight, fearing that the controversy that had sprung up around him following the first Johansson match and the conflict with the New York State Athletic Commission over his license might hurt ticket sales. D'Amato felt confident that Patterson was making progress and would win the rematch. "After the fight," he said, "I'll climb into the ring as the crowd acclaims Floyd Patterson as the first heavyweight champion to regain his title." Perhaps it was D'Amato's snaky logic, or perhaps it was simple rationalization, but he'd come to believe that it had been necessary for Patterson to lose to Johansson. He'd always promised Patterson that he would be the greatest champion in the history of the heavyweight ranks: "How could Floyd be the greatest champion unless he lost the crown and then regained it?"[26]

The Polo Grounds and the neighborhood surrounding it seemed as if they might turn into a battleground. The Eighth Avenue entrance was jammed with people, many of whom were shoving their way toward the ticket stand, when it was announced over the loudspeaker that all ten thousand upper-stand seats (going for $5 each) had been sold. Only thirty-five ticket takers were on hand to serve the people who did manage to get a ticket. Finally, the frustrated fans — both those who'd failed to get tickets and those with tickets who were upset with the slowness of the ticket takers — had had enough and a riot broke out. Two gates were broken down, and outraged fans desperate to see the fight attempted to scale the walls of the stadium. Within a few minutes, though, the two hundred New York City police officers on hand, aided by contract security forces, managed to get the unruly crowd under control.

Just prior to the opening bell, the Polo Grounds went surreal as fashion models passed out orchids and perfume samples to the women at ringside. To the men they distributed samples of Wash 'N Dri, "the miracle moist towelette." "This is what I call class, really class," said a woman upon receiving the perfume and orchid. "This is what's needed to bring people like us back to boxing."[27] The fedora-wearing gangsters who'd dominated boxing behind the scenes in previous years must have been stupefied.

The two fighters met at the center of the ring. For the first time, Floyd weighed 190 pounds going into a fight, 8 pounds heavier than he'd been when he first battled Johansson. All the new weight was muscle, giving Floyd an imposing presence. Patterson glanced up at Ingo and saw something that surprised him: fear. "I could see it in his eyes," Floyd said. "His eyes told me that he knew I meant business . . . He knew. He just knew."[28] When the bell rang, Floyd came out in a conventional stance instead of the peek-a-boo. This was no surprise. His intentions had been reported in the papers weeks before the fight. Yet Johansson was perplexed by the change. Patterson followed Joe Louis's advice and crowded Ingo from the beginning, while Ingo flicked jabs and awkwardly stepped backward to avoid Floyd's inside attack. But Floyd's punches were finding the mark. After just three minutes, Johansson's left eye was red and swollen.

In the second round, Johansson unleashed a heavy right that crashed into Patterson's jaw. The crowd roared its approval and delight when Patterson absorbed the blow and continued to throw down, fazed but unbroken. Patterson resumed his attacks after the brief setback. At times, Johansson looked defenseless against Floyd's speed — lightning besting toonder. Floyd effectively landed combinations of left hooks to the body followed almost immediately by left hooks to the head. He was able to slip many of Johansson's responding punches. Chris Schenkel, providing the commentary for TelePrompTer's film of the fight, said, "It's obvious Patterson's chances ride on his left hook. It's not only his best punch, but it is also forcing Johansson to use his best hand, his right, defensively."[29]

In the fifth round, Floyd stunned Ingo with a hard left hook to the body. Johansson flipped a couple of ineffective jabs in Patterson's direction, allowing his right hand to slip downward. Patterson immediately pounced on the opportunity. He smashed a left hook into the right side of Johansson's head and sent the man who'd taken his crown a year earlier tumbling to the floor. On his knees, Johansson gulped air while the referee counted to nine. Then Johansson rose to his feet, his eyes wide open, shock painted on his face. Floyd went into full attack mode—all the anger, all the hatred, all the resentment now on full display. He battered Johansson viciously, showing a side of himself that he'd never before revealed in the ring. A stunned Ingo could do nothing more than attempt to tie up Floyd in clinches, but the referee refused to allow Johansson to get away with it.

Then, with just over a minute left in the fifth round, Patterson struck Ingo squarely on the jaw with a picture-perfect left hook—one that boxing historians would marvel at for decades to come. Johansson went down like a stricken steer at a slaughterhouse. Even before he hit the canvas, it was clear he would not be able to get up. He lay there, completely out, one foot trembling. Patterson knew what he had accomplished with that blow. The man who'd suffered so much self-torture over the previous year could not contain himself. Floyd danced briefly in the neutral corner, electric with the knowledge that the title belonged to him once more. When the count was over, Patterson shouted, "I showed you!" to the naysaying press at their posts along the apron.

After that, he rushed to Johansson, who had yet to move except for that shaking foot. Patterson knelt, gave him a quick embrace, and promised him a rematch. But there was no way Johansson could have heard him. Cosell, who'd scurried into the ring, nabbed Patterson for an interview. Then the sportscaster turned and saw Johansson, still out, blood oozing from his mouth. Cosell became alarmed. "For God's sake, Whitey," he said to Whitey Bimstein, who had again worked as Johansson's cornerman, "is he dead?"

"The son of a bitch should be," Bimstein answered. "I told him to look out for the left hook."[30]

Cosell stared down at Johansson's twitching foot. He saw not a top-rank champion but a demolished, overmatched fighter. Patterson, who had spent months training with a burning loathing for Johansson, was staring at the fighter he'd just crushed. Floyd's jubilation from just moments earlier gave way to horror. With trainers and the ring doctor tending to him, Johansson spent four minutes stretched out on the canvas before he began to stir. Johansson was alive but far from well. Another three minutes followed with the deposed Swedish champ planted on his stool in his corner of the ring, oblivious to what was going on around him. Finally he was helped to his dressing room, where he remained unresponsive, though at least conscious. Patterson told author and *Sports Illustrated*'s pro sports dilettante George Plimpton that he resolved to never again inflict as much damage on another fighter as he had on Johansson at the Polo Grounds.[31]

Floyd's dominance in the fight suggests that he possessed a thorough confidence that he would defeat Johansson. But Floyd hadn't been at all sure that he would win. He even had a plan in place in case he lost. Two autos waited outside the Polo Grounds—one that would allow him to make a very public exit if he won, another that would whisk him away in stealth if he lost. Also, in the weeks leading up to the fight he had become obsessed with disguises and had employed the services of several makeup artists to create fake beards and mustaches. Floyd had them at the ready in his Polo Grounds dressing room. If he lost, he planned to disguise himself so he could flee the stadium unrecognized. But there would be no need for subterfuge on this occasion. Instead, the night was for celebrating.

Floyd was now the first man ever to win the heavyweight championship for a second time. The next morning, the new champ arrived at the postfight press conference beaming and feeling confident enough to take verbal jabs at the boxing writers who had predicted his annihilation at the hands of Johansson. Later, he rode in a parade in Brooklyn that snaked its way from Grand Army Plaza to Borough Hall, with the borough president, John Cashmore, seated beside him.

A few days after the fight, New York City mayor Robert F. Wagner Jr. declared World Championship Day for the city and, on the steps of City Hall, presented Floyd with an award. A two-hour parade took place in Harlem, where Patterson basked in the sort of adoration the African American community had earlier bestowed on Joe Louis and Sugar Ray Robinson. Jackie Robinson and Ed Sullivan cochaired a testimonial dinner for Patterson at the Commodore Hotel, with the proceeds going to the Wiltwyck School for Boys. Dinner guests ranged from government figures such as Mayor Wagner and Justice Justine Wise Polier to sports luminaries like retired Dodgers and Cardinals general manager Branch Rickey, the man who had integrated Major League Baseball by signing Jackie Robinson. Pope John XXIII sent a congratulatory telegram. The president of Ghana sent a ceremonial robe. Patterson also delivered a speech to a graduating class at his alma mater: "I'm proud to bring back the championship to America and to PS 614," he spoke into the microphone, a huge photograph of himself hanging behind him.[32]

But there was more. For the first time, Patterson began to admit that race was elemental in the contest. He told *Ebony* magazine that he believed he regained the championship for himself, his country, and his race. "Joe Louis," Patterson said, "did a lot for Negroes. He did more for our race than almost anybody. Every person, every Negro in boxing, is trying to get somewhere near the record set by Louis." That Louis backed Floyd in this contest stoked Patterson's sense of racial pride. "It was a victory for us!" proclaimed the *Ebony* editors.[33]

Finally, Floyd's victory was celebrated in verse by a self-styled poet then little known outside the world of amateur boxing. Like bards of old, he carried his poems in his head, ready to recite at the appropriate occasion, rather than write them down. This particular poem he delivered while performing sit-ups as the *New Yorker*'s A. J. Liebling scribbled the lines:

> You may talk about the Swede,
> You may talk about Rome,
> But Rockville Centre is Floyd Patterson's home.

> A lot of people say Floyd couldn't fight,
> But you should have seen him on that comeback night.

> He cut up his eyes, he mussed up his face,
> And that last left hook knocked his head out of place!

> A reporter asked: "Ingo, will a rematch be put on?"
> Johansson said: "Don't know. Might be postponed."

> If he would have stayed in Sweden,
> He wouldn't have taken that beatin'.

The poet's name was Cassius Marcellus Clay Jr.[34]

10

Standing at the Peak

F OR NOW, FLOYD was back on top of the world, and he lost little
time making a deal to give Johansson a rematch. After a contorted
process to work out the details, the rubber match in their series
was set for March 13, 1961, in Miami. Before Floyd began training in
earnest, he took time off to travel to Rome, where the American team
was competing in the 1960 Olympics. There he ran into Cassius Clay,
who had dazzled Olympic spectators with his boxing skills while winning the light-heavyweight gold medal. Clay was as proud of his Olympic win as Patterson had been of his own eight years earlier — maybe
even more so. Clay had not taken off his medal since he received it on
the victor's platform, wearing it even when sleeping.

While being interviewed by Earl Ruby of his hometown newspaper, the *Louisville Courier-Journal*, Clay spotted Patterson and said,
"Good Lord, there's the champ!"[1] Clay ran over to greet the recrowned
heavyweight king. Patterson was Clay's hero. It was Patterson who had
showed it was possible for a heavyweight to possess a middleweight's
hand speed and fluidity in the ring, and Clay was building his own
career around those qualities. After Clay saw Patterson's fight with
Brian London on TV, he became obsessed with winning the heavyweight championship someday. At one point, Clay had traveled to
Indianapolis with his father and brother, Rudolph Valentino Clay, to

seek out D'Amato, who was in the city with Patterson for an exhibition. Clay's father inquired whether D'Amato might consider managing his son Cassius, who was already showing a lot of promise as an amateur. D'Amato passed, but Clay did get to meet Patterson briefly.

Now in Rome, Patterson recognized the hyperanimated eighteen-year-old boxer with the medal around his neck and the nonstop mouth. "Hi, boy, how's your dad?" Patterson said. For the benefit of the reporters who had ambled up to the scene, Clay, who stood six feet, three inches, said, "Look, I'm three inches taller than him. When I fill out, I'll be bigger all around. That's something good to know. You see, I may have to fight him some day."

That same day, Clay stood in the Quonset hut that served as the dining hall, carrying on with a group of African American boxers and track athletes. Clay spied Patterson strolling through the building and said, "Watch this, I'm going to get this guy. Watch this!" As soon as Patterson reached Clay and the others, Clay jumped up on a table with a knife and fork and proclaimed to the heavyweight champion, "I'm having you next! I'm having you for dinner!"[2] Patterson laughed. From the beginning, he understood Clay's shtick in a way some later fighters never could.

While in Rome, Floyd took part in another meeting of significance, but this one included no levity whatsoever. Pope John XXIII had granted him an audience. It was an important moment in his life as a Catholic, and Floyd was nervous, fearful of making a mistake as, sweat trickling down his face, he kneeled and kissed the pontiff's ring. The audience was a success. Floyd left the Vatican relieved that he had not messed up.

Promoters wanted Johansson to train for a while in Miami to boost ticket sales, and made arrangements for him to work out at the Fifth Street Gym, which was run by Chris Dundee, a Philadelphia-born promoter with deep ties to bigtime boxing. Publicist Harold Conrad arrived at the gym with Johansson and Whitey Bimstein in tow. Only after arriving did they realize that they had failed to line up sparring partners for Johansson. So Conrad asked Dundee's brother, trainer Angelo Dundee, if he had anyone the ex-champ could work with. Angelo called to a young boxer, who turned out to be none other than Cassius Clay. Clay had wasted little time in turning pro after his Olympic triumphs. The coterie of Louisville businessmen who managed Clay had hired Dundee as his trainer, who then moved Clay to Miami so he could train at his brother's gym.

Clay's performance against Johansson left Conrad and Bimstein flabbergasted. Johansson looked helpless against the fast young man who never stopped talking. "Johansson was furious," Conrad said. "I mean, he was pissed. He started chasing Clay around the ring, throwing right hands and missing by twenty feet, looking ludicrous."[3] All the while, Clay kept chanting that he was the one who should be fighting Patterson for the championship, not Johansson. After just two rounds with Clay, the gasping Johansson was unable to continue. Gil Rogin, then a young writer for *Sports Illustrated,* having witnessed the scene, told skeptical editors back in New York that he was confident Clay was a future heavyweight champion of the world.

Without question, Clay was sharp at Miami's Fifth Street Gym that day. But it was easy for him to look good against Johansson, who, despondent after his loss to Patterson, had let himself fall out of shape. Ingo was twelve pounds over his prime fighting weight. All twelve of those pounds seemed to be nothing but flab. For the sake of his own reputation, Floyd hoped for an impressive win over Johansson, something that would prove that what had happened at the Polo Grounds was no fluke. Boxing prognosticators agreed that Patterson was likely to get just that against such an ill-prepared opponent.

A couple of weeks before the fight, Robert H. Boyle of *Sports Illustrated* reported on discord in the Patterson camp. He described Floyd's extended group of associates as being the "most bizarre cast of characters to hit the road since Jack Kerouac and buddies careened across the country." The article focused on Julius November, Roy Cohn, Bill Fugazy, Irving Kahn, and, especially, D'Amato: "The sole tragic figure in the lot is Cus D'Amato, entangled in all sorts of legal snares. The press often reviles him as a crook. A crook he is not; a kook he may be."[4]

Boyle exposed the diminished role D'Amato had in all matters pertaining to Floyd Patterson. "Most of the time I just lay around," D'Amato told Boyle. "I read. I play with the dog. Anything to avoid boredom." Boyle reported that with D'Amato all but out of the picture, the management power had shifted to November, whom Boyle described as a big, bald, baby-faced Brooklynite, a boastful man who liked to tell people about the honors he won in law school. Fugazy confirmed to Boyle what a lot of outside observers had decided: D'Amato was all but completely out of the Patterson picture. "He is not calling the shots," Fugazy said.[5]

The article seemed to be a truthful assessment of the situation, with the people controlling the promotion of Patterson's fights speaking honestly if somewhat harshly. But November did not take it that way. He sued *Sports Illustrated* for libel, saying the article defamed him as an attorney and a man. (The suit never went to trial, so presumably was settled out of court.) Patterson's followers were about to learn that the tumult wasn't limited to Patterson's professional associates. It was affecting the champ as well.

A week later, the *New York Times Magazine* ran one of the most in-depth profiles of Patterson yet published. Not surprisingly, its author was Gay Talese. Patterson opened up to Talese more than he ever had to any other writer about how his shyness and insecurity had left him petrified as a child, unable to hold his head up, and how those things still affected his life. "I'm a lot better now," Patterson told Talese, "but I remember the funny feeling I had in Rome last year as I waited for my audience with the Pope."[6] Floyd recounted how he'd sweated in the presence of John XXIII.

Readers also learned about Patterson's growing affection for Sweden. After his loss to Johansson, Floyd received hundreds of letters from Swedish fans saying they were sorry he'd lost: "Not so many encouraging letters came from people in this country." To repay that kindness, Patterson visited Sweden following the second Johansson fight, where he was received with adoration. The nation impressed him: "Everywhere I went in Sweden, I saw there was no color line."[7] Mixed-race couples were able to walk down the streets there without fear.

Floyd told Talese that while he was enjoying the racial equity overseas, his wife was having trouble getting an appointment back home at a Rockville Centre beauty salon. When Julius November's wife, who was white, experienced no difficulty at the same salon, it was all too apparent that Sandra was a victim of prejudice. "I wanted to make this incident known," Patterson told Talese. "I didn't want colored people to go there and receive the embarrassment my wife received." Then Patterson learned that the shop was operated by a Swedish family. He couldn't believe it. But Sandra double-checked, and, yes, it was true. "And I didn't know what to say."[8]

The heavyweight champion divulged that he struggled with racism every day. Patterson shared with Talese that he'd been thinking about moving his family to the upscale suburb of Scarsdale but had been warned that it would be unwise for him to do so because black people weren't welcome there. As for the fight in Miami, a city that in early 1961 was primarily southern in its attitudes, Patterson said he would take part in the Johansson rematch there only if he could be guaranteed that seating would be totally desegregated, holding true to a promise he'd made to himself when he fought the exhibition match in Fort Smith. The promoters agreed to Patterson's stipulation, certainly the first time such a demand from an African American athlete had ever been granted in the South.

"I used to think Jesus was a white man," Patterson said. "All the pictures I've ever seen of Him showed Him white. But I no longer can accept Him as a white man. He either is a Jesus of no color, or a Jesus with skin that is all colors."[9] It was a bold thing to declare in America in 1961. Patterson told Talese he'd learned a lot from Johansson during the year Ingo was champion. He'd hear Johansson saying things at press conferences, mostly dismissive statements about his opponents, that Floyd thought one wasn't supposed to say. Patterson decided to speak his mind more readily. He wouldn't resort to insulting other boxers. He would, however, speak out — in his subtle way — about matters of racial injustice and fair play. Long gone were the days when Floyd would depend on Cus D'Amato to do all the talking.

If Floyd had practiced self-denial at his training camps and in his choice of accommodations at earlier fights — a freezing jockey's room, a rat-infested abandoned dancehall — he now indulged himself. He lodged at a villa in an upscale Miami neighborhood, apart from his wife and daughters and his recently born son, Floyd Jr. He trained at Miami Beach's Hotel Deauville, a fabulous MiMo structure that was one of Sinatra's favorite hangouts. At the villa, he greeted the *New Yorker*'s

A. J. Liebling while wearing a silk dressing robe. To Liebling's eye, it appeared Patterson had fleshed out to a full heavyweight, with ropey muscle showing around the base of his neck. But the champ exuded anything but confidence. Patterson said a bad dream was haunting him, so bad he couldn't describe it. "It's lucky I'm not superstitious," he said. "If I was, I wouldn't go through with this fight."[10] Liebling could hardly believe his ears. Neither fighter seemed particularly hungry for the title.

D'Amato, arriving in Miami with his position in the Patterson entourage reduced to little more than that of hanger-on, considered the fight to be a no-win situation for Patterson. D'Amato thought Johansson would be as good as ever in the ring, gluttony aside. Floyd would have to fight his best fight to win. But D'Amato thought the boxing press would refuse to recognize the situation as such. If Patterson won, D'Amato believed, the press would report it was because Johansson was fat and out of shape. If Johansson won, well, then that would prove that Patterson was really a bum all along, a bum who lost to another bum who wasn't even in condition. No doubt the fighters themselves held similar concerns. For the average boxing fan, the bout promised to be a ho-hum affair.

Early on, ticket sales were as soft as Johansson's expanding gut, only picking up once promoters resorted to fire-sale pricing: $100 ringside seats could be had for as little as $20. Matters were better organized than they had been at the Polo Grounds — there were no riots. This time, since the bout was taking place in Miami instead of in New York State, where he remained banned as a manager, "adviser" D'Amato was among those working Patterson's crowded corner. The others were Dan and Nick Florio and Buster Watson. Liebling, watching from ringside, wasn't sure having D'Amato as a second was such a good idea. He feared D'Amato's presence made Patterson jumpy — "It must be like having your old man in your corner."[11]

Patterson certainly seemed jumpy during the hours before the opening bell. Perhaps he was still haunted by the indescribable nightmare. He remained on edge when he climbed through the ropes for the fight's first round. He had good reason to be anxious. The jab Patterson had been trying to improve in recent weeks was ineffective as the fight got under way. After throwing one, Floyd committed the cardinal sin of failing to follow it with another jab or with a right cross. He also failed to step out of Johansson's range. Ingo may have been soft and already breathing hard, but he reacted to the amateurish opening Patterson provided him. Johansson's toonder flew, and Floyd, a four-to-one favorite, collapsed. The crowd gasped. Patterson shook off the blow and was back on his feet after just two seconds.[12] The referee, a local fireman, signaled for the boxers to resume fighting. Just a few seconds later, Patterson went down again. For the moment, it seemed as if the bloated Johansson was somehow going to pull it off again, floor Patterson over and over until Floyd could no longer fight. But then Patterson surprised Johansson with a left hook that floored the ex-champ. Like Patterson, Johansson refused to stay down. The bell rang to end the round and the audience applauded crazily, certain an out-and-out donnybrook was in the works.

In the second round, the fight quickly became boring. Patterson boxed carelessly, leaving himself vulnerable to attack, but Johansson, his energy already spent, couldn't exploit the openings Floyd offered him. All Ingo seemed to be able to do was trudge ponderously after Floyd. It went on like this through four rounds, the audience growing ever more discontented by the lack of action. "When they came out for the sixth," said Liebling, "Johansson made his last charge, and Patterson backed away, as if to gauge the force left in the harpooned, dying porpoise."[13] Patterson hit him with a left hook to the body, followed by two rights. The fireman ended the fight at two minutes and forty-five seconds of the round, declaring Johansson knocked out, as the fans booed referee and boxers alike.[14] Patterson paid them no heed. But he did do something no one could ever remember seeing in a boxing ring before. He kissed Johansson on the cheek after his defeated opponent stood back up. Floyd said later, "I think I called it 'girlish' when they asked me about it, but it was my expression of admiration for a man who had fought me well."[15]

The fight reviews were anything but expressions of admiration. Even sympathetic writers like Liebling determined that Patterson was a second-rate heavyweight champion. For Howard Cosell, the second Johansson fight had been "the zenith of Floyd Patterson's career."[16] He believed the third meeting was the beginning of some sort of decline. Floyd was just too vulnerable to right hands. Even harsher criticism came from Jimmy Cannon, who ridiculed Patterson at length for his inability to take a punch and remain on his feet: "At first, I thought he would be the first heavyweight champion with a cauliflower tail but he still is able to sit in hard-seated chairs during television interviews without squirming . . . the champion has become a master of the pratfall. Only Red Skelton challenges him in this line." Cannon listed Patterson as no better than the tenth best of eleven heavyweight champions since Max Schmeling won the title in 1930, rating even mediocrities like Primo Carnera and Jack Sharkey above him. The only solace Patterson could take from Cannon's heavy-handed column was that Johansson was ranked eleventh.[17]

Yet, with the public beyond the boxing ring, Patterson stood at the peak of his popularity. He may not have sung duets with Dinah Shore on TV, but he had learned from Johansson how he could make the most of his heavyweight crown in terms of generating publicity, and he planned to use it for causes he valued. A little more than a month after the fight, NAACP Executive Secretary Roy Wilkins introduced Floyd as the chair of a membership and fundraising drive for the civil rights organization's New York City operations. The goal was to raise $1 million for legal, legislative, and educational programs while boosting membership from twenty-seven thousand to fifty thousand. Cochairing the effort with Floyd was Jackie Robinson. In addition to the NAACP project, Patterson raised money to create a halfway house for Wiltwyck boys transitioning from the school to life back in the city. He put up $12,500 of his own money and secured pledges for an additional $12,500 to help establish what would become known as the Floyd Patterson House.

There was also opportunity for Floyd to make some money for himself. A deal was struck with Bernard Geis Associates to publish Floyd's autobiography. Bernard Geis, described by sportswriter and broadcasting legend Dick Schaap as "a large-sized middle-aged cherub who can quote sales figures and Shakespearean sonnets with equal ease," issued only ten or twelve titles a year, cutting deals with major publishers to distribute the books for him. Because Geis published so little, he aimed for bestseller status for each of his titles. "He is a home-run swinger in a league of bunters," Schaap said.[18] Geis published sensational racy runaway hits like *Valley of the Dolls* and *Sex and the Single Girl*. Patterson's life story was in no way a salacious matter, so it was hard to imagine it as a "home run" along the lines of *Valley of the Dolls*. But Geis moved ahead with the project, which Patterson insisted be told in a dignified way though Geis books typically weren't well written. Patterson lacked the writing skills to pen the book without assistance. Finding the perfect collaborator proved to be a tricky task.

The first ghostwriter to audition — whose identity has been lost — failed to produce a manuscript acceptable to anyone involved. Next came Arthur Mann, an author who wrote for newspapers and magazines. He had also worked under Branch Rickey as a publicist for the Dodgers and the Pirates. Mann's manuscript pleased Geis, who enthusiastically sent it to Patterson along with a letter of congratulations. It wound up at Julius November's office for review. A November associate, Joel Weinberg, shared excerpts with Floyd, who didn't like Mann's heroic portrayal of D'Amato. Floyd told Weinberg it should be retitled "Cus D'Amato's War against the IBC." November ordered that Mann be fired from the project. The third and final ghostwriter was Milton Gross, who proved to be the perfect match for Patterson.

At the time, Gross was a significant figure in American sportswriting. The *New York Post* boasted the best sports section in New York, and Gross became its star in the late 1950s and early 1960s when he replaced Jimmy Cannon to write the five-day-a-week column, which was syndicated to scores of other newspapers. Gross was one of the first sportswriters to probe the troubled souls of athletes. One of his most famous — and most influential — columns was "The Long Ride Home," about Dodger pitcher Don Newcombe, who lost the deciding game of the 1956 World Series. Gross also was among the first journalists to tackle issues of race as they pertained to bigtime sports.

Gross sensed that he was on to something big with the Patterson autobiography, and he certainly worked hard at it. He went through his personal files and found he'd written more than a hundred columns and articles about Patterson already, which he organized for use in the text. Then he taped interviews with Patterson, some thirty hours of them, after which he went to work writing. Patterson worked closely with Gross during the composition stage of the project and took his part in it seriously, sometimes referring to the big dictionary that was always at hand when reading or writing. "Once I used 'that' instead of 'which,' and he corrected me," Gross said, "and he's very conscious of 'me' and 'I.'"[19]

Fundraising and writing a book took time and energy, which might have been fine if Floyd were content with what he had accomplished as a boxer. But he wanted to continue to fight. Looming were heavyweight challengers who were much more dangerous than any he'd faced so far. Patterson would have to fight better than ever if he wanted to retain his heavyweight crown.

11

Camelot Denied

NOVEMBER 8, 1960, was a day of celebration for Floyd Patterson, as it was for many African Americans. John Fitzgerald Kennedy was elected president of the United States. Kennedy was young, still in his forties, and for Patterson and other black Americans, Kennedy's ascendancy to the White House promised a break with past practices, especially in terms of race relations. It was the dawn of a new era in America, and Floyd was a product of the brand of liberalism that Kennedy embraced. Poor and otherwise disadvantaged as a child, Floyd had undergone a life-changing experience at Wiltwyck, the very sort of social experiment that true believers in progressive policies could point to as a success. As an adult, Floyd was, like Kennedy, well mannered, well dressed, and well spoken — always conscious of his public image. Floyd was willing to speak out against social ills, and he did so in a forthright yet polished manner, never allowing his emotions to take charge. Many Kennedy supporters, even those with no interest in sports, were Patterson fans. As Kennedy took office in January 1961, Floyd stood as something of a symbol of the New Frontier, a living, breathing answer to the problems of ignorance and prejudice, poverty and surplus that Kennedy had addressed during the campaign. Floyd would carry more than just himself into the boxing ring as he continued to defend his title.

Three contenders seemed to be obvious choices as Patterson positioned himself for his next contest: California's Eddie Machen and two Texas-born fighters, Cleveland "Big Cat" Williams and Zora Folley. All three boxers had good records of quality wins mixed with the occasional embarrassing loss. Machen was a puzzle, both in and out of the ring, but when he was emotionally sound, he could fight very well. Williams was a power hitter who'd racked up an impressive number of knockouts. Folley possessed the best boxing skills and ring savvy of the three. Cus D'Amato had been scolded by the boxing press for not lining up these fighters earlier in Patterson's career. Now that Floyd was in charge, he could have assuaged that criticism and signed to fight one of them.

Or he could have gone a step further and signed the man nearly everyone now conceded as *the* best of the heavyweight contenders — a fierce fighter who seemed to bring the force of a tsunami into the ring with him. His name was Charles "Sonny" Liston, a convicted felon with a reputation for beating anyone who stood in his way, in or out of the ring, cops included. In the previous year, he had scored impressive knockouts against Williams and Folley and won a unanimous decision over Machen. (Liston had also dispatched Roy Harris in just one round.)

Patterson ended up choosing . . . *Tom McNeeley?* McNeeley hardly seemed a worthy opponent for the world heavyweight champion.

Tom McNeeley was a tall, thin, Boston-based fighter who sounded something like Rocky Marciano when he spoke but possessed very few of the Rock's boxing skills. He was athletic enough to have played football under Duffy Daugherty at Michigan State, and, since leaving college, had defeated twenty-three prizefighters. But he was not a true contender for the heavyweight championship. Even Boston newspaper writers dismissed their hometown boy as nothing more than an embarrassingly inept ring mauler.[1] Fighting McNeeley seemed like a sure-fire win for Floyd, an easy payday against yet another white boxer.

The original intention was for Patterson and McNeeley to clash at the fabled Boston Garden. Although Cus D'Amato had been relegated to the status of adviser, he nonetheless wound up deeply involved in making decisions about the fight's details. D'Amato insisted on a nonresident-referee clause in the contract, fearing that a Massachusetts ref would favor McNeeley. The Massachusetts State Boxing Commission refused to accept that condition. D'Amato dug in his feet over the matter. With neither side budging, promoters began looking for another host city. In early October 1961 they announced that the fight would occur in Toronto on December 4, 1961, nine months after Patterson-Johansson III. Ex-champ Jersey Joe Walcott would be the referee. A sellout at the Maple Leaf Gardens was expected to garner around $300,000, with Patterson guaranteed to get 40 percent of the gate. More important, he would receive half the money TelePrompTer paid for closed-circuit TV rights. Cautious Cus demanded that McNeeley's manager, Boston blue-blooded sportsman Peter Davenport Fuller, put up a million dollars in escrow to serve as a guarantee for a return bout, in the event Patterson lost. (If Patterson lost and Fuller failed to arrange the rematch, Fuller would lose the million dollars.) Once that was agreed upon, the contracts were signed.

The oddsmakers expressed solid confidence in Patterson; he was a ten-to-one favorite. The other star of the closed-circuit broadcast was Sonny Liston, fighting German Albert Westphal in Philadelphia immediately prior to Floyd's fight. The pairing of Patterson's and Liston's fights on the same broadcast was tantalizing to fight fans, since Liston was now the number one threat to Floyd. Viewers would have the chance to compare the fighters' performances and speculate what a battle between the two might be like — *if* such a contest could ever be lined up. Like Patterson, Liston was a ten-to-one favorite, though Westphal was a better boxer than McNeeley. Despite the odds, bettors found both fights boring prospects and stayed away from bookmakers. Ticket sales were dismal, too, enough so that promoters allowed only sixteen locations in the Toronto metropolitan area to carry the closed-circuit broadcast — earlier the area had been blacked out.

Those closed-circuit viewers watched Liston demolish Westphal in the first round of their Philadelphia fight, with a few jabs followed by a massive one-two combination. Westphal stayed down for well past the count of ten. Liston wasn't in the ring long enough to start breathing hard. Patterson's victory in Toronto was just as one-sided, although McNeeley's agony at the Maple Leaf Gardens lasted four times as long as Westphal's. This time, it was the challenger, not the champ, who hit the canvas over and over — so many times, in fact, that there is dispute over just how many knockdowns there were. It took ten minutes before McNeeley was able to exit the ring after Floyd knocked him out in the fourth round. Another half hour passed before his trainers allowed anyone except family members into his dressing room. When the press finally managed to interview him, McNeeley said, "If anybody tells you Patterson can't hit, you tell them to come see me. He's the fastest puncher I've ever faced, and one of the hardest punchers."[2] No one cared much about the assessment of a nobody like McNeeley. Boxing fan President Kennedy, who watched on a closed-circuit feed at the White House, said he thought that fight-night fans would have been better served if Patterson and Liston had fought each other, although he would soon take a different view of the matter.

It seemed logical that Kennedy and Patterson should meet, given their common stance on civil rights and Kennedy's love of sports. Influential newspaper columnist Drew Pearson set about to arrange such a meeting in early 1962. Pearson wrote to Kenneth O'Donnell, who was part of the so-called Irish Mafia of White House officials who had Kennedy's ear, and urged O'Donnell to set up a photo opportunity and brief conversation between the champ and the president centered around Big Brothers of America, a charity Patterson supported.

On January 12, a month after the McNeeley fight, the White House gave Pearson and Patterson ten minutes between the president's Oval Office meetings with the ambassador to Ireland and the ambassador to the Republic of China. At 12:25 P.M. Patterson shook hands with President Kennedy.[3] The champ and the president posed for photos with Pearson, District of Columbia commissioner John Duncan, and a ten-year-old "little brother," Freddie Cicala. At one point, Kennedy grasped Patterson's arm and said he was impressed by the shape Patterson was in. For his part, Patterson found Kennedy's knowledge of boxing to be a "pleasant revelation." During their conversation, Kennedy asked Patterson who his next challenger would be. Patterson replied that he had Sonny Liston in his sights. Kennedy suggested that Floyd avoid Liston, citing Justice Department concerns about Liston's ties to organized crime. But Floyd was resolute. Liston was the man, even though he was not ready to make that official. Not just yet.

After the meeting, Patterson told members of the press that he had confided to the president whom he would fight next. When pressed for a name, Patterson nodded toward the president's office and suggested the reporters ask Kennedy. (When Kennedy was asked about it at a subsequent press conference, he referred reporters to Patterson.)

When a reporter mentioned Liston, Floyd suggested two other possible contenders, Zora Folley and Roy Harris.

That night Patterson was feted at a banquet, where Attorney General Robert Kennedy also asked Patterson not to fight Liston. Robert Kennedy had positioned himself as a crusader against organized crime, and Liston's alleged mob connections must have made him especially unsuitable as a potential heavyweight champion. But Patterson was firm with Bobby Kennedy as well. After his meetings with the Kennedy brothers, Patterson left Washington, his spirits soaring. He wrote to the younger Kennedy that the Oval Office visit made for the "most memorable day in my life"—more important than anything he'd accomplished in the ring.[4]

A little more than a week later, Floyd attended opening ceremonies for the Floyd Patterson House, 208–210 East Eighteenth Street in New York. The halfway house for Wiltwyck boys reentering New York City public schools and life on city streets had become a project close to Floyd's heart. He devoted both money and time to it. At times he provided tickets for his New York fights to house residents. He also brought special guests by to meet the boys, some of them celebrities like movie director John Huston. The house helped many boys make a successful transition. For others, the outcome was less positive. Some of the boys were violent, still "maladjusted" even after their time at Wiltwyck, and counselors could be overwhelmed by the extent of the problems they faced. Drugs sometimes made their way into the facility. But while there were failings, there were also victories.

While at the opening ceremonies, Patterson discussed his next fight with reporters. This time, he was less coy. Yes, Liston would be the likely challenger, he said, but the deal wasn't set. In 1961 the New York State Athletic Commission had announced it would not grant Liston a boxing license, citing his multiple police arrests and prison terms. The NAACP and other prominent organizations and individuals agreed with the commission's decision. Less well-known groups weighed in as well, such as the Susquehanna Valley Lodge No. 52 of the Fraternal Order of Police: "We strongly object to Mr. Liston getting an opportunity to influence young people toward a way of life which is not only un-Christian but diametrically opposed to all that is good in America."[5] Floyd understood that he would be perceived as a much more appealing champ than someone like Liston. But he also believed that Liston deserved to be a licensed fighter. In Patterson's opinion, Liston had paid his debt to society, and fair play demanded that Sonny be allowed to compete like everyone else. "One night in bed," Patterson said, "I made up my mind. I knew if I wanted to sleep comfortably, I'd have to take on Liston even though the NAACP and the Kefauver Committee didn't want me to take on the fight. Some people said: 'What if you lose and he wins? Then the colored people will suffer.' But maybe if Liston wins, he'll live up to the title. He may make people look up to him."[6]

By Saint Patrick's Day 1962, Patterson and Julius November had made it official: Sonny Liston was to be his next opponent. Floyd said he hoped the fight would occur in the summer. "The mere fact that there is going to be a fight shows how D'Amato has lost rank," Red Smith commented, "for Cus wanted no part of Liston."[7] But D'Amato wasn't out of the picture entirely. In fact, Patterson still sometimes referred to him as his manager. In announcing the fight, Patterson said that he and D'Amato would choose the location, which most likely would not be New York City.

After announcing the Liston fight, Patterson boarded an airliner in March 1962 for a far-flung trip in support of the Kennedy administration. Patterson along with his brother Raymond, November, boxing promoter Tom Bolan, Dan Florio, Buster Watson, and others flew to Egypt for a State Department–sponsored tour of what was then officially called the United Arab Republic. Egyptian president Gamal Abdel Nasser was no friend of the United States, but the Kennedy administration wanted Patterson to visit the UAR as part of the State Department's "Good Neighbor" efforts.

Thousands of people greeted Patterson and company at the Cairo airport. Riding with an aggressive driver through the crowded streets, Patterson asked his host, Colonel Mahmoud Safwat, director of the UAR Amateur Boxing Federation, if there were many automobile accidents in the city. "No," Safwat replied, "it is forbidden to have accidents."[8] Such was Egypt under the dictatorial gaze of Nasser. Patterson did meet with the Egyptian dictator for an amiable photo opportunity. He also visited the pyramids and the Great Sphinx of Giza, riding horses and camels, mugging with Egyptian officials at each turn.

The high point of the trip came when Patterson attended an amateur boxing tournament sponsored by the UAR Boxing Federation, which included participants from across Africa. The winning team of boxers received a newly named Floyd Patterson Cup.[9] Here, as elsewhere in Egypt, Patterson was mobbed by enthusiastic fans. "When Floyd was spotted as he walked into the Alexandria Arena," wrote Bolan, "the roar of the fans was deafening. The cheering lasted ten minutes."[10] As he prepared to spar as part of an exhibition, Floyd enjoyed fan reaction the likes of which he'd never experienced. When he took off his robe, the crowd erupted into applause. Each movement he made while sparring drew a similar reaction from spectators. When he tried to leave the arena afterward, the crush of the crowd became too much. Patterson escaped only with the aid of a police escort. He returned to the United States tired and nursing a sprained ankle but beaming from the reception he'd received.

There was another matter for Patterson to deal with that spring before he could turn his full focus on Liston: his autobiography. Completing *Victory over Myself* had been a painstaking task. Milton Gross had polished the final manuscript and presented it to Floyd, who read it carefully, then passed it on to Julius November and, finally, to Sandra. Gross, Patterson, and November then set up a marathon session in a Midtown hotel suite and went over the manuscript page by page, with Patterson referring to a list of corrections he'd made on the back of an envelope. November suggested removing material about Floyd's complicated relationship with Cus D'Amato, but Patterson insisted that it remain: "He's part of my life. He's got to be in."[11] Patterson also wanted the book to "sound" like him, and Gross rewrote passages the way Patterson would actually phrase them.

When the writing was complete, Gross thought that he and Patterson had accomplished something special. "This is the story of a boy who's mentally disturbed, who runs from his friends, who finds the only identity he's ever known in the violence of the prize ring," he said. "Tennessee Williams could play with a theme like this." He added, "This is not a sports story or a boxing story. This is the story of a man."[12]

"The story of a man" was picked up by *Sports Illustrated,* which serialized it starting in May 1962. Sections of the book were published in newspapers as well. Bernard Geis personally obtained permission from the White House to use one of the photos of Patterson with President Kennedy on the dust jacket. Thus adorned, the book had its official coming-out party at Toots Shor's saloon on May 25. Geis and *Sports Illustrated* cosponsored the publication party, which required attendees to purchase a $50 ticket for admission, with Wiltwyck as the beneficiary.

Victory over Myself received accolades as soon as it hit the shelves, and from some unlikely corners. The poet Marianne Moore said, "I regard [it] as a manual for descriptive writing — how to exhibit yourself without repelling the reader. I read the book very carefully and annotated it at the back. It was delicately done."[13] In his *New York Times* review of the book, Gay Talese praised it in part because of what it wasn't — another "sweaty thriller" about the kid from the slums who slugs his way to the top "to reign in Hamburger Heaven."[14] In the *Los Angeles Times,* influential sports columnist Jim Murray called *Victory over Myself* a "remarkable book," adding, "It's a fascinating insight into an essentially sad and gentle human being which lifts it above the realm of a sports book and is a testimony of human spirit which would probably do more good if read than all the sermons you and I will hear today or this year."[15] If it fell short of the blockbuster status of other Geis titles, it nonetheless proved popular enough and was translated for several foreign editions.[16]

But the book's release, along with the White House visit and the trip to Egypt, distracted Patterson from his primary business at hand: preparing to fight Sonny Liston. A win over Liston would require more from Patterson physically and emotionally than any other previous fight — more even than the second Johansson fight. Yet Floyd took time away from training to attend to matters surrounding the book's publication.

Family concerns were also diverting his focus. When Milton Gross visited the Highland Mills training camp, Floyd blurted out to him,

"My daughter [Seneca] is six years old and I don't know her."[17] The comment surprised Gross. If Floyd didn't know his oldest child, he was certainly a stranger to the others. Floyd had painted a rosy picture of his relationship with his wife and kids in *Victory over Myself.* In fact, his marriage was deteriorating even as the size of his family increased. In addition to his two daughters and Floyd Jr., he now had another son, Eric. Gross asked whether Patterson was contemplating retirement in order to devote more time to his family. Patterson admitted that his wife had been demanding he spend more time at home, but assured Gross that retirement wasn't on his mind. Floyd explained that before he met Sandra, he had fallen in love with boxing. Boxing was his first love. Floyd didn't want to give it up, not the one thing he could do best in life. The implication was clear. If it came down to it, he'd choose boxing over his wife and children, however painful that decision might be, especially for a man who embraced the Catholic Church's teachings on honoring marriage and family.

There was a further complication that would affect Patterson's family life. As heavyweight champion, Floyd received thousands of letters and had relied on an assistant to help with his correspondence and other business matters. When his secretary married and left the job, Floyd asked his close friend, the singer Mickey Alan, if he knew of someone who could replace her. Alan recommended his sister-in-law Janet Seaquist. The attractive blonde proved to be efficient, and she showed an interest in Floyd's career and business dealings. Over time, she and Floyd grew closer.

The Patterson family residence only added to the problems on the home front. Floyd and his family had moved to an upscale neighborhood on Troublesome Brook in northeastern Yonkers, near the town's border with Scarsdale. Until their arrival, the neighborhood had been inhabited exclusively by whites. The name of the brook turned out to be prophetic: the newcomers did not receive a warm welcome. The Pattersons' next-door neighbor was a dentist. He built a redwood fence along the property line dividing the backyards of the two houses. Floyd was certain his neighbor built the fence to keep the families' children from playing together. On a visit home from training camp, Floyd responded by hiring workmen to construct a fence between the front yards of the two homes. When construction began, the dentist's wife faced off with the workmen and Floyd in the front yard. Later in the day, the dentist himself threatened Patterson with a lawsuit if the fence builders touched anything in his yard. Patterson replied that if the dentist touched anything in his yard, he had better have an ambulance waiting.

Yet a further distraction for Floyd in the weeks leading up to the Liston fight was a business deal he'd entered at Cus D'Amato's urging. In 1959 D'Amato had met handball champion Jim Jacobs. Jacobs had amassed a collection of fight films, the sheer size of which (five thousand films) made him a somebody in the world of boxing. He and D'Amato hit it off and quickly became tight friends and eventually roommates.

In 1962 Cus encouraged Floyd to participate in a project that Jacobs had concocted. Jacobs would produce a one-hour retrospective about Patterson's career that Jacobs would syndicate to television stations. Floyd would receive a fee for interviews and a percentage of the profits. Patterson entered into an oral agreement with Jacobs; the actual letters of agreement were signed by D'Amato. The "fee" Floyd received for the interviews was $1, according to the letters D'Amato signed. After expenses were settled, there was no profit. Or at least that was what Jacobs told Patterson. Floyd made nothing out of the deal. "Cus couldn't give away those rights to my life, in 1962 — only I could do that, or only I should've been able to do that," Patterson later said. "And it wasn't what Jacobs promised me. No percentage of what the film made, no fees, nothing . . . Who knows what that film made? Jacobs had the records."[18] For Floyd, it was the last straw. Cus still had a written contract in place with Patterson that gave him a percentage of Floyd's purses. But after the Jacobs incident, Floyd was ready to part company with D'Amato for good.

It all made for a bad state of mind for Patterson as he readied himself to face a man considered the most dangerous heavyweight the sport had known. One thing was certain about Sonny Liston: he never kissed anyone in the ring.

It was in his family's cypress-board shack that Charles "Sonny" Liston came into the world. The boxing publicist and promoter Harold Conrad once said of Liston, "I think he died the day he was born."[19] Liston himself never knew where or when that dying birth occurred, but he actually drew his first breath on a large farm called the Morledge Plantation in the Mississippi River region known as the Arkansas Delta. Liston's father, Tobe, worked as a tenant farmer, renting fifty acres on a part of the plantation known as Sand Slough. As was the case with Patterson's birth in North Carolina, Liston's was not registered with state officials.

One story holds that his father carved the date on a tree, but the tree eventually was felled, eliminating the only record of Sonny's birth. As a consequence, his actual age was disputed during his boxing career, with many saying he was much older than advertised. He was an adult in 1953 when a birth certificate listing May 8, 1932, was filed. It is likely incorrect, though Liston grew threatening whenever someone challenged it to his face. But US Census records reveal that Tobe and Helen Liston's family did not include Charles among their children in 1930. This suggests that he was born in that year or sometime after. What is clear is that his hard life made him seem older than he was. He suffered vicious abuse at the hands of his father. St. Louis trainer Johnny Tocco once noticed something akin to bird tracks on Liston's back. He asked Liston about the scars and Liston said, "I had dealings with my father."[20] At other times he remarked, "The only thing my old man ever gave me was a beating."[21]

The Liston family, like Floyd's, was part of the Great Migration. In the case of the Listons, they didn't travel as a family unit. Sonny's mother moved from Arkansas to St. Louis to find work. Liston couldn't stand being left behind to labor in the cotton fields under the glare of his father. Eventually, Sonny showed up at his mother's door. He was illiterate. The public schools failed to teach him to read and write. Unlike Floyd, he was offered no opportunities akin to Wiltwyck to help him overcome his troubles. So he went to work, taking short-lived jobs at a poultry-packing plant and an icehouse. By 1949 Liston had turned to crime, in the company of two other thugs. Eventually Sonny was arrested, and he pleaded guilty to three counts of first-degree robbery and two charges of larceny. He received a sentence of five years in the Missouri State Penitentiary in Jefferson City, commencing June 1, 1950.

It was in prison that Liston became a boxer, learning to fight under

Manager Cus D'Amato, who guided Floyd Patterson to the heavyweight championship of the world, advises his fighter during a Yankee Stadium bout in 1959. D'Amato was the most significant professional influence on Floyd, though Patterson later split with him.
George Silk/Time Life Pictures/Getty Images

In 1952, the American boxing team made its best showing to date in the Olympics when five black fighters, seventeen-year-old Patterson (center) among them, brought home five gold medals to a still largely segregated United States. *Bettmann/Corbis*

Floyd floors the legendary Archie Moore to become the youngest heavyweight champion. The 1956 title fight in Chicago—Floyd's best as a pro—was so one-sided that Moore had to defend himself against charges of a fix. *AP Photo*

Dan Florio (right) was Floyd's most important trainer, refining the fighter's famous peeka-boo stance, then later encouraging him to abandon it. Here Florio and his brother, Nick (left), also a trainer, hoist Floyd in victory after the Moore knockout while D'Amato looks on from behind. *AP Photo*

Recently crowned heavyweight champ Floyd and his first wife, Sandra, step out in style as VIP guests at an Atlantic City prizefight. They presented an image of a happy couple in public, but Floyd spent most of his time away from home, and eventually the marriage crumbled when Floyd refused to retire from boxing. *AP Photo*

Swedish heavyweight Ingemar Johansson was not expected to present much of a challenge to Floyd when they fought in Yankee Stadium for the heavyweight crown in 1959. But Ingo proved to be a hard-hitting contender who surprised the experts. He became Floyd's greatest ring rival. *STF/epa/Corbis*

Johansson went into the second fight with Patterson, at the Polo Grounds in 1960, as the solid favorite, believed by many insiders to be the next Dempsey. But Floyd landed one of the great left hooks in boxing history and watched as Johansson collapsed, unconscious. Patterson became the first man ever to win the heavyweight crown twice. *AP Photo*

In 1962, Patterson met with President Kennedy, along with Washington, DC, commissioner John Duncan, syndicated columnist Drew Pearson, and "Little Brother" Freddie Cicala to boost the national Big Brother program. Floyd used the occasion to tell Kennedy he planned to go against the president's wishes and fight Sonny Liston.
Courtesy of the John F. Kennedy Presidential Library and Museum

Floyd and baseball legend Jackie Robinson (right) traveled to Birmingham, Alabama, in 1963 to show support for Dr. Martin Luther King Jr. and the Reverend Ralph Abernathy as the city suffered through bombings and other violence aimed at supporters of the civil rights movement. *AP Photo*

Floyd went against many of his fans, including the president, representatives of the NAACP, and Cus D'Amato, in agreeing to fight Sonny Liston. The 1962 fight became a literary event, but Floyd lasted less than a round before Liston knocked him out. *AP Photo*

Patterson was so humiliated by the loss that he wore a "beatnik beard" and a hat and shades to disguise himself from fans and the press. *AP Photo*

The war of words between Muhammad Ali and Patterson grew heated as their 1965 fight approached, particularly over the topic of the Nation of Islam. Ali publicly dismissed Floyd as an "Uncle Tom," but in fact the two men had a complicated relationship built on a kind of respect. *Bettmann/Corbis*

Patterson entered that fight injured and lost to Ali. Floyd's final fight, in 1972, was also a loss to Ali, yet The Greatest later ranked Floyd with Sonny Liston, George Foreman, and Joe Frazier as the best boxers he ever fought. *Bettmann/Corbis*

As the 1960s progressed, Floyd became increasingly politically conservative. In 1972, he paid a second visit to the Oval Office, this time at the invitation of Richard Nixon. Accompanying Patterson are his second wife, Janet, and their two young daughters, Jennifer and Janene. *WPHO 9741-02. Courtesy of the Richard Nixon Presidential Library and Museum*

Patterson stayed in shape and loved boxing, just as he loved America, to the end of his days. Here he is in 1995, at his gym in New Paltz, New York, where he trained many aspiring upstate fighters after he left the ring. *Michael Brennan/Corbis*

the approving eye of the institution's Catholic chaplain. Liston's good behavior and his dedication to boxing earned him parole in late 1952. Back home in St. Louis, he took a job at a steel plant and roomed at the YMCA. He began boxing in earnest. His managers and trainers were connected to John J. Vitale, the boss of the city's Italian mob. Vitale had connections to Frankie Carbo, Blinky Palermo, and, ultimately, the IBC. Liston won seven straight pro fights in 1953 and 1954, including a split-decision victory in Detroit that was broadcast nationwide on television. After his sole stumble against Marty Marshall in September 1954, Liston accumulated win after win, mostly in the Midwest and mostly against opponents who never came close to being contenders. Nevertheless, he seemed destined to one day fight for the heavyweight championship.

Two obstacles loomed on Liston's road toward a title fight. He drank heavily, and when he was loaded he tended to get into trouble. The St. Louis police didn't like him and arrested him at every opportunity. In the five years after his release from prison, Liston was jailed fourteen times. Things took a serious turn one night in 1956 when a St. Louis police officer argued with a soused Liston over a parking ticket. The dispute turned physical. Liston wrested the cop's service revolver from him and aimed it at him. Although Liston did not shoot the officer, he did manage to split open the cop's head and break his leg before he fled. The police arrested Liston the next morning. In January 1957 Sonny pleaded guilty to assaulting a police officer and was sentenced to nine months in the city workhouse. After serving his sentence, he encountered a St. Louis police captain who gave Liston some advice. If Sonny wanted to stay alive, he better leave the city, because if he remained in St. Louis, the cops planned to kill him. Liston heeded the warning and began fighting out of Philadelphia.

Liston fought eight times in 1958, lunching on fighters whose names are now largely forgotten. In 1959 and 1960, however, he carried his campaign of annihilation to the best contenders in the heavyweight division. They all learned that Liston was a tremendously talented heavyweight with extraordinary reach, devastating power, and hands so large that he required custom-made gloves. Liston could knock someone out with a single jab. His punching ability was so overwhelming that most fight spectators failed to note that he had also mastered all the technical intricacies of a topflight boxer. He possessed outstanding footwork. No boxer in history could cut off a ring better than Liston in his prime. Sonny stood six feet even, and typically went into the ring weighing between 210 and 220, yet he had a way of gliding across the canvas as if he were skating on ice. Once he appeared on Ed Sullivan's television show and jumped rope to the accompaniment of his favorite song, "Night Train," his feet as deft as a modern dancer's.

When D'Amato was in complete control of Patterson's career, Sonny had no chance to challenge for the heavyweight crown, which frustrated Liston and his handlers to no end. Liston never would part company with his mob connections. Sonny actually confronted D'Amato in a surprise visit to Cus's office. The enraged heavyweight towered over D'Amato, demanding to know if he'd ever be allowed a shot at Patterson's title. It took a moment or two for D'Amato to compose himself before telling Liston it would be possible once Liston made a management change, meaning once Liston aligned himself with a manager and a trainer who had no organized crime connections. D'Amato knew that wasn't about to happen and watched as Liston stormed away.

Even as people in the boxing world called Liston a menace, a thug, and a "bad nigger," Floyd regarded Sonny differently. Patterson saw much of himself in Liston. Floyd believed he could have ended up just like Liston — threatened by cops, doing time in prison, answering to gangsters — if life hadn't provided him opportunities Liston never received. But Patterson also knew he was going to have to put together the best performance of his career if he was to defeat this challenge to his crown on September 25, 1962, at Chicago's Comiskey Park.

Patterson-Liston was set to be a huge heavyweight championship bout, no two ways about it. Promoters planned to reconfigure seating in Comiskey Park so that the venerable stadium could accommodate fifty-seven thousand fans. Transforming the "Baseball Palace of the World" into a boxing venue would be a chore; the White Sox would finish their season there just two days before the September 25 bout. Tickets went on sale for between $10 and $100. The promoters predicted the fight would earn substantially in excess of $6 million, which, they proclaimed, would make it "the greatest fight in history." Patterson was guaranteed 45 percent of the net live gate and 55 percent of the ancillary income, including money from closed-circuit and broad-cast rights. Liston had to yield a lot of money for his shot at the title. He would receive just 12½ percent of the live gate and 12½ percent of the ancillary income, both against guarantees of $200,000. That was fine with him. "I don't care where or how much," Liston said, "just as long as we fight."[22]

Once the contracts were signed, the boxers set up their respective training camps. Patterson chose Elgin, Illinois, somewhat hidden from the media glare. Six years earlier, Patterson had trained at Sports-man's Park racetrack to prepare for his only other pro match in Chi-cago — the fight in which he defeated Archie Moore to become heavy-weight champ. Perhaps ominously, Liston chose to train at Aurora Downs, an abandoned racetrack that was even more rundown than Sportsman's Park had been. Patterson's camp in Elgin was typical of his other camps. The atmosphere was friendly, and Patterson attempted to answer reporters' questions as best he could. Liston's camp was more like a reverse prison: it had barbed wire and an armed guard posted to keep people out.

As Patterson and Liston worked out at their training camps, publicist Harold Conrad began his job in Chicago: generating hype. No one could do a better job of that when it came to bigtime boxing events. Conrad realized that the Patterson-Liston battle was weighted with sociological and political implications, not the least of which was that Patterson was going against President Kennedy, his political hero, by agreeing to the bout. But Patterson believed fair play trumped even presidential requests, that Liston had earned the right to fight for the crown. Floyd could see no reason to deny Liston. The fight had cap-tured the fancy of many, many Americans, making it the most talked-about heavyweight title bout since Louis-Schmeling in the 1930s and Dempsey-Tunney in the 1920s. But this fight was different in one very important respect: both Patterson and Liston were African American. No event in American history, in or out of sports, had focused so much attention on an event in which the leading players were black.

Conrad knew writers would be attracted by everything the clash between Floyd and Sonny symbolized — not just the sports reporters, who would be there anyway, but big-name literary writers. Conrad was right. Prize-winning novelists and highbrow essayists elbowed their way into Chicago's Sheraton Hotel, the fight headquarters, where they joined the sportswriters in churning out fight-related verbiage at the rate of "ten thousand words a minute," in the words of Norman Mailer, one of the authors who'd come to town. No self-respecting writer turned down Conrad's offer of press credentials, not for something this big. So the writers came to Chicago in droves, turning this prizefight into a genuine literary event. Mailer's appearance was particularly significant. He was covering the fight for *Esquire*, the magazine that was defining the New Journalism of the 1960s, Mailer being one of the creators of the new form, which used techniques of fiction — scene-by-scene constructions, subjective points of view, interior monologues — to make nonfiction more lively and relevant to readers. The New Journalism was so popular that some prognosticators predicted it would spell the death of the Great American Novel. That didn't happen, but the New Journalism left a lasting mark on American nonfiction prose, making it less stodgy and more accessible. In addition to its literary contributions, *Esquire* also served as the arbiter of what was cool by early 1960s standards. By dispatching Mailer, arguably the most famous writer of his time, to Chicago, *Esquire* was giving the Patterson-Liston bout a stamp of hipness that no previous prizefight had received.

But Mailer was not the most compelling presence in Chicago. That nod belonged instead to novelist James Baldwin, who had been assigned to cover the Patterson-Liston fight by Seymour Krim, the brilliant essayist who was then editing *Nugget* magazine, a rival of *Playboy*. Assigning the championship fight to Baldwin was one of Krim's finest decisions, though at first glance, Baldwin seemed to be the most unlikely of boxing writers. While other Harlem adolescent boys had been playing stickball or basketball, Baldwin had been a teenage Pentecostal preacher, concerning himself with matters of the soul, not of the body. Baldwin admitted that he knew "nothing whatever about the Sweet Science or the Cruel Profession or the Poor Boy's Game."[23] Yet he seemed to be more in tune with the deeper implications of the Patterson-Liston fight than anyone else in Chicago.

Baldwin knew a good deal about pride, especially "the poor boy's pride," and he saw that as being the elemental dispute at hand in

Chicago. He bristled when he heard criticism from the mostly white sportswriters about how the black champion Patterson had mishandled his affairs since taking control of his career away from D'Amato. Baldwin writes:

> "In the old days," someone complained, "the manager told the fighter what to do, and he did it. You didn't have to futz around with the guy's *temperament,* for Christ's sake." Never before had any of the sportswriters been compelled to deal directly with the fighter instead of with his manager, and all of them seemed baffled by this necessity and many were resentful. I don't know how they got along with D'Amato when he was running the show — D'Amato can certainly not be described as either simple or direct — but at least the figure of D'Amato was familiar and operated to protect them from the oddly compelling and touching figure of Floyd Patterson, who is quite probably the least likely fighter in the history of the sport. And I think that part of the resentment he arouses is due to the fact that he brings to what is thought of — quite erroneously — as a simple activity a terrible note of complexity. This is his personal style, a style which strongly suggests that most un-American of attributes, privacy, the will to privacy; and my own guess is that he is still relentlessly, painfully shy — he lives gallantly with his scars, but not all of them have healed — and while he has found a way to master this, he has found no way to hide it; as, for example, another miraculously tough and tender man, Miles Davis, has managed to do. Miles's disguise would certainly never fool anybody with sense, but it keeps a lot of people away, and that's the point. But Patterson, tough and proud and beautiful, is also terribly vulnerable, and looks it.[24]

Baldwin witnessed the tough and vulnerable aspects of Patterson when he accompanied Gay Talese to a press conference, where Patterson was asked questions likely never asked of earlier champs. *Do you feel you've ever been accepted as champion?* "No," Patterson said. "Well, I have to be accepted as the champion — but maybe not a good one." *Why do you say the opportunity to become a great champion will never arise?* "Because," said Patterson, "you gentlemen will never let it arise."

Why are you greeted with much greater enthusiasm in Europe than in the United States? "I don't want to say anything derogatory about the United States. I am satisfied."

Later, Patterson spoke with Talese and Baldwin as the three men strolled around Floyd's training camp. "I can't remember all the things we *did* talk about," Baldwin said later. "I mainly remember Floyd's voice, going cheerfully on and on, and the way his face kept changing, and the way he laughed; I remember the glimpse I got of him then, a man more complex than he was yet equipped to know, a hero for many children who were still trapped where he had been, who might not have survived without the ring, and who yet, oddly, did not really seem to belong there."[25]

Although Talese had helped gain entrée for Baldwin into Patterson's camp, he could not get Baldwin into Liston's camp. Baldwin was on his own for that. So Baldwin turned to journalist Sandy Grady, who put in a good word with Liston's manager of the moment. Baldwin was granted time with Sonny and showed up knowing that Liston had no use for the press: "I was sure he saw in them merely some more ignorant, uncaring white people, who, no matter how fine we cut it, had helped to cause him so much grief . . . The press has really maligned Liston very cruelly, I think. He is far from stupid; is not, in fact, stupid at all. And, while there is a great deal of violence in him, I sensed no cruelty at all."[26] Liston reminded Baldwin of other African American men the writer had encountered, big men who encouraged a reputation of toughness to conceal an inner softheartedness.

Baldwin found himself liking Liston from the moment he sat down with him, even though Liston seemed leery of the novelist. Baldwin sensed that Sonny was prepared for verbal blows to start coming. But Baldwin felt only empathy for Liston and saw in the silence of his face a man who had suffered. Baldwin told Liston that he had not come to ask questions, because he believed all the questions had already been asked. The only thing Baldwin had to say was that he wished Sonny well.

This prompted Liston to open up to Baldwin, and, speaking black man to black man, Liston confessed that he was hurt by the fact that relatively few African Americans seemed to be backing him in the championship bout. "Colored people," Liston said, "say they don't want their children to look up to me." Liston and Baldwin discussed the civil rights movement and the role prominent people like heavyweight champs should play in it. Then they talked more about the "respectable" black people who did not want Liston to be champion. Liston believed that blacks needed to come together and stop "fighting among our own."[27]

"I felt terribly ambivalent," Baldwin said, "as many other Negroes do these days, since we are all trying to decide, in one way or another, which attitude, in our terrible American dilemma, is the most effective: the disciplined sweetness of Floyd, or the outspoken intransigence of Liston."[28] In the end, Baldwin laid down money on Patterson to win the fight. Oddsmakers had it three-to-one in favor of the challenger, but Baldwin put his money on Floyd, knowing there was more at stake than just who would be the heavyweight champion of the world. It was the right thing to do, from a moral and ethical standpoint.

Liston may have had little use for white reporters — after all, some columnists had referred to him as a gorilla — but one white writer did get to sit down with him. Edwin "Bud" Shrake, a *Dallas Morning News* sports columnist, didn't press Liston about his inner feelings. Instead, Shrake asked Liston about Patterson's speed. Shrake shared with Liston that there was some belief that Patterson would be able to cut up Liston with his fast punches and that Liston would be too slow to lay a solid blow on Floyd. Liston, trademark glare firmly in place, suddenly shot one of his huge hands into the air, then brought it back, his fingers clenched into a fist. Liston slowly opened his fist in front of Shrake's face to reveal that he'd just captured a fly in flight. "Do you think that will be fast enough to take care of that skinny-assed son of a bitch?" Liston growled.[29]

Shrake left the interview a Liston believer.

Many boxing insiders held out for Patterson, never mind the odds. Daniel M. Daniel, writing for *The Ring* magazine, said, "They will fight, and I will be surprised if Patterson does not beat him." The Cinderella Man, James J. Braddock, also liked Patterson in spite of what the bookmakers were prognosticating: "I have news for you — being an underdog makes you a better fighter . . . Patterson is most dangerous when least is looked for from him." Braddock predicted a decision in favor of Floyd, with Patterson controlling the final rounds of the bout. The crusty old fight manager Jack Kearns saw Patterson winning, as did former heavyweight champ Ezzard Charles and one-time Floyd foe Archie Moore. Ingemar Johansson seemed torn: "I am confused. In Sweden I pick Liston and in a magazine, Patterson. Now I don't know."[30]

Partying at the Chicago Playboy Club, Mailer and *New York Post* columnist and Patterson confidant Pete Hamill agreed that Floyd would win the fight. Both men thought Patterson would claim victory during the sixth round. Mailer said, "I think Liston is going to have Patterson down two, three, four times. And Patterson will have Liston down in the first, second, or third and end it with one punch in the sixth."[31] But Mailer also understood that Patterson would carry into the ring a burden quite unlike anything any other fighter had endured:

> Patterson was a churchgoer, a Catholic convert . . . Patterson was up tight with the NAACP, he was the kind of man who would get his picture taken with Jackie Robinson and Ralph Bunche (in fact he looked a little like Ralph Bunche), he would be photographed with Eleanor Roosevelt, and was; with Jack Kennedy, and was; with Adlai Stevenson if he went to the UN; he would campaign with Shelley Winters if she ever ran for Mayor of New York; he was a liberal's liberal. The worst to be said about Patterson is that he spoke with the same cow's cud as other liberals. Think what happens to a man with Patterson's reflexes when his brain starts to depend on the sounds of "introspective," "obligation," "responsibility," "inspiration," "commendation," "frustrated," "seclusion" — one could name a dozen others from his book. They are a part of his pride.[32]

Pride — as both Baldwin and Mailer intimated — more than anything else was on the line for Floyd as he went to Comiskey Park. The members of his team argued with officials about Liston's custom-made gloves. They weighed the prescribed eight ounces, but there was little padding over the knuckles, making them a dangerous knockout tool. But Patterson was more concerned about letting down all those people who had done so much for him over the years. Living up to their expectations of him in the ring was his pride. As he sat in his dressing room, he drifted into what he later described as a kind of blindness. It was apparent to people in the room with him that something was wrong. Joseph Triner, chairman of the Illinois State Athletic Commission, said that Patterson turned to ice in those minutes before he left for the ring.[33]

It was in that frozen blindness that Patterson climbed between the ropes in Comiskey Park. He heard his longtime friend Mickey Alan sing "The Star-Spangled Banner." He heard Liston loudly booed when he was introduced as the challenger. He heard his own name cheered when he was introduced as the champion. As always, Patterson stared downward as the referee read the fight instructions. Meanwhile Liston glared at Patterson as if Floyd were responsible for every whipping delivered in the Delta cotton fields, every swollen knot rendered on the skull by some cracker St. Louis cop.

During those opening seconds, Floyd was fluid, bouncing on the balls of his feet as usual, attempting to set up his left hook. But as the round progressed, Floyd planted his feet and tried to slug it out with Sonny up close. It was a huge mistake. Liston saw his opportunity and went on the attack. At around the two-minute mark, Sonny battered Patterson to the ropes with lefts to the body and shoulders. Floyd reacted in a bizarre way. Rather than use his speed to escape further punishment, Patterson stood up straight and allowed his left hand to slide down the top rope, leaving his head totally exposed, almost as if he were offering himself up as a sacrifice. No one who watched the fight knew just why he did this. Maybe Floyd himself didn't know. It gave Liston a chance to hit Floyd with a left and a short right, neither particularly sharp but both effective enough. Patterson was collapsing on himself when Liston slammed Floyd's undefended head once more, this time with a massive left hook. Floyd attempted to wobble back to his feet in vain. The fight was over, in near record time for a heavyweight championship bout.[34]

Baldwin, stunned, joined A. J. Liebling at a bar to mourn the "very possible death of boxing, and to have a drink, with love, for Floyd."[35]

12

♦

Confronting a Certain Weakness

T HE NEXT MORNING, the traditional postfight press conference
turned into a farce as a soused Norman Mailer tried to upstage the
new champ. Mailer, who'd been drinking steadily at the Playboy
Club since the end of the fight, had determined that there should be
a rematch: in grandiloquent Mailer style, he indicated that his cos-
mic understanding of what *really* transpired during the fight would
allow him to turn such a contest into a multimillion-dollar success.
He continued to believe Floyd was the better boxer.[1] In the throes of
spirits and lack of sleep, Mailer concocted a fantastic theory about why
Patterson had lost: the Mafia had cast some sort of Sicilian evil eye on
Patterson that caused him to surrender before the fight even began.
Cus D'Amato, Mailer reasoned, was well schooled in matters such as
warding off evil eyes. Patterson's mistake was that he'd distanced himself from D'Amato, thus making himself vulnerable to supernatural
threats.[2] After tolerating this lunacy for a few minutes, the police literally carried Mailer out of the room.

Patterson saw none of it. By that time, he was closing in on New
York.

A week or so before the fight, promoter Al Bolan asked Harold Conrad
if he knew the name of a good makeup man in Chicago — Patterson

had requested one. Conrad contacted the Chicago CBS affiliate, where he had a friend who agreed to take care of whatever Patterson needed. Conrad made an appointment for Patterson to see the man. Later, the friend called Conrad and said, "What the hell's playing with Patterson? He asked my man to fix him up a beard." Conrad quickly figured out it was for a disguise. He swore the man at the TV station to secrecy about the affair. But he knew that Patterson was planning an escape from Chicago.[3]

In fact, Patterson had taken the fake beard and mustache he'd had made prior to the second Johansson fight with him to Chicago. The mustache was still in good shape, but the beard had become somewhat unraveled, so he paid the makeup artist $65 and gave him a $50 ticket for the fight to make him a new beard. After he lost the fight, Floyd dispatched a trainer to the hotel to fetch his disguise. Just as he had for the second Johansson fight, Patterson had two cars waiting. One was the official one, his Lincoln, to be used to drive him back to the hotel if he won. The other was hidden away and pointed toward New York, just in case Patterson wanted to make a clandestine escape. Once he had the beard in hand, he fled with his friend Mickey Alan. His regular driver, Ernest Fowler, waited with the Lincoln for Patterson to show up. Because of that, reporters assumed Floyd was holed up somewhere in the stadium.

Patterson and Alan's hurried drive was almost identical to the one he had made across the dark Midwest following his triumph over Archie Moore in Chicago almost six years earlier. Then he'd been hailed as the newly crowned champion on his way home to see his newborn daughter. But now, he traveled in disgrace. The night was his friendly protector as Floyd sat behind the wheel, navigating the lonely highways. Other than Alan, no one knew what Patterson was up to that night, not even his friends and family. In fact, Floyd had told Sandra that he would pick her up at Chicago's Bismarck Hotel, and they would drive back to New York together. She learned about the change in plans only after he called her from a phone booth on the road to tell her to catch a plane home.

Just before dawn, somewhere in Ohio, Patterson pulled the car off the road for a break. Floyd stepped out to stretch his legs. Almost immediately, a state trooper pulled in behind them. Patterson quickly attempted to attach his beard disguise. But by the time the cop reached him, he had secured only the mustache in place; the beard hung loosely from his chin. Naturally, the trooper was suspicious and demanded to see Patterson's license. Patterson stiffened. His driver's license was back in Chicago, still in the hotel with the rest of his personal effects. He did have the registration for the car, which he had borrowed from a relative, and he showed that to the trooper.

"If you don't have a license," the trooper said, "I have got to take you in."

Not knowing what else to do, Patterson dislodged the mustache and beard to reveal himself for who he really was. At first, the trooper didn't recognize him and wondered aloud if he was an actor. Patterson removed the cap he was wearing, and the cop shined his flashlight into Floyd's face. Now it registered with him.

"Aren't you—" he began.

"Yes," said Patterson. "I lost a fight last night. Do I have to lose again? Wouldn't it be all right if I mail you my license when I get home? I just forgot it."

The trooper squeezed Patterson's shoulder in a friendly way and said, "You won't have to do that. You won't have to lose again. You'll get him the next time."[4] Patterson and Alan were free to go on their way.

With Alan now driving, Patterson told him to head directly to the place where he felt most comfortable—not his home in Yonkers, but the training camp in Highland Mills. After twenty-two hours on the road, he and Alan collapsed into sleep. The next morning, Floyd asked Alan to leave. Floyd wanted only solitude. He spent the day alone, mindlessly watching TV. He avoided the radio because he didn't want to hear any news reports about Liston. Late in the day, he went for a walk and wound up entering the gym on the property. Suddenly he felt an overpowering desire to start training. But all his gear remained back in Chicago. So Floyd resumed his walk, chastising himself for throwing away all the training he'd done to prep for Liston in two minutes and six seconds.

A few days after the fight, Patterson finally made the drive to Yonkers. He arrived wearing the mustache, having discarded the beard because it irritated his chin. Sandra scarcely recognized him. Floyd stayed for a short while to play with the kids, but then left to meet with

Julius November, who had just flown in from Chicago. The two men discussed business and concluded that they should exercise Floyd's option for a rematch. It was all-important to Floyd. "I've got to prove to myself that I'm a better fighter than I was that night," he said.[5]

In fact, Patterson had plenty of self-doubt. Within a few days, he arrived at an airport ticket counter wearing a fake beatnik beard and carrying a suitcase. He peered up at the departures board and saw that a flight for Madrid was leaving soon. Madrid seemed to be as good a place as any to escape to, so he purchased a ticket for the Spanish capital. In Madrid, he booked himself into a hotel under Buster Watson's real name, Aaron Watson. He had decided to affect a limp to complement his disguise, so for the next few days he hobbled around the city's poorest neighborhoods and took stock of the people who stared at him, this seemingly disabled black American with the odd beard. He was certain they thought him insane. He allowed himself to eat only soup, a dish he hated because he considered it fit only for old men. Why did he do all this? He later explained that it had to do with confronting a certain weakness that came out only when he was alone. "And I have figured out that part of the reason I do the things I do, and cannot seem to conquer that one word — *myself* — is because . . . is because . . . I am a coward."[6]

A coward in his own mind, perhaps. But he showed no cowardice as he agreed to a July 1963 rematch with the new heavyweight champion. And he showed no cowardice when he agreed to travel to the bloodied heart of the American civil rights movement in May 1963 to lend support to Dr. Martin Luther King Jr. King welcomed Patterson's backing, even as many of Patterson's own backers were beginning to abandon him, John Kennedy among them. After Liston beat Patterson, Floyd learned that the president threw away an autographed photo of Patterson he kept in the Oval Office.

In the spring of 1963 King organized a protest campaign to break down the walls of segregation in Birmingham, Alabama. The city's police chief, Eugene "Bull" Connor, ordered that demonstrators were to be dispersed with fire hoses and vicious guard dogs. Americans outside the South registered horror as they watched TV news images of men, women, and children knocked from their feet by water blasts and attacked by snarling German shepherds. Officers arrested more than two thousand demonstrators, half of whom were jailed. Jackie Robinson, determined that something must be done about violence in Birmingham, organized an emergency meeting of civil rights supporters to raise money for King's activities. The meeting took place at Sardi's in New York and was attended by leaders and celebrities alike, including actresses Diahann Carroll and Ruby Dee. Patterson did not attend the meeting in person, but he agreed to travel to Birmingham.

A year earlier, Robinson and Patterson had traveled to Mississippi to champion rights for African Americans. Also on that trip were Archie Moore and Curt Flood, of the St. Louis Cardinals. (Flood eventually played a pivotal role in establishing free agency in baseball, which freed players to negotiate with different teams once their contracts expired.) At a regional NAACP meeting in Jackson, Patterson spoke to four thousand attendees and faulted himself for staying in the North while blacks in the South sacrificed personal safety while fighting for racial integration. "I feel extremely guilty sitting there in the North," said Patterson, "reading and hearing about the things you are going through down here. You people are the ones going through all the danger."[7]

But in May 1963, Patterson was ready to head south once again, even if it meant breaking training camp fewer than ninety days before his return match with Liston. When asked by a WSB-TV reporter why he was going, Floyd echoed the sentiments he expressed a year earlier: "Well, sitting up here in my training camp, watching television and reading the newspapers, I felt I wasn't doing my job, at least my share of it anyway. And then I heard that Jackie Robinson was going down and I thought it was a good opportunity for me to go down with him. And when I go down there, I'm going down prepared to be arrested." The TV reporter asked Patterson what he would do if he were arrested, and Floyd responded that he would go to jail. What if they turned the fire hoses or attack dogs on him? The hose was OK, Patterson said, "But an animal, it's a dog, see? I'm not used to standing by like the people in the South, who are much stronger than I am when it comes to this type of thing. I can't stand around and let an animal bite me. So I will have to do something."[8]

The situation in Birmingham was growing more dangerous by the day. Three weeks before Patterson and Robinson's trip to Alabama, the Reverend A. D. King, Martin Luther King Jr.'s brother, had called for a nationwide boycott of stores operated by Sears, Woolworth, W. T. Grant, and Walgreens because of the segregation practiced by their southern stores. A. D. King topped the enemies list of many southern segregationists. Racists bombed King's house and also the Gaston Motel, an all-black establishment that Martin Luther King used as his Birmingham headquarters. The explosives went off in the predawn hours of the very day Patterson and Robinson were to arrive in Birmingham.

Thousands of enraged African Americans took to the streets and battled hundreds of city police, firemen, state highway patrolmen, and county sheriff's officers. It was the worst violence of the crisis. Authorities used an armored car and police dogs to no avail to disperse the crowd near the motel and Kelly Ingram Park, a half block away. One police officer was stabbed in the back, and others were injured by the showers of bricks, rocks, gravel, and bottles as the crowd chanted, "Kill 'em, kill 'em!" With violence-deafened ears, the rioters even refused to heed Dr. King's executive assistant, Reverend Wyatt Tee Walker, who implored them to disperse. Walker's own wife was clubbed with a rifle butt by a policeman.

Walker called Robinson, who was in New Jersey, to tell him what to expect in Birmingham. Walker also asked Robinson if he could persuade the White House to offer assistance to prevent another assassination attempt. Robinson agreed to contact a Kennedy aide he knew. That afternoon Patterson joined Robinson and eleven others at the airport in Newark for the flight to Birmingham. They were greeted in Alabama by Walker, who told them that death threats had been issued from white citizens against Robinson and Patterson.

While in Birmingham, Floyd and Robinson spoke at two Baptist churches, eliciting joyful responses from the crowds. They also toured the city and saw the dynamited house. At one point, they came across a set of drinking fountains, one marked "colored" and the other marked "white." Floyd drank from the latter, then turned to some whites watching him and said, "Tastes like the same water."[9] Patterson and Robinson spent the night at the Gaston Motel, in rooms that had not been damaged by the earlier bomb attack. They departed the next day.

The trip was applauded by most supporters of the civil rights movement. One black activist, Mable Roberson from San Antonio, sent a telegram to President Kennedy urging that he include Patterson and Robinson among the personal representatives he planned to send to Birmingham. "The Negroes of America feel one or both of these men will represent them with dignity," she said.[10] But the trip also received a fair amount of criticism. The *New York Daily News* questioned its wisdom. Conservative blacks like Olympic hero Jesse Owens wondered if the appearance of Patterson and Robinson had only stirred up more trouble for Birmingham. On the other end of the political spectrum, Nation of Islam minister Malcolm X criticized the two men as being dupes of white liberals.

But Patterson didn't have time to pay much heed to Malcolm X and those who were then commonly called the Black Muslims. Now that the trip was history, Floyd returned his focus to regaining his crown. "My chances of winning the title are good," he said. "The chances of my putting up a better fight are better. If I go down again, I will be able to get up proudly this time."[11] Floyd believed the pressure would be on Liston this time. "All that good guy versus the bad guy stuff," Patterson said. "Everybody was pulling for me and I felt it. That's over with. Now Liston is the champion and the weight is all on his shoulders this time. Now he has to make the fight."[12]

Sonny Liston was of a mind to make the fight. He had intended to carry himself as the world champion in much the same way that Joe Louis and Patterson had. But Liston was not treated to cheering crowds at airports or plaudits from politicians. His public image hardly improved after he became the champion. To the minds of most people, he remained some kind of dangerous beast. So Liston retreated into anger and booze. He was asked once if he planned to go south like Floyd to show support for the civil rights movement. His famous response was, "I ain't got no dog-proof ass."[13] Instead, he set his sights on crushing Patterson once more.

The fight would take place in Las Vegas, and the location itself became one of the most significant things about the rematch. "Where else but in that razzle-dazzle capital of Suckerland," wrote Budd Schulberg, "could you fill a large hall for a rematch of the felling of an apprehensive, thoroughly rehabilitated delinquent by a very tough prison-hard-ened man?"[14] The second fight between Patterson and Liston was the first heavyweight title fight ever held in the city. It allowed Las Vegas to begin to stake its claim as the boxing capital of America. The city went all out to promote the venue. Its brand-new, spic-and-span, $6 million domed Convention Center and Exhibit Hall was futuristic in design by 1960s standards, with palm trees out front and eighty-five hundred seats inside. It was a far cry from the dingy, often rat-infested halls and arenas that played host to bigtime matches on the East Coast.

Norman Mailer and his newest wife arrived in razzle-dazzle land at the end of a cross-country drive. Mailer was in the process of writing his first novel in years, *An American Dream*. His early designs called for the book to be structured around the second Patterson-Liston fight. Once in Vegas, Mailer gave Patterson proofs from a collection of his journalism called *The Presidential Papers*, which included his account of Patterson's first fight with Liston. Mailer regretted that he'd done so. He said, "I was glad to hear that Floyd had never read it, because I felt spooked by the Las Vegas fight, as if Floyd had read it, and it had gotten him thinking of other things . . ."[15]

Ever the good reporter, Mailer kept thorough notes about his time in what Schulberg called "Syndicateville, U.S.A." Mailer ran into Cus D'Amato, now all but completely squeezed out of Patterson's team. D'Amato told him, "Everything points to an upset. The other man is ca-sual, Patterson has been working hard, all the signs are there."[16] Mailer scribbled this down and perhaps believed it. No one else was holding out much hope for Floyd.

Patterson was training hard at his makeshift camp outside Las Vegas at Hidden Well Ranch, a getaway catering to celebrities like Elizabeth Taylor and Eddie Fisher. Hidden Well Ranch may have been a movie-star retreat, but Floyd didn't indulge himself in much luxury there. Instead he practiced the asceticism he learned from D'Amato all those years ago. He rose at 4 A.M. to get in his roadwork, running with two German shepherds while tossing a red rubber ball ahead of him-self. "It's nice for a change," Patterson said, "to have police dogs on your side."[17] When Mailer paid Patterson a visit, he noticed that Floyd ate steak and liver for breakfast. "He hates it but does it," Mailer recorded in his notes.[18]

Patterson promised that he'd fight better than he did in Chicago. "I'm not making excuses for that other time," he said. "I'm in just as good physical condition and, as I told you, more mentally alert."[19] Yet Floyd's psychological state was hardly picture-perfect. Howard Cosell and his wife, Emmy, visited Patterson at Hidden Well Ranch a few days before the fight. They spent an hour with Floyd, and Cosell was struck by the former champ's lack of confidence. Floyd had a hangdog air about him. It wasn't the first time Cosell noticed it. Cosell believed that the defeated expression was on its way to becoming a Patterson trademark. When two visitors departed, Emmy said to Cosell that she thought Patterson seemed already beaten. "He is," Cosell said.[20]

Liston, meanwhile, spent a good deal of his training time gambling and drinking hard at the casino tables, scowling at anyone who interrupted him. Most people kept their distance. There were exceptions, of course, and one of them was notable. Past champions and top contenders typically are invited to title bouts, and Cassius Clay, as one of the latter, was in Vegas. He realized that Liston would be the man he would have to defeat someday to become champion. Clay saw Liston at the Thunderbird Hotel craps table. The champ was on a losing streak, so he was already steaming when Clay spoke up after Sonny threw craps and watched a pile of his chips raked away. "Look at that big ugly bear; he can't even shoot craps," Clay said. Liston turned and glared at the young fighter, then picked up the dice and proceeded to roll another craps. "Look at that big ugly bear. He can't do nothing right." Liston slammed down the dice, walked over to Clay, stuck his face in Clay's face, and said, "Listen, you nigger faggot. If you don't get out of here in ten seconds, I'm gonna pull that big tongue out of your mouth and stick it up your ass." Clay was truly frightened.[21]

Such was Liston's psychological state on July 22, 1963, as he fought Floyd for the second time. In the first round, Liston smashed a seemingly defenseless Patterson with a right uppercut, followed by a left hook. Then he put Floyd down with a right cross. The referee sent Liston to a neutral corner and asked a dazed Patterson if he wanted to continue. Patterson nodded. The fight resumed with Patterson trying to clinch Liston. The champ used his free right hand to pound Floyd's kidneys. After the ref broke them apart, Liston had his way with Floyd. Liston staggered Patterson with an enormous roundhouse left. Somehow, a wobbly Patterson remained on his feet. Liston unloaded shot after shot, then floored Floyd with a massive right to the temple. During the mandatory eight count, the ref asked Patterson again if he wanted to continue. Floyd again said yes. Liston next hit Patterson with a paralyzing left to the body, then slammed him with a right followed by a crisp left hook to the head. Again, Floyd fell. As the referee signaled a knockout, Floyd pushed himself to his feet and went into a boxing stance. That he was beaten registered with Floyd only when Liston embraced him. It was all over in two minutes, nine seconds — just three seconds longer than the Chicago fight had taken.

Patterson again left boxing experts scratching their heads. "He made no use of those skills he had," commented columnist Melvin Durslag of the *Philadelphia Inquirer,* "and he gave a performance that was scandalously unsatisfactory."[22] Even more critical was matchmaker Teddy Brenner, who was a true believer in Floyd back in the early days. In Patterson's dressing room that night, Brenner unloaded: "Any man on that card tonight — from welterweight up — could have taken Patterson. The man just doesn't know how to fight anymore."[23]

This time, there would be no clandestine escape for Patterson after his failure in the ring. Floyd dutifully arrived at the press conference at eleven the next morning. He appeared to be still addled from the previous evening's beating as he uttered sentences that confounded the assembled reporters. There was a general agreement in the room that Floyd should not postpone retirement. Later in the day, Patterson left Vegas on a private plane. The plane overheated not long into the flight and had to return to the airport. Floyd booked passage on a commercial flight. The airport was crowded with departing fight fans. Try as he may, Floyd couldn't hide from their prying eyes.

That fall, *Ebony* published its list of "America's 100 Most Influential Negroes," and Floyd's was among the names. He no doubt appreciated the honor, but the words written about him had a valedictory air: "Unlike many fellow celebrities who have lent their support for the betterment of the race as 'checkbook citizens' from behind the scenes, Floyd not only gave freely of his money but also of his effort and time." The editors lauded him for his trips to the South on behalf of the civil rights movement. They especially gave him credit for demanding that the seating in Miami Beach for the third Johansson fight not be segregated and for having African Americans seated at ringside "where I can see them."[24] But the magazine also judged Patterson to be finished as a fighter of prominence.

Over the span of just a few months, Floyd had gone from being a symbol of the successful "Negro" in America to a relic of a bygone time. As Patterson prepared to fight Liston in 1963, America seemed to be coming apart at the seams. There was the violence in Birmingham, followed by the June assassination of NAACP field secretary Medgar Evers in Jackson, Mississippi. The idealism of Dr. King's "I Have a Dream" speech, delivered at the March on Washington a month after Floyd lost in Las Vegas, was shattered in September when four young black girls died in a hideous church bombing in Birmingham. Then, on a sunny Friday in November, an assassin's bullet blew the side of President Kennedy's head off in Dallas, a city rife with reactionary hatemongering. With the racial strife, the nation's growing military presence in Vietnam, and the continuing cold war, America appeared headed toward some sort of Armageddon. A respectable, well-spoken hero like Floyd Patterson suddenly seemed out of place. This was a time for angry stridency. In the months to come, Floyd would find new purpose in the boxing ring as he took it upon himself to silence the shrillest voice coming from this America in turmoil.

13

A Title for America

"S AY, AREN'T YOU Floyd Patterson?" asked the driver of the car that pulled over. Floyd, trotting along a country road outside Highland Mills at dawn, insisted he was not the ex-heavyweight champion of the world, that he was in fact Raymond Patterson. The car moved on. A while later, another man stopped him. "Hey, Floyd Patterson!" Patterson again said no, he was the boxer's brother Raymond. The man didn't buy it and told him so. He asked for an autograph. Patterson accepted the paper and pencil that was offered, and signed it "Raymond Patterson."

The incident occurred while Gay Talese was shadowing Floyd, gathering material for a profile to run in *Esquire*. Talese found a fighter who was frustrated and bewildered by what had happened during his two encounters with Sonny Liston. He did not want a rematch — "Who would pay a nickel for another Patterson-Liston fight?"[1] — but he wished for a way for him and Liston to square off where no one would see them, a fight in which Floyd would be free of all the pressures he had felt going into their two meetings. In this fantasy fight, Patterson did not want to find out if he could win. He just wanted to find out if he could get past the first round.

"It's not a *bad* feeling when you're knocked out," he said. "It's a *good* feeling, actually. It's not painful, just a sharp grogginess. You don't see angels or stars; you're on a pleasant cloud. After Liston hit me in Nevada, I felt, for about four or five seconds, that everybody in the arena was actually in the ring with me, circled around me like a family, and you feel warmth toward all the people in the arena after you're knocked out. You feel lovable to all the people. And you want to reach out and kiss everybody — men and women — and after the Liston fight somebody told me I actually blew a kiss to the crowd from the ring."[2] But the love evaporated. Floyd realized where he was, what had happened. What ensued was a confused pain combined with anger. There was no avoiding it.

Floyd could not seem to escape conflict, especially on the home front. The Patterson children were having a difficult time with the white kids in their neighborhood. Floyd's children were "stoned, literally," on the way to school, according to Milton Gross's daughter, sportswriter Jane Gross.[3] In addition to throwing rocks, the white kids called the young Pattersons "nigger, chocolate drop, and Sambo."[4] Now, a new problem had arisen. "I'm not going to work out today," an upset Patterson said to Talese. "I'm going to fly down to Scarsdale.[5] Those boys are picking on [Floyd's daughter] Jeannie again. She's the only Negro in this school, and the older kids give her a rough time, and some of the older boys tease her and lift up her dress all the time. Yesterday she went home crying, and so today I'm going down there and plan to wait outside the school for those boys to come out, and . . ."[6]

Talese in tow, Floyd stormed off to the airport, threatening to deal with the offenders with a left hook. Patterson had always been afraid of flying, and he was addressing that fear by taking flying lessons. Accompanied by his pilot friend Ted Hanson, Patterson flew a Cessna to the airport in Westchester, where Sandra was waiting for him. They drove to the school. There, Patterson confronted the boy who had been lifting his daughter's skirt. Despite his earlier chest-thumping, Floyd threw no punches. In fact, he did nothing more than tell the boy to stop it. "I won't tell your mother — that might get you in trouble — but don't do it again, okay?"[7] The boy calmly walked away. Patterson retreated to his airplane and flew back to training camp.

Floyd found himself dealing with conflict even at his inner sanctum, the place he felt most secure, his training camp. For several days in a row, Cus D'Amato drove to Highland Mills to visit his former fighter's camp. Each time, D'Amato banged on the door, expecting Floyd to step out and greet him. His knocks went unanswered, but Cus knew that Floyd was inside. Miffed, D'Amato would linger, sometimes for as long as an hour. Still, the door remained closed. Finally, D'Amato would leave. "We had an agreement," D'Amato would say, "that I never was to believe anything he supposedly said until he told it to my face. He has never told me to my face that I am not his manager. I have no idea why he won't see me."[8]

Unable to penetrate the wall of silence from the Patterson camp, D'Amato began legal action against Patterson for money he believed was contractually owed him from the two Liston fights. D'Amato claimed he was flat broke, even though he was now guiding José Torres up the light-heavyweight ranks. He maintained that his battles with the IBC had used up every dime he'd earned off Patterson, leaving him busted. He estimated he was owed at least $250,000 from the first Liston fight alone. D'Amato asked Julius November for a full accounting of the proceeds from the first Liston fight but November refused him — or at least did not provide enough of an accounting to satisfy D'Amato. So D'Amato hired famed attorney Edward Bennett Williams to find remedy in the legal system. But there was more than just money involved.

"I am the only man in this business who has made flat and uncompromising statements about fighters I've been associated with," D'Amato said. "When Patterson won the Olympics, I said that Floyd would be rookie of the year in boxing and that he would become a heavyweight champion, and he was still a middleweight! My predictions were based on knowledge and analyses of Patterson and his potential. I was derided. When Patterson was knocked out by Johansson I saw what happened and why, and I knew what had to be done. So I went into the ring and made a flat statement that Floyd Patterson would be the first heavyweight champion to win back the title. The critics said that if Dempsey couldn't do it, how could Patterson? But then look what happened. My record, damn it, is certainly worth some respect."[9]

But none was forthcoming for the barrel-chested, white-haired man who soon began fading from public sight, as did the lawsuit.

• • •

Though written off by all but his staunchest American fans, Patterson started to slowly recover a measure of respect for himself as a fighter. Wisely, he chose Sweden as the location for his next two fights. There, never mind what had happened with Liston, he was a beloved figure, someone who could attract a crowd of adoring fans just by walking down the street — "I'm kind of a one-man Beatles," he said.[10] He would not have to deal with a cynical press or cynical fans. His Italian opponent for the first fight was no world-beater, but that hardly mattered. After two humiliating knockouts, Floyd wanted a win. And he notched one in early 1964.

After that time, Patterson was the ninth-ranked contender in the heavyweight category. Cassius Clay had risen to number one. If Patterson wanted to get a shot at the title any time soon, he needed to beat someone of higher standing than a virtually unknown Italian boxer to lift his ranking. That opportunity came along when he was scheduled to fight Eddie Machen, the fourth-ranked contender, in July 1964.

But before that fight could take place, Talese's profile of Patterson appeared in *Esquire*. It was a stunning example of the New Journalism, the result of Talese's dogged reporting during the weeks he spent with Floyd. Talese would return to his motel room after following Patterson through the day and dump out page after page of notes and impressions that he would later use to compose an article as tightly constructed as the best short story. The long article was a hit from the moment it showed up on newsstands. It was destined to be anthologized for years to come, ensuring that Patterson's name lived on. But the *Esquire* editors used a title for it that Talese never approved of — "The Loser" — which consequently served to reinforce Patterson's failings over his successes. Floyd had plenty of pressure on him to become the winner in his fight with Machen.

In 1958 Eddie Machen had suffered an upset in a bout with Ingemar Johansson, which opened the door for Ingo to fight Floyd for the world championship. Before that, Machen was considered one of the best contenders for the crown. Machen hailed from Redding, California. After a few amateur fights in his late teens, he served three years in prison for armed robbery. When he was released, he began boxing in earnest and entered the pro ranks in March 1955. Fighting often in the

Bay Area or elsewhere on the West Coast, Machen won twenty-four straight bouts, including two wins over Joey Maxim, before fighting Zora Folley at the Cow Palace in San Francisco in 1958. The two men battled to a twelve-round draw. Then Machen fought Johansson.

After the Johansson loss, Machen fought at a furious pace, recording win after win with only occasional losses. One of the defeats was to Sonny Liston in 1960, but Machen stayed in the ring for the full twelve rounds of the fight, which was a kind of moral victory. After that Machen scored an impressive win over contender Doug Jones in December 1961 and a draw with Cleveland "Big Cat" Williams in July 1962. In December 1962, however, authorities committed Machen to the Napa State Hospital after he threatened suicide. He was diagnosed as an acute schizophrenic. At the time, he was the third-ranked heavyweight in the world. His inactivity in the ring while he was institutionalized caused his rating to fall. Finally released, he resumed fighting in early 1964. Machen smashed Duke Sabedong to the canvas in just one round to boost his world ranking to number four and set up his fight with Patterson in July of that year.

In spite of Machen's contender status, the fight elicited mostly yawns back in the United States. Arthur Daley of the *New York Times* dismissed the bout between a defrocked champion and a "quondam contender" as a stop on the road to nowhere. He said of the Patterson and Machen matchup, "They are a pair of emotionally entangled men with enough psychoses and neuroses to have fascinated Freud. They have totally bewildered those amateur psychiatrists, the boxing experts. Neither ever realized his full potentialities as a fighter and the irony is that a fight between them might have straightened out the winner at least. Now it is too late."[11]

Still, it was a contest between two of the ten highest-ranked heavyweights. Floyd's friend Pete Hamill thought it could be the most important fight in his career. "For Patterson," Hamill said, "the money he can earn from prizefighting is no longer of prime importance. What is important is his pride. He wants to erase the image he fears he will leave behind when he retires: that as heavyweight champion he was an elaborate fraud with no ability to take a punch, a fraud whose true measure could be found in the total of four minutes and sixteen seconds he lasted in two fights with Sonny Liston."[12]

The bout in Råsunda, Solna, Sweden, on July 5, 1964, turned out to be dull, with Patterson and Machen spending much of the time locked in clinches. When they weren't hugging each other, Patterson managed to knock Machen down two times. In the end, Floyd was awarded nine rounds, two were judged even, and just one round went to Machen. Floyd thought the Machen bout proved that he could still battle the best in the world and win. Patterson, who planned to retire if he lost to Machen, announced he wanted to fight the man formerly known as Cassius Clay.

Muhammad Ali was now the heavyweight champion of the world, having pulled off one of the greatest upsets in boxing history when he dethroned Liston earlier in 1964. Liston, overconfident, perhaps, as a seven-to-one favorite, trained with little intensity before that fight. He certainly looked like an older, slower fighter than he had against Patterson. Liston quickly learned that the larger, faster Ali was not going to be an easy man to defeat. After three rounds, Liston and his cornermen conspired to end the fight by disabling Ali. When Liston came out for the fourth round, his gloves were coated with a caustic substance — no one outside Liston's corner was ever sure exactly what it was — that he smeared into Ali's eyes. His vision blurred, Ali insisted to his corner between rounds that he could not go on and asked that his gloves be cut off. Ali's corner wizard Angelo Dundee was able to flush out Ali's eyes and instructed him to stay away from Liston until his vision cleared. At the midpoint of the fifth round, Ali could see clearly once more and began to take charge of the fight. In the sixth round, Ali ripped Liston's face to hamburger with his whip-snap jabs. Liston, like a twelve-year-old bully who has run into someone willing to stand up to him, feigned a shoulder injury and refused to answer the seventh-round bell. With that, Ali became the new king of the world.

In the weeks after the Machen fight, Patterson became obsessed with beating Ali for reasons having more to do with Floyd's ideas about patriotism and religion than with the challenge the young Ali presented in the ring.

In October 1964 Patterson began to stir up controversy when he collaborated with Milton Gross for a *Sports Illustrated* essay entitled "I

Want to Destroy Clay." Patterson struck out at the dethroned Liston, expressing dismay that Sonny refused to keep fighting in his championship bout with Ali. "A champion doesn't quit," Patterson said. That was certainly true for Floyd. He did have fights stopped because of injuries, but they were always halted by the referee. Floyd never once failed to answer the bell on his own. In the article, Floyd slammed Ali for telling Dundee that he wanted to quit when his eyes were burning and his vision went blurry. Floyd questioned the character of the men who had claimed the title he once proudly held. Patterson said, "There's a tremendous responsibility on the champion that Clay and Liston obviously don't understand — to themselves, to the sport and to the public, especially in these times of such great social changes in our country and in the way the people all over the world look at us."[13]

But Ali's religious conversion irked the good Catholic Patterson even more. The Nation of Islam, an American religion that embraced teachings contrary to orthodox Islam, stood in opposition to all that Patterson believed when it came to issues of race. He once told Pete Hamill, "It's not a fight for *friendship;* it's a fight for equality. As long as I can sleep in the same hotels as you, as long as I can eat in the same restaurants as you, as long as I can read in the same libraries and swim in the same swimming pools and watch movies in the same section as you and vote with the same rights as you, then we can consider friendship."[14] Black Muslims under Nation of Islam leader Elijah Muhammad believed that that was all folderol. They demanded that American society be segregated because they believed the races had no business intermingling.

At the base of the Nation of Islam's belief system was the tenet that black people were not equal to white people but *superior* to them. Whites, in their view, were devils, the creations of a mad scientist intent on releasing evil on the world. By expressing this kind of attitude toward whites, the Black Muslims had exposed a nerve that ran throughout black communities in the United States at the time. James Baldwin's *The Fire Next Time* is one of the most important books written about race in America and grew out of his own meditations on the Nation of Islam. "There appears to be a vast amount of confusion on this point," Baldwin wrote, "but I do not know many Negroes who are eager to be 'accepted' by white people, still less to be loved by them; they, the blacks, simply don't wish to be beaten over the head by the whites every instant of our brief passage on the planet."[15]

The message of the Nation of Islam resonated with blacks who were growing increasingly frustrated and angry by the slow progress America was making in ending the virtual apartheid that had existed since the end of Reconstruction. The Freedom Summer of 1964 may have been when Lyndon Johnson signed the landmark Civil Rights Act, but it was also when sheriff's officers in collusion with the Klan killed three civil rights workers in Neshoba County, Mississippi, and dumped their bodies beneath a rural earthen dam. These killings and other violent incidents reinforced Black Muslim concepts about why the races should remain apart. Since he was born, Cassius Clay had been exposed to his father's disdain of white people. The young boxer made for a rapt acolyte when he learned about the Nation of Islam's teachings from Malcolm X and others. And he stunned and outraged much of America when he announced his conversion and name change after he became heavyweight champion in February 1964.

Floyd could not abide a Black Muslim holding what he considered to be the most prestigious title in sports. He said of Ali, "He has a right to believe what he believes, but harm has been done to the Negroes' cause and the way the rest of the world regards it by the one who calls himself Muhammad Ali." Patterson went on to say:

I am a Negro and I'm proud to be one, but I'm also an American. I'm not so stupid that I don't know that Negroes don't have all the rights and privileges that all Americans should have. I know that someday we will get them. God made us all, and whatever He made is good. All people — white, black and yellow — are brothers and sisters. That will be acknowledged. It will just take time, but it will never come if we think the way the Black Muslims think.

They preach hate and separation instead of love and integration. They preach mistrust when there must be understanding. Clay is so young and has been so misled by the wrong people that he doesn't appreciate how far we have come and how much harm he has done by joining the Black Muslims. He might just as well have joined the Ku Klux Klan.[16]

Floyd said that he hoped Ali would defeat Liston in their rematch. Then, if Patterson were successful in his upcoming fights, he wanted to battle Ali to, at least in his mind, reclaim the title for America. Ali responded by calling Floyd an Uncle Tom and criticized him for moving into an affluent, predominately white neighborhood. Ali also questioned just how much Floyd cared about black people, saying that the only time Patterson was ever seen in Harlem was to ride in a parade. "The big shot didn't have no time for his own kind," Ali said, "he was so busy integrating. And now he wants to fight me because I stick up for black people."[17]

Before he could attempt to return the title to America, the thirty-year-old Patterson had to best a tough Canadian. George Chuvalo was nearly three years younger than Patterson and grew up in a rough part of Toronto known as the Junction. He began boxing when he was eighteen. He was a big man, six feet tall, typically weighing around 210 pounds for his fights. He hit hard, but the thing he was best known for was his chin. If Patterson had a chin made of china, as critics often alleged, Chuvalo's chin was cast iron. He had gone the distance with the very best boxers of his time, never once getting knocked down. But he was more than a pair of fists. Though he quit school before graduating, Chuvalo read Freud and Jung as well as Greek and Asian philosophers. He said that if he weren't a boxer, he'd have become a lawyer.

By the beginning of 1965 Chuvalo had risen to be the third-ranked heavyweight contender.[18] Patterson was rated number two following his victory over Machen. The winner of the Patterson-Chuvalo bout would be in line to fight for the heavyweight crown. "Should I be victorious against Chuvalo," Patterson said, "I look forward to meeting Cassius Clay. It will be a great opportunity to vindicate myself. Of course, once I do that I want to fight Liston again. I must do that. I have a lot of things to prove — to myself and to everybody."[19]

Floyd trained with particular intensity. He also put on weight, knowing that he would have to be ready to brawl with Chuvalo if necessary. As Floyd's training camp was winding down, he had muscled up to 197 ¼ pounds, which was the most he'd ever weighed as a boxer. Oddsmakers took heed of Floyd's impressive size and the determination he'd shown at training camp. Patterson was a seven-to-five favorite, but one very noticeable voice was proclaiming that Chuvalo would win: Muhammad Ali.

The fight stirred much interest in New York. Madison Square Garden sold out, which was the first time it had done so for a boxing contest in more than two years, suggesting to some that the involvement of a white combatant who stood a chance to win was boosting sales. But no doubt Ali played a role as well. Ali was a genius at creating publicity, and he actively involved himself in the promotion of Patterson-Chuvalo. One day he showed up at Patterson's Marlboro, New York, training camp. Ali carried two heads of lettuce and a half dozen carrots.

"Hey," he shouted to the reporters and others in the makeshift gym, "anybody seen the Rabbit?"[20] Ali's nickname for Patterson derived from his belief that Floyd was timid and scared. (Ali also gave Chuvalo a nickname: the Washer Woman. The moniker came from an earlier fight in which Ali thought Chuvalo, working on an opponent pinned against the ropes, looked like a woman washing laundry with a scrub board.) Patterson came downstairs into the gym. Ali, flanked by two Black Muslims, immediately approached Floyd with the lettuce and carrots. Patterson extended his hand to the brash young champ, who knocked it away as members of the press looked on. Ali declared to Floyd that if he could defeat the Washer Woman, he might cease to be a nobody in the young champion's eyes and get a chance to reclaim the heavyweight title. The performance continued for a while, and then Patterson began to address some of the reporters present: "Despite the lettuce and the carrots, I am glad that the heavyweight champion, Mr. Cassius Clay . . ."

"That's not my name — call me by my right name Muhammad Ali!" Ali said. Some banter followed, ending with Ali saying, "Cassius Clay is a slave name . . . I'm free . . . you got a slave name . . . you ain't nuthin' but an Uncle Tom Negro . . . You Uncle Tom, I'll jump right in there on you now."

"Well, do it," Patterson said.[21]

Ali, employing soon to be all-too-familiar antics, made an exaggerated attempt to free himself from his Black Muslim handlers and climb into the ring. But of course no fisticuffs were exchanged. Patterson sparred for a couple of rounds to the accompaniment of disparaging remarks from Ali about his abilities. Then Patterson left the circus, and Ali climbed into the vacant ring to dance and shadowbox for the benefit of the reporters.

No doubt all this was a distraction for Patterson, who still had to defeat a very tough Chuvalo before he'd get a chance to fight Ali. But at the same time, he understood Ali's underlying purpose for the performance, which was to build up publicity for the Patterson-Chuvalo bout. About these kinds of encounters with Ali, Patterson would say, "I guess it all helped sell tickets to the fight. But in that split second that Cassius Clay's eyes met with mine, I could sense that he was a little embarrassed about it all. He seemed to be apologizing, saying, 'This is what I have to do.'" (Later still, Ali was at a press conference with Patterson, screaming and bragging as was his wont. But then he leaned over to Patterson and whispered, "You want to make some money, don't you, Floyd? You want to make lots of money, don't you?"[22] Yes, Patterson did, and he understood what his role was, there alongside Ali. "This is only one of the peculiarities of the fight promotion in the era of Muhammad Ali," said the *New York Herald Tribune*'s boxing sage Jesse Abramson, "who, on the one hand, claims all the credit for building the gate and stirring interest in boxing, and then airily asserts, 'I'm going to be the last of the champions. There will be no boxing after me.'"[23]) One thing was clear. As Cassius Clay, growing up in Louisville, Ali had idolized Patterson. But that was all long in the past. Ever since he became a professional boxer, Ali idolized only himself.

Ali did not limit his promotional efforts to Patterson alone for the Patterson-Chuvalo fight. He made a similar stop at the Washer Woman's camp. Only this time, he bore buckets and mops instead of carrots and lettuce and was joined by a retinue of reporters who'd ridden on Ali's beloved red-and-white tour bus. They almost didn't make it. Ali, notorious for his lack of skill behind the wheel, had been driving the bus when it ran off the road and into a ditch. He and the reporters were forced to walk from the scene of the accident to Chuvalo's camp outside Monticello, New York. Chuvalo played along, asking, "When do I get my bucket?" After Ali gave it to him, Chuvalo said, "Thanks, Popeye."[24]

Having crashed their training camps, Ali wasn't through with Patterson-Chuvalo. He signed on to provide the between-rounds commentary for the closed-circuit broadcast of the February 1, 1965, fight. At ringside before the opening round, Ali said he'd visited both camps, and to him both "boys are in tip-top condition." He pronounced Patterson's punches as looking sharp, adding that Floyd was determined to win back the championship. For Chuvalo, Ali saw the contest as a do-or-die affair. "This should be a great, great fight," he said. He picked Chuvalo to win, "because Floyd has a rather glass jaw." He added that the boxer who won at Madison Square Garden that night deserved a shot at his crown.[25]

In the first round, Chuvalo seemed to have little defense against Patterson, especially his left jabs. Chuvalo tried to tie up the faster Floyd and slip in some punches. Patterson opened up Chuvalo's nose before the two-minute mark. Although Floyd didn't seem overly dominating, it was clearly Patterson's round, and it impressed observers at ringside. An excited Ali shouted between rounds, "Floyd Patterson surprised me and I believe I have to change my mind. I'm a man who tells the truth, and I believe that this man won — he won the first round. He surprised me. I believe that George is fighting a little rough, a little dirty as far as boxing is concerned, hitting behind the head, holding, hitting on the clinches, and he's not doing like I thought he would. But Floyd is determined, and I believe he is a threat to my title."[26]

Patterson's resolve was impressive. Floyd was the most intense he'd been in the ring since the second Johansson fight. But Chuvalo was his match in that department. Chuvalo's team had devised a good plan: attack Patterson's body repeatedly in the early rounds, and when he started lowering his elbows to protect his belly, attack his exposed head. Chuvalo pursued Patterson relentlessly, forcing Floyd to back-pedal, and that disallowed him from throwing left hooks effectively. "He slammed Floyd in the belly with the impact of a man tamping dirt with a four-by-four," said *Sports Illustrated*'s Tex Maule. Chuvalo also landed some of his jackhammer shots to Patterson's vulnerable chin, but this time, Patterson kept his feet. "I think I proved after thirteen years tonight that I can take a much better punch than you gentlemen have given me credit for," Patterson would say to reporters afterward. "He hit me well at times — in the belly and on the chin. Several times these punches hurt me, but never seriously. I thought at one time in the fight I was behind, and my corner told me so — I guess somewhere around the eighth or ninth round. They told me — I guess it was just before the tenth round — that if I would start punching and become more aggressive I could win."[27] Patterson was indeed particularly aggressive in those later rounds and finished with a flourish in the twelfth and final round to bring the Madison Square Garden crowd to its feet.

Floyd wept in his corner as the closely scored but unanimous decision in his favor was announced, in part because of the appreciative applause from his hometown fans in the Garden but also because he felt he had redeemed himself.[28] At least to a degree. He told Chuvalo afterward, "You gained more prestige in defeat than I did in victory."[29] In fact, both combatants gained prestige. *The Ring* magazine named the hard-fought bout its fight of the year for 1965. The never-say-die Patterson, who seemed washed up after the second Liston fight, moved to the top of the list of heavyweight contenders. Now he set his aim on Ali.

Shortly after the Chuvalo fight, D'Amato reemerged in the boxing headlines. José Torres, Patterson's longtime friend and gym mate, defeated Willie Pastrano to become world light-heavyweight champion, with D'Amato guiding the way. Sort of. D'Amato functioned as a manager without portfolio at the time of the fight, because he still had not regained a New York license. Also, the matchmakers in charge of the title fight had told Torres that they would not let him participate if D'Amato were involved — bad blood from the old IBC days. Moreover, Torres was encountering some of the same frustrations with D'Amato that Floyd had, and was in the process of pushing Cus aside. But to the boxing press, Cus was regarded as the new champion's overseer, and after Torres won, Cus was newsworthy again. Cus used the opportunity to defend himself for his handling of Patterson and to state his belief that he had been treated unfairly by Floyd and the people now surrounding him. He even took a swipe at Floyd's victory over Chuvalo. Yes, he said, Patterson had been successful in the ring, but he'd been technically unsound. Floyd had deteriorated as a boxer because Cus had not been allowed to pressure him in training to keep his skills sharp. Floyd made no public comments on Cus's statements. The spotlight on Cus following the Torres victory amounted to one of the last times D'Amato basked in the glow of New York media. Over the next eighteen months, Torres would successfully defend his title three times, but by the end of that time, he and D'Amato had gone their separate ways.

Before Patterson could challenge the champion, Ali had to give Sonny Liston a rematch. This had been delayed for six months after Ali developed a hernia. Liston said that Ali's hernia was the result of all the champ's hollering. During that six months, Malcolm X, who had proselytized Ali to the Nation of Islam, was assassinated by individuals loyal to Elijah Muhammad after a particularly acrimonious split between the Black Muslims and Malcolm X. As the most famous member of the Nation of Islam, Ali conceivably was a likely target for Malcolm X loyalists seeking revenge. With violence outside the ring a real possibility, the fight was rejected by city after city until tiny Lewiston, Maine, agreed to host it. The glittery throng that normally flocked to heavyweight championship bouts stayed away, fearing the possibility of gunfire in the arena. On May 25, 1965, just 2,434 fans showed up at St. Dominic's Hall in Lewiston, the all-time-record low attendance for a heavyweight championship fight. One of the people who braved whatever might happen in Lewiston was Floyd Patterson.

At 1:42 of the first round,[30] Ali clipped Liston's chin with a fast straight right. To many spectators, it seemed like nothing more than a glancing blow, but it was enough to knock Liston down. Was it enough to knock him out? That question has been the subject of intense debate for nearly half a century. Liston's wallowing on the mat seemed exaggerated. While Liston was on his back, Ali preened over him, refusing to go to a neutral corner as referee Jersey Joe Walcott struggled to get him to do so, losing track of the count in the meantime. After Ali had retreated, Liston stood up and appeared set to resume fighting. Walcott readied the fighters to continue. But an official had ticked off twelve seconds while Liston was down. Fight writer Nat Fleischer shouted this information to Walcott. Walcott stopped the fight and raised Ali's arm as the victor.

The few spectators in the arena became irate, shouting, "Fake! Fake! Fake!" It certainly had the look of being fixed. Floyd was not focused on the question of whether the fight was legitimate. He knew what Liston had to be feeling. This knockout was much more humiliating than either of the ones Floyd had experienced at Liston's hands. Patterson decided to seek Liston out:[31]

I went in the back, in the dressing room, and he was all by himself. I said to him, "I know how you feel. I've experienced this myself." And he didn't say one word. He didn't say anything. He just kept looking and looking, [and] he had that mean look on his face. I don't think he knew he had the mean look. But I kept on talking anyway. And finally I said [to myself] I don't think I'm reaching him. So I said, "Okay, I'll see you later." So I went to walk out the door and before I could get out the door, he ran up and put his arms on my shoulder and I turned around, and he said, "Thanks." I knew then that I'd reached him.[32]

Thereafter, the one-time rivals were friendly for the few years remaining in Liston's life.

Once Ali had finished with the fighter he dismissed as the Big Ugly Bear, the road was clear for a matchup with Floyd. The fight was set for the same convention center in Las Vegas where Patterson had lost to Liston for the second time. The date was to be November 22, 1965, exactly two years after President Kennedy's murder in Dallas. America seemed a very different place from what it had been before that tragic Friday. Hope had given way to chaos.

In the summer of 1965, racial violence spread beyond the South to Los Angeles.[33] What seemed to be a simple traffic stop involving a white California Highway Patrol motorcycle officer and a black driver evolved into a riot in the Watts section of the city. Matters worsened gravely when the city's longtime powerful police chief, William Parker, referred to the rioters as monkeys in a zoo. Soon, dozens of buildings were burning. Black rioters targeted white-owned businesses. The Watts violence received massive media coverage, and, in ways, the riot came to symbolize the state of race relations in America. LA was no backwater burg run by vicious, ignorant Dixie crackers. In the mid-1960s, many Americans viewed the city as a kind of dream land, offering freedom from the kinds of prejudices that hobbled much of the rest of the nation. If a race riot of this magnitude could happen here, it could happen anywhere. Watching the flames and bloody confrontations on the evening news, many white Americans who had been fervent supporters of the civil rights movement were appalled by what they perceived as the unbridled violence of black rioters in Watts.

The heavyweight title fight in the fall of 1965 came to mirror the Watts riots in some ways. Ali became the face of the black anger that had erupted in Los Angeles. Floyd, who just a few years earlier had stood as the groundbreaking liberal who demanded and received fair treatment as a black athlete, became the representative of the establishment. At the time, Ali was an unpopular champion among fight fans, who thought him to be a loudmouth who eschewed time-tested fundamentals, a brash young man who deserved a comeuppance. They turned to Floyd to deliver it — none more so than Frank Sinatra, the best-known fight fan in the world. Sinatra had grown closer to Floyd since the two had met a few years earlier, and he urged him to bring respectability back to the heavyweight crown by defeating Ali. Ali had a response to the Sinatras of the world: "I am America. Only I'm the part you won't recognize. But get used to me. Black, confident, cocky; my name, not yours; my religion, not yours; my goals my own — get used to me! I can make it without your approval! I won't let you beat me and I won't let your Negro [in this case, Patterson] beat me!"³⁴ Floyd now appeared to be a cultural leftover, a man still listening to Billy Eckstine and Patti Page at a time when Soul Brother No. 1 James Brown topped the R & B charts.

Many radicalized young African Americans felt free at this time to load negative symbolism on Patterson. Poet, playwright, and essayist LeRoi Jones, soon to drop his "slave name" to become Amiri Baraka, found Patterson to be a disgusting presence: "Patterson was to represent the fruit of the missionary ethic; he had found God, reversed his underprivileged (uncontrolled) violence, and turned it to work for the democratic liberal imperialist state. The tardy black Horatio Alger offering the glad hand of integration to welcome twenty million into the lunatic asylum of white America . . ." Baraka loved to see Patterson get knocked down in a fight. "And each time Patterson fell, a vision came to me of the whole colonial West crumbling in some sinister silence."³⁵

Even from the grave, Malcolm X weighed in on Floyd. Malcolm X's autobiography was compiled from a series of interviews Alex Haley conducted over the two years prior to his assassination. It hit the bookstores just weeks before Patterson's fight with Ali. It included Malcolm's take on the contest, which he believed would be a battle over the *truth:* "Nothing in all the furor which followed was more ridiculous than Floyd Patterson announcing that as a Catholic, he wanted to fight Cassius Clay—to save the heavyweight crown from being held by a Black Muslim. It was such a sad case of a brainwashed black Christian ready to do battle for the white man—who wants no part of him."[36]

In prison in California, black radical Eldridge Cleaver noted that many black Americans supported Ali because Patterson "was an anachronism light years behind" Ali, who was "more in harmony with the furious psychic stance of the Negro today." Cleaver also said: "The white hope for a Patterson victory was, in essence, a counterrevolutionary desire to force the Negro, now in rebellion and personified in the boxing world by Ali, back into his 'place.' The black hope, on the contrary, was to see Lazarus crushed, to see Uncle Tom defeated."[37] Ali himself began to refer to Patterson as the "black white hope" as the fight approached.[38] Like Cleaver, Ali viewed pro–civil rights activists like Patterson as Lazaruses—dead men who had not been brought to life through the teachings of Elijah Muhammad.

Such was the surface rhetoric. But both Patterson and Ali also understood how they could use their dispute over religion and the civil rights movement to ensure their bout would be a box-office success, starting with the issue of Ali's name. Floyd's insistence on referring to Ali as Cassius Clay unquestionably was a suitable device for adding tension to the morality play about to take place in Las Vegas. But during a private moment around this time, Patterson said to Ali, "It's all right if I call you Cassius, isn't it?" Ali smiled and said, "Anytime, Floyd."[39] Patterson once told W. C. Heinz that he continued to call the new champ Cassius Clay because he found it difficult to pronounce "Muhammad." It sounded suspicious—Floyd wasn't known for having trouble pronouncing other words—but perhaps it was true. And perhaps Ali knew that and permitted Patterson to call him Cassius in private moments for that reason. But all that was indeed in private.[40] In public, Ali roiled when Floyd referred to him by his old "slave name," because it played into the idea that Floyd wasn't anything but an Uncle Tom, subservient to his white Christian masters. Ali promised to punish Floyd in the ring and "give him a good beating."[41]

The approaching Patterson-Ali fight generated hostility among fans unlike anything since the black champion Jack Johnson battled the "Great White Hope" Jim Jeffries on July 4, 1910. That fight led to race riots after the black champion Johnson handily defeated the past-champion Jeffries, who'd come out of retirement to attempt to win back the title for the white race. As his bout with Ali approached, Floyd feared that he might be shot by an irate Black Muslim in the audience. If not that, who knew what the contest's outcome would ignite once the final bell sounded in Las Vegas, 272 miles across the desert from the burned-out hulks in Watts? But one thing was certain. The prefight brouhaha was translating into ticket sales, especially in the closed-circuit TV market.

In the month before the fight, Dan Florio developed abdominal pain and sought out medical care. He underwent intestinal surgery in New York. A week later, to the shock of the boxing world, the sixty-nine-year-old Florio died from complications from the surgery. Suddenly, Floyd was without his trusted mentor — the man who had been with him since the very beginning of his professional boxing career, the architect of his comeback victory over Johansson. In recent fights, Patterson had even listed Florio as his manager of record. Floyd announced that he would not allow Florio's passing to delay the Ali fight. But he had to find a new trainer to work his corner, and he had to do so fast. Patterson received a call from his biggest supporter, the Chairman of the Board, who recommended a friend of his, Al Silvani.

At the time, Silvani was working for Sinatra's production company, but he possessed plenty of boxing credentials. He learned the business at Stillman's Gym under legends Whitey Bimstein and Ray Arcel — for the latter, he was said to have been his "right-hand man and left-hand man, too."[42] Silvani had trained champions Rocky Graziano, Henry Armstrong, and Jake "Raging Bull" LaMotta, among others. In the mid-1940s, Silvani met Sinatra, who asked the trainer to teach him how to box. Silvani took Sinatra to Stillman's, where the young crooner began to learn the fundamentals of sticking and moving. A second career of training famous entertainers how to box began for Silvani. He prepped Paul Newman for his role as Graziano in *Somebody Up There Likes Me* and worked as an assistant director on the Elvis Presley boxing-themed film *Kid Galahad*. Still, Silvani was unknown to Patterson, and Floyd hesitated before agreeing that Al was the man.

Silvani shortly discovered that he had more to deal with than he expected. From time to time, Floyd experienced pain from a slipped disc. It always seemed to go away or at least become tolerable. But as Floyd trained for Ali, he suffered a major flare-up. At times, the herniated vertebra made it all but impossible for Floyd to walk. It was apparent to everyone in his training camp that he was in bad shape, but Floyd refused to speak of his condition publicly. For him, the fight had to go on, regardless of the pain he suffered. It fell to Silvani to try to get Floyd in good enough shape to fight Ali, through stretches, massage, and manually popping the herniated disc back into place.

When the two fighters entered the ring in November, Ali, at twenty-three, was seven years Patterson's junior and in his athletic prime. He was the one heavyweight of the time who could match Patterson's hand speed. Beyond that, Ali was faster than Patterson when it came to moving around the ring. He stood three inches taller than Patterson, possessed longer reach, and, at 210 pounds, weighed around 15 pounds more. Like the former light-heavyweight champion Tommy Loughran, Ali fought from the outside, circling his opponents, attacking them with slicing jabs, only Ali was much better than Loughran. It was a style guaranteed to cause many problems for Floyd, who was used to battling much more ponderous heavyweights.

As the bout began in Las Vegas, Floyd seemed to match up well with Ali, catching jab after jab, with the resulting distinctive snap of leather on leather. Patterson also proved deft at slipping Ali's punches, and he seemed aggressive, as if sensing he needed a quick knockout if he were to win. Meanwhile, Ali seemed more interested in talking than in hitting. His mouth never stopped flapping, taunting Floyd with "What's my name?" and "Come on, White America." He repeatedly called Patterson "Uncle Tom" and "White Man's Nigger" when they were in clinches.

After the first two rounds, Patterson's back started to spasm. Be-

tween rounds, Silvani and Buster Watson began playing amateur chi-
ropractors. "So I just snapped his back into place," Silvani said. "He
couldn't sit down."[43] But the tricky disc refused to stay put. To Silvani
and others at ringside, it quickly became clear that Patterson had no
business being in the ring. His back injury prevented him from punching effectively, and he appeared at times to be all but defenseless. Yet
Floyd remained on his feet, puzzling those who'd seen him fall so easily at the hands of Roy Harris, Ingemar Johansson, Sonny Liston, and
even Pete Rademacher. Ali later claimed that through the first six
rounds, he threw "everything in the book but [Floyd] just wouldn't
fall."[44]

After the sixth round, Patterson was scarcely able to move. Ali believed the referee would call a stop to the contest, but it continued. Ali
decided that the immobilized Patterson was at risk for serious injury,
so he contained whatever aggressive impulses he felt and backed off
for the rest of the fight. "When a man is whipped and in the physical shape [Patterson was] in now," Ali told Howard Cosell during a
largely overlooked postfight interview, "it's just not worth the money
[to harm him]. I don't want to hurt nobody. Patterson's a nice fellow, a
clean-living fellow." After the eleventh round, Patterson's back was so
tight he had to hobble to get to his corner. Some perceptive sportswriters at ringside picked up on the problem, but most thought Ali was
slowly and methodically beating Floyd into submission. In the twelfth
round, Patterson was tottering, but, as Ali said, "He still was ducking
many of my jabs. I have to say, he took a lot from me. He was really
determined."[45] At long last, the ref stopped the bout and awarded Ali
a TKO. But Floyd shook his head no: "I really was protesting his stopping those punches. I wanted to be hit by a really good one. I wanted
to go out with a great punch, to go down that way."[46] But it was not to
be. Patterson left the ring unmarked and surprised. He couldn't understand why Ali had not knocked him out. In his years as a prizefighter,
Floyd had never felt such soft punches.[47]

The fight began to take on the stuff of legend the next day, when
Robert Lipsyte's account of it ran on the front page of the *New York
Times*. Lipsyte likened Ali to a little boy pulling off the wings of a but-
terfly piecemeal. Lipsyte wrote that Ali "mocked and humiliated and
punished" Floyd.[48] The next week *Life* called the match a "sickening

spectacle" in a headline, and said that Ali had delivered on a "promise
to degrade the former champion and 'make him suffer.'"[49] After that,
the bout became a keystone in the mythology of The Greatest — it was
the fight in which Ali cruelly tortured Patterson for round after round
for Floyd's sin of refusing to call him Muhammad Ali. Few accounts
since have mentioned Floyd's slipped disc.[50]

Patterson appeared at the press conference the next day and saw
Gay Talese among the reporters. At the time, Talese was working on
the celebrated article that would be published in *Esquire* as "Frank
Sinatra Has a Cold," which is often referred to as one of the best magazine articles ever written by an American writer. Patterson asked Talese
if he'd ever been able to get an interview with Sinatra. Talese was surprised that Floyd would have that on his mind, given all Patterson had
just gone through the previous night. Talese said he had not been able
to interview Sinatra. Patterson said he planned to see Sinatra later and
that he'd put in a good word for him.[51]

But Patterson never had a chance. As soon as Sinatra admitted
Floyd to his suite, Floyd could tell that the Chairman of the Board
was no longer his biggest fan. Patterson apologized for letting Sinatra
down, but Sinatra didn't want to hear it. He silently turned his back on
Floyd and walked to the other side of the large room, too far away for
Patterson to talk to him. Patterson understood the message. After a few
awkward moments, Floyd left the suite.

Although Sinatra gave Floyd the cold shoulder, the man who had publicly called him an Uncle Tom and the White Man's Nigger began to
treat him cordially. When Patterson met up with Ali in New York to
pose for photos for *Esquire* a few months after the fight, it was as if two
old friends had come together. "He gave me a big bear hug," Patterson
said, "when I walked to the door, had a big smile on his face, and there
was real warmth there." They discussed the possibility of an exhibition
tour with Ali, Patterson, and Liston to make some extra money. Ali said
he needed money because he had alimony and other debts to settle.
To Patterson he seemed like the lovable teenager he'd known in Rome
during the 1960 Olympics, not the man who delivered the ugly verbal
barrage in Las Vegas. "He was very polite and gentle through the evening," Patterson remembered.[52] This, Floyd would say, was the real Ali.

The photo shoot was held to secure illustrations for a cover piece that eventually ran in the August 1966 issue of *Esquire*. The article was called "In Defense of Cassius Clay," and it was one of the earliest major media pieces to present a somewhat sympathetic view of the postconversion Muhammad Ali. Its author was none other than Floyd Patterson, who'd written it with the assistance of Talese. Ali was extremely unpopular in the United States, receiving resounding boos every time he was introduced at an American boxing event. Patterson called on Americans to try to understand Ali and to stop heckling him. "Right now," Floyd said, "the only people in America who are not booing him are the Black Muslims, and maybe that is one reason he prefers being with them. Maybe if there were a few cheers from the other side of the fence, and a little more tolerance, too, people would realize that Cassius Clay is not as bad as he seems."[53] Floyd had not changed his mind about the Black Muslims in general, but he believed that Ali should be allowed the freedom to speak as he pleased. However much it might have stung inside, Patterson was conceding that Ali had, in his own way, proved to be the man who had actually won the title for America.

14

A Boxing Man

B
Y 1966, FLOYD WAS thirty-one years old, with fourteen years of prizefighting behind him. He was on the downhill side of his career. He certainly was not the fighter he'd been at the time of his second fight with Ingemar Johansson, let alone what he was against Archie Moore. It seemed like an appropriate time to retire. He could perhaps defeat other contenders and pick up a paycheck here and there, but as for being able to best Ali — well, that was something else entirely. Still, he needed to earn a living, and boxing was what he knew. By his own description, he was a boxing man. So he kept on training and looked for the next fight.

Sandra Patterson, however, had had enough. She had been raising their four children in the relative affluence of, first, Yonkers, living in a big house surrounded by manicured lawns and white neighbors who had never accepted them — an environment Floyd didn't particularly like — and then Great Neck. Floyd stayed at training camps for weeks on end, and Sandra was on her own. She was an attractive woman who drew the attention of other men. A grocer made a pass at her. A dishwasher repairman called her "baby" when he worked at their house. Floyd warned Sandra about white men who just wanted a "good time" — they'd never commit to a relationship with an African American woman.[1] Floyd shared his concerns with Gay Talese. "I think Sandra really resented Patterson," Talese said, "and you could well be on her side, to a degree, because I think a prizefighter is not going to be ideally suited to be a husband."[2]

It was uncommon for a Catholic couple to divorce at the time, especially when small children were involved. So Sandra officially ended the marriage in Mexico. The house in Great Neck went up for sale. Sandra and the children moved to Springfield, Massachusetts.[3] Floyd later admitted that, although he did not regret marrying Sandra, he felt that they wedded too young, when neither of them was capable of giving serious thought to the future. As time went on, Floyd and Sandra discovered that they were different sorts of people. "My former wife, Sandra," he said, "is an outgoing type who loves crowds and parties. I'm exactly the opposite. It was a matter of an introvert being married to an extrovert. It was doomed to fail. There was never any viciousness in our marriage or divorce because we realized our differences and couldn't help how we felt."[4]

Though he chose not to discuss it publicly for two more years, Floyd got married again around this time, to the woman who had been working as his secretary, Janet Seaquist. The dates of the divorce and remarriage are murky. Julius November maintained that Sandra's divorce from Floyd was finalized in Mexico in July 1966.[5] Floyd told *Jet* magazine in 1968 that he had wed Seaquist in February 1966. Floyd indicated to other publications in 1968 that the marriage occurred in the summer of 1966.[6] "We definitely haven't been secretly married," Floyd said.[7] But neither did he and Janet seem eager to let the world at large know that they'd tied the knot.

Given the tenor of the times, it was a marriage that could have provoked controversy. Janet was white. Muhammad Ali and the members of the Nation of Islam would not have approved, nor would the followers of the segregationist George Wallace, nor would much of middle-class white America. Janet was born to Swedish immigrants in Rosedale, New York, and grew up in Greenwood Lake. For years, writers repeated the falsehood that she herself was from Sweden.

In Janet, Floyd found a romantic partner who took a more active role in his boxing career than Sandra ever had. Patterson eventually established a training gym at the rural home they purchased outside New Paltz, New York, so he did not have to leave home to train. Most important, Janet and Floyd had similar temperaments. "She doesn't care for publicity at all," Floyd said, "and just wants to live a quiet life. So, the fewer people who come up our driveway, the better we feel. She's a financial whiz and was quite well off when we met. So she watches the financial end and I take care of the boxing part."[8]

For his first post-Ali fight, Patterson signed to meet a boxer who lacked nothing when it came to moxie or his ability to spill blood — especially his own. Henry Cooper was enormously popular with UK fight fans as the first British boxer to seriously contend for the heavyweight title in a half century. The high point of his career came in 1963 when he came close to derailing Muhammad Ali's climb to the championship.[9] During the closing seconds of the fourth round of their fight in 1963, Ali was showboating, his hands down at his side, daring Cooper to hit him. Cooper, who seemed to be out on his feet from the pummeling Ali had already given him, suddenly clubbed The Greatest with a left hook to drop Ali. Ali seemed unlikely to answer the count. But then the bell rang to end the round, saving Ali from being counted out. Ali's trainer, Angelo Dundee, was able to work his magic in the corner to revive his fighter. Ali was able to end the fight in the next round, but Cooper had come close to knocking Ali out.

So "Our 'Enry," as Cooper's cockney fans called him, was a threat to a boxer like Patterson, who had a history of allowing himself to be hit. "'Enry's 'Ammer" had led him to some quality wins, including victories over Zora Folley and Brian London. But Cooper had lost to Ali a second time in May 1966. To get his career back on track, he needed to score a win. Patterson told reporters that he would retire if he lost to Cooper, and he seemed to mean it.

Staged at Wembley Stadium in London, the September 1966 contest had respectable marquee value. Cooper remained the British champion, and he had been ranked as the number eight contender by *The Ring*, even after his loss to Ali. Patterson was the number nine contender, according to the sanctioning organization known as the World Boxing Association (WBA), which did not rank Cooper. Patterson entered the fray as a two-to-one favorite.

This was a rare fight for Patterson in that he didn't surrender a weight advantage to his adversary. He weighed 193 pounds to Cooper's

1913⁄4. Patterson's back didn't seem to bother him at all as he danced around the ring, adopting the old peek-a-boo style from time to time to block Cooper's hard shots. In the third round, Patterson dropped Cooper with a left hook. Patterson floored him again in the fourth round, smashing his nose. Cooper arose one more time, but Patterson knocked him flat again with a deft combination of punches. That was it for Our 'Enry. True to form, Floyd helped Cooper up from the mat after the referee called an end to the bout. Floyd was apologetic about the cut he gave Cooper on the side of the nose, but he also believed he had redeemed himself after the Ali fight fiasco. Patterson hoped his performance might help get him a rematch with the champ down the line. "I hope I'm one step closer toward Cassius Clay," Floyd said. Ali agreed that Floyd was just that. "He is another step closer," the champ, who had expected Cooper to win, said. He declared that Floyd had been "impressive" in defeating the British battler.[10] Floyd dropped any talk of retirement, and Ali said he would be willing to negotiate with Patterson for a rematch, but soon, events beyond Floyd's control rendered moot any talk of Ali-Patterson II. At least for the time being.

Even as talk made the rounds about an Ali-Patterson rematch, Cus D'Amato was back in the news. Like Floyd, Cus was eyeing Ali's title. Though he remained unlicensed to manage boxers in New York, Cus had entered into an agreement to prepare a man-mountain of a fighter named Buster Mathis for a possible title shot. As he had with José Torres, D'Amato functioned as Mathis's de facto manager. Mathis was a somewhat promising young heavyweight. He had won the 1964 Olympic trials, but a broken hand prevented him from representing the United States in the games; instead, alternate Joe Frazier fought in the Olympics, winning the heavyweight gold medal. In January 1967, his broken hand a distant memory, Mathis was an experienced pro ready to contend for a title. His career was under the control of a syndicate of young, rich men, none of whom was out of his twenties. The syndicate brought in D'Amato to prepare Mathis for a title shot and did so with a media splash. D'Amato set about getting the three-hundred-pound Mathis ready for the big time, putting him on a diet. D'Amato told the press that he was confident that a slimmed-down Mathis would destroy top contender Smokin' Joe Frazier, and then, in the fall of 1967, be ready to knock out Ali to claim the heavyweight title. But Mathis would have no more chance of fighting Ali that year than Floyd did. And Cus's involvement with Mathis did not last long. Shortly Cus would leave the city to live in obscurity in a small upstate town.

In early 1967 the heavyweight boxing world entered a chaotic state with the ring exile of Muhammad Ali. Years earlier, Ali had been declared ineligible for military induction by his local draft board after he failed what was essentially a writing and spelling test. The board reversed itself after the Pentagon relaxed eligibility standards. Ali could be drafted after all. In April 1967, citing his standing as a minister in the Nation of Islam, Ali refused military induction on religious grounds. The government's response was that Ali's motivation for refusing the draft was political, not religious. Criminal proceedings were initiated against the heavyweight champion. Ali was found guilty of draft evasion. As soon as the verdict was in, the various professional boxing sanctioning organizations lost little time in stripping Ali of his heavyweight title.[11] His professional boxing licenses were revoked. Floyd was somewhat conflicted by what had occurred to Ali. He agreed that the government should prosecute Ali for refusing induction: "I feel that if a man lives in a country and enjoys the fruits of the country, he should be willing to fight for it. Clay should serve his country. If not, he should go to jail or be driven out of the country." Floyd said he could understand the rationale of the sanctioning bodies for lifting the title. But in spite of that, Floyd believed, "Clay is the heavyweight champion, there are no two ways about it. Regardless of what he is outside the ring, inside the ring he is the champion, and titles are won and lost inside the ring."[12]

It would be three years before Ali returned to boxing. In the meantime, various sanctioning organizations and promoters attempted to capitalize on the vacant throne. A new promotional group called Action Sports Inc. appeared on the scene with a proposal to conduct an elimination tournament to determine a replacement champ, at least for the World Boxing Association's version of the heavyweight crown. Eight top contenders were scheduled to take part, but the tournament lost much of its luster when the fighter who was emerging as the best of the contenders, Joe Frazier, pulled out. Further diminishing the tournament's legitimacy was the absence of other top heavyweights, such as Sonny Liston, George Chuvalo, and Zora Folley. Still, the tournament moved forward, with Leotis Martin taking Frazier's place. Floyd was included, as was an impressive young California contender, Jerry Quarry. Floyd and Quarry had agreed to fight each other before the tournament was announced, so they would meet to fulfill that contract first.

Quarry was a decade younger than Patterson, with a thick neck, ridged abs, and a chin that could withstand a heavy shot. Quarry was often promoted as an Irish fighter, but he was, in the words of *Sports Illustrated*'s Mark Kram, "pure Okie."[13] Quarry had turned pro at his parents' urging, and it certainly beat his former job of changing tires at a Greyhound bus garage. He was no fighter to take lightly, and Patterson knew it. He was a tough, young, legitimate heavyweight contender with an effective right hand. He no doubt received more press than he otherwise would have because he was a promising white fighter at a time when heavyweight boxing had largely become a black man's realm. But Quarry had put together a record of 23-1-3, losing only to Eddie Machen in 1966.

The first Patterson-Quarry fight took place on June 9, 1967, at the Los Angeles Memorial Coliseum, and the twenty-three thousand fans there cheered when Quarry won the first two rounds. He floored Patterson twice in the second round alone. But Floyd came back to win the next four rounds. Then, in the seventh round, Quarry landed a stiff right to Patterson's head. Patterson seemed groggy for a few seconds, but he surprised Quarry with a left hook that sent the younger fighter tumbling just before the bell. Floyd seemed to control the remainder of the fight. Quarry was bleeding, bruised, and swollen when the final bell rang. But the fight was ruled a draw. The referee's calls in particular were suspicious, outraging many at ringside, including Joe Frazier. Floyd was so sure he had won, he stood in the ring with his mouth agape at the announcement of the decision.[14]

Patterson swallowed his disappointment and left on a USO tour of Vietnam. He supported the American war effort there, and he was well received during the trip. Floyd was impressed by how well blacks and whites in the military interacted with each other. "There's no race problem here," he said. "It would be a fine example for the entire country to live together like these guys do here. Everybody helps everyone else out all the time." He expressed to the troops he met that he supported their mission. Patterson may have fully backed civil rights protests earlier in the decade, but he had no use for Americans who protested against the war. "I made it a point not to wait for them to ask about these peace demonstrations back home," he said. "Every place I went, I told them not to be discouraged, that it was only a minority, a handful, and that fifty percent of that minority don't have any understanding of what's going on." Floyd added that he went to Vietnam to see if he could do some good. "I believe in my country," he said, "and I just came over to see what I could do."[15]

When he returned, he prepared to take on Quarry again, this time as part of the heavyweight championship elimination tournament. (Floyd may have disagreed with the decision to remove the title from Ali, but he was nevertheless willing to fight for the vacant championship.) Once again, Patterson and Quarry would fight in Los Angeles. Quarry promised a different outcome this time, pledging he would be more aggressive in his attempt to defeat Floyd. As if to prove his point, Quarry was particularly brutal with his sparring partners leading up to the match.

As it turned out, however, Quarry failed to fight much better in October than he had in June. In the early going, he had Floyd in trouble twice but couldn't put together the punches to knock out the former champ. Just as he had in their previous fight, Quarry wilted against Patterson during the later rounds. Yet Quarry was awarded a split decision. Again, the verdict was controversial. Quarry "stole the return fight," said Mark Kram, "thanks to the munificence of the officials."[16] The sparse crowd at the Olympic Auditorium shouted boos and pelted the ring with beer cups. With Patterson out of the elimination tournament, Quarry progressed to the finals, where he was decisioned by Jimmy Ellis, the man crowned WBA heavyweight champion.

Almost a year passed between Patterson's split-decision loss to Quarry and his next fight. Those months included some of the most turbulent times the United States has ever known. Disagreement about the war in Vietnam and the civil rights movement led to strife throughout the country, from college campuses to urban ghettos. The gap between black and white Americans seemed to grow with each passing day, as did the gap between the World War II generation and its baby boomer offspring. "Things fall apart; the centre cannot hold," William Butler Yeats had written in an apocalyptic poem nearly fifty years earlier, yet those words seemed particularly appropriate for America in 1968.

At no time did the center seem less likely to hold than in April, when an assassin's bullet felled Martin Luther King Jr. in Memphis. A grieving Patterson made plans to go to Atlanta to attend the funeral for the man who symbolized the dream Floyd and other moderates held for a peaceful, integrated American society. While post-assassination violence erupted across the United States, Floyd arrived in an Atlanta that was unprepared for the funeral, an Atlanta that was in a state of shock, an Atlanta whose population had swelled with the influx of as many as a quarter of a million mourners.

The crowd at the funeral was so large that Ebenezer Baptist Church could not accommodate all who had come to pay their respects. A second memorial service was scheduled at King's alma mater, Morehouse College, but many of the grief-stricken insisted on witnessing the service at the church where King served as co-pastor with his father, Floyd among them. Patterson had to elbow his way through a throng to get close to the building. Other dignitaries, including Robert Kennedy, Richard Nixon, Bill Cosby, Marlon Brando, Betty Shabazz (the widow of Malcolm X), and Jacqueline Kennedy, did the same. The widow of the slain president was pulled and then pushed through a narrow doorway, a frightened look on her face. Inside, the church was packed, but people kept coming — "Clear the way for Wilt!" someone shouted as Wilt Chamberlain, the seven foot, one inch center for the Philadelphia 76ers, ducked through the door. Like Floyd, renowned NFL running back Jim Brown used his size and strength to squeeze in.[17]

After the Reverend A. D. King threatened to remove the casket and conduct a private burial service, the jostling and tumult lessened, and the funeral commenced. From his post inside the church, Patterson heard Dr. L. Harold DeWolf, dean of Washington's Theological Seminary, say, "It is now for us, all the millions of the living who care, to take up his torch of love. It is for us to finish his work, to end the awful destruction in Vietnam, to root out every trace of race prejudice from our lives, to bring the massive powers of this nation to aid the oppressed and to heal the hate-scarred world."[18]

That torch of love seemed nowhere to be found in America in 1968.

Improbable as it seemed to many fight fans, Jimmy Ellis was recognized as heavyweight champion in most states in the United States. Ellis was a fellow Louisville fighter roughly the same age as Muhammad Ali, and it was Ellis's fate to always be in the more famous Kentuckian's shadow. While Ali's career was sublimely plotted and executed by his management, Ellis had to take what he could get when he could get it. He was a natural middleweight and spent three years fighting in that category before moving up in weight. As a light-heavyweight, and then as a heavyweight, he won ten straight fights, including victories over formidable challengers like Leotis Martin and Oscar Bonavena. But during that time, he was better known for being one of Ali's sparring partners. He even knocked Ali cold during one of their sparring sessions. Still, almost no one considered Ellis to be championship material, right up until April 27, 1968, when he decisioned Jerry Quarry to win the WBA world heavyweight title.

Once Ellis was champ, Teddy Brenner attempted to match him with Joe Frazier, whom the New York Athletic Commission recognized as world heavyweight champion. The winner would emerge with an essentially unified title. But Ellis turned down Brenner's $250,000 offer, most likely because Ellis stood little chance of beating Frazier. Ellis's handlers then contacted Patterson, who readily accepted an offer to fight Ellis in a title match. Nearing thirty-four years of age, considered a has-been after his loss to Ali, Patterson suddenly had a chance to be a world champion for a third time.

Las Vegas and the Swedish city of Stockholm bid on hosting the fight. In the end, Stockholm won out, the package put together by none other than Edwin Ahlquist, Ingemar Johansson's old manager. The contract offered Patterson a good payday, $60,000 (Ellis would receive $125,000), and Floyd's kid brother Raymond would fight on the undercard; Ray had turned pro in March 1963 and the following year began fighting regularly in Sweden, where he became a fan favorite. Harold Conrad was promoting the fight. But there was a catch.

Floyd, intrigued by Hollywood for years, had agreed to play a small role on the popular TV series *The Wild, Wild West*. Patterson told Conrad that the fight's original date had to be postponed until he could film his scenes for the TV show. Conrad was flabbergasted. How could anyone put a bit TV part ahead of a title fight? "I'm not going to be fighting forever," Patterson said. "I'm going to become a movie star. If Jim Brown can do it, I can do it."[19] Conrad feared that this was not going to sit well with the Swedes involved in the fight's promotion. He contacted *The Wild, Wild West*'s star and producer, Robert Conrad (no relation), and asked him to persuade Patterson to change his mind. The actor, a fight fan, agreed with Harold Conrad that Patterson was nuts to postpone the Stockholm fight, and said he would try to talk Patterson out of it. He failed. "It's no soap," the *Wild, Wild West* star reported to Conrad.[20] Patterson insisted on shooting the series. So the fight was rescheduled for September 14, 1968.

The date wasn't the only sticking point, however. Choosing a referee caused controversy as well. The Swedish prizefighting rules held that the referee would be the only official scoring the fight. No judges would be involved in scoring. So both fighters' camps attempted to get a ref in place who would not be inclined to favor the other side. Harold Conrad produced a list of five referees. Harold Valan, who'd boxed out of Brooklyn in the 1930s before beginning a distinguished career as a ring official, topped the list. Angelo Dundee, who was acting as Ellis's trainer and manager,[21] nixed him immediately. Dundee believed that a New York–based referee like Valan would be inclined to favor Patterson. When Conrad contacted Patterson and told him that Dundee did not want Valan, Floyd said, "Then I want [Valan]." Conrad went back to Dundee and said Valan was Patterson's choice. A great deal of back-and-forth bickering occurred before Dundee finally accepted Valan.[22]

Patterson was an eleven-to-five underdog, according to London oddsmakers, one of whom sniffed that betting on Patterson to win would be like betting on the Communists to win the upcoming British national elections. The weigh-in was unlike any the boxing reporters on hand had ever witnessed. It occurred at a hotel ballroom that had the air of an art gallery, as soft music played and vases of roses adorned the tables. Patterson arrived at the weigh-in at a svelte 188½ pounds. Ellis outweighed him by 10 pounds. Floyd seemed relaxed. He had a ref of his choosing making the decisions, and he knew he would have an enthusiastic Swedish crowd supporting him at the fight.

The Swedes had plenty to cheer about. In the first round, Patterson landed a right-hand punch that fractured Ellis's nose, sending blood cascading down Ellis's chest. Patterson later opened a large cut above Ellis's right eye. Floyd clearly seemed to be winning, ready to make history as the first man to win the heavyweight title three times. Back in America, his fans watching ABC's live broadcast were starting to celebrate.

But then a curious thing occurred. Howard Cosell's audio commentary from Sweden suddenly went dead. An ABC sportscaster in New York was quickly enlisted to provide a voice-over. The sportscaster in New York reported that Patterson was winning on the scorecards kept by boxing writers at ringside. In the fourteenth round, Patterson hammered Ellis with two left hooks that knocked the champ off his feet. In the fifteenth and final round, the video feed failed, leaving televisions in America blank. ABC scrambled to recover the lost signal. American viewers at home were unaware of how the last round played out, though it appeared certain, barring a knockout, Floyd would win. Finally the decision was announced, and it was a stunner: Jimmy Ellis had won, and won big. Valan scored it a lopsided nine rounds for the sitting champion to just six rounds for Patterson.

The decision caused a near riot among the pro-Patterson fans in the Stockholm soccer stadium. Police had to provide Valan with protection as he departed the venue. The fight's outcome outraged Floyd's followers in America as well. Arthur Mercante, a boxing referee who worked some of the biggest fights of the late twentieth century, was watching the bout on TV and nearly choked on his beer when he heard the decision: "It was clear to anyone with 20/200 vision that Floyd Patterson was the clear winner."[23] Mercante thought Valan was lucky to get out of the stadium alive. Cosell said he saw fear on Valan's face as the cortege of Swedish cops swept the referee past the sportscaster.

Cosell interviewed Floyd, who came across, as always, as the perfect gentleman once he knew he was on camera. Patterson refused to admit he believed he had won the fight. But it was a different story once Patterson was out of range of the camera. "Patterson is screaming in his dressing room after the fight that he was jobbed and blames it all

on the referee," said Harold Conrad, who was rendered incredulous by
what Patterson was saying. After all, Harold Valan had been the Patterson camp's top choice. Conrad's incredulity grew as Patterson's rant
continued: "He makes no bones about it and says that Valan is in the
pay of the Dundees [Angelo and his brothers]. He also says that Valan
is hanging out with the Dundees and living at their hotel — which is
not true."[24]

Conrad scheduled a press conference to allow Patterson to air his
grievances. The reporters showed up, but Patterson did not. Conrad
discovered that Patterson was at the airport, literally helping Cosell
with his baggage. Cosell said, "He personally carried our bags to the
trunk of his car and drove us to the airport. He had about him a sense
of elation. He admitted to me, now, that he indeed thought he had won
the fight. I asked him why he wouldn't say so in the ring. He shrugged
that little shrug of his. When we got to the airport Floyd carried our
bags to the ticket counter. The Swedish people looked at him with love.
Some would reach out and touch him, softly, gently, as he would bow
his head."[25] Back in the United States, Patterson finally asserted, during interviews with Cosell on ABC and with Johnny Carson on NBC's
The Tonight Show, that he believed he had beaten Ellis. But there was
to be no third crown for Patterson.

Legend has it that Patterson carried a grudge against Harold Valan
for years. Such was not the case. Charles Valan, Harold's son, said that
his father and Patterson actually dealt with each other amiably in the
years after the fight: "Floyd Patterson was always a gentleman and understood that boxing is a judgment sport and the referee goes by what
he sees in the ring. I have had the opportunity to view the fight and am
amazed at how one-sided the crew of ABC were and how from the start
they favored Floyd."[26]

Cosell no doubt believed Floyd had every right to be angry at Valan.
The sportscaster was growing weary of what he believed was Floyd's
perfect-gentleman act. "There is no question that this posture continu-
ally appealed to the public . . . ," Cosell said. "But equally in my mind
there had been no question it *was* a posture, and this was confirmed
for me forevermore in 1968 . . . It was exactly what the fans wanted

to hear, and Floyd instinctively knew it. He always did know how to appeal to the public." Cosell eventually dismissed Floyd as a fighter "whose career had been a fantasy."[27] Cosell's gift for hyperbole was clear when he made that statement — Floyd's career was far from a fantasy, and Cosell had to know that. But, in fact, Cosell was finished with Patterson, in spite of their earlier close relationship. Floyd had become yesterday's news to Cosell, who by this time had inextricably wed his career to Muhammad Ali. Ali was brash, hip, part of the baby boomer generation. Floyd was none of these things. Patterson could no longer be of benefit to Howard Cosell.

At the end of 1968, Floyd fired Julius November as his attorney. November, Patterson said, had made four large investments of Patterson's money, all of which had failed. Patterson said he was suing November for a full accounting of his money. With November now gone, all of Floyd's old entourage had fallen by the wayside. Floyd plodded onward to whatever inevitability awaited him.

Floyd fought ten more times over the next four years, but none of the bouts were title shots. They were just paydays. Floyd might have been only a shadow of the boxer he'd been at his peak, but as a man, he had not lost the capacity to surprise people he met along the way. In May 1971 he battled Terry Daniels. Daniels's cornerman that night was Doug Lord, a Dallas-based trainer and manager who'd earlier guided Curtis Cokes to the world welterweight title. Patterson won a unanimous decision. After the fight, Floyd found Lord and asked if he would mind staying up to talk for a while. Patterson didn't feel like sleeping just yet. Lord said he'd be glad to. He accompanied Patterson to the apartment where Floyd was staying while in Cleveland for the fight. Patterson introduced him to Janet and the couple's two small daughters, Jennifer and Janene. Once Janet and the girls retired, Lord and Patterson began talking and continued to do so until dawn. The conversation centered around Terry Daniels's ring possibilities. Patterson was certain that Daniels had no chance to win the championship, but he was also convinced that Daniels could make some money out of boxing if he handled his career the right way, and Floyd shared his opinions about how that could happen. After dawn, Lord left the apartment amazed. In all his years in boxing, he had never met an opposing boxer who wanted to talk the night away after a fight.[28]

In 1972 Floyd was thirty-seven, well beyond the typical retirement age for most boxers of the time; Rocky Marciano retired at thirty-two, for instance. Yet Floyd kept on fighting. Nine months after the Daniels fight, Patterson took on Argentinean Oscar "Ringo" Bonavena, a heavyweight whose career was both colorful and controversial. Bonavena had emerged as one of the division's top contenders. He was the first boxer to knock down Joe Frazier. *The Ring* editor Nat Fleischer called Bonavena the most powerful fighter he'd ever seen. Bonavena used that power to defeat contenders like George Chuvalo, Zora Folley, and Karl Mildenberger. In December 1970 Bonavena gave Muhammad Ali (back in the ring after his three-year banishment) a very tough fight for the North American Boxing Federation's heavyweight title. Ali won the bout, but it took him fifteen rounds to do so. Bonavena was a born brawler, and his passion for fisticuffs was not confined to the ring. Once, Bud Shrake traveled to Argentina to profile Bonavena for *Sports Illustrated.* The piece was never finished because Argentinean authorities mistook Shrake for a political opponent of the regime then in power and jailed him. While he was there, though, Shrake was able to see Bonavena in action on the Buenos Aires streets. One night Ringo, given the nickname because of his Beatles-like haircut, abruptly floored a man. When Shrake asked him why he'd done it, Bonavena explained that the man was standing where he wanted to stand.[29]

Bonavena was the clear favorite going up against Patterson, a hellion with the capacity to rough up the older boxer. "The ghost of Floyd Patterson walked in Madison Square Garden last night," said Red Smith of the February 1972 fight, "and the sad part of it was that the ghost won. Looking no more like a two-time champion of the world than one would expect of a thirty-seven-year-old in his twentieth year as a professional fist fighter, Patterson still had enough to win a unanimous decision in ten rounds with rough, inept Oscar Bonavena."[30] The 17,958 fans present were euphoric about the decision. Although, as Smith mused, some must have had misgivings about the outcome, because it would encourage Patterson to keep fighting. Patterson had let it be known that he wanted a fight with Joe Frazier. But such a contest was not in the works. Instead, Patterson would get one more shot at Muhammad Ali.

As he was training for his September 1972 match with Ali, Patterson took a break to make another visit to the White House, this time to meet with a Republican president, Richard Nixon. Over the previous ten years, the United States had changed greatly on the political front. Floyd had changed little. In the early 1960s, the Left had embraced Kennedy's military action in Vietnam, which Floyd supported. By 1972, liberals had turned against Vietnam. But Floyd continued to support American involvement. In the early 1960s, the Left dismissed radical organizations like the Nation of Islam and the Black Panthers. But by the early 1970s these groups had gained credibility among liberals. Not so with Floyd, however. Many on the Left accepted Muhammad Ali's jabs that Floyd was just an Uncle Tom. So, largely abandoned by liberals, Floyd had no qualms about meeting with the politician who stood as their fiercest bogeyman. Nixon, facing reelection in November, no doubt welcomed the opportunity to meet with a high-profile African American like Patterson; few black voters supported the president. By the time of their meeting — just past noon on August 8, 1972 — Nixon hardly needed to fear losing the election to George McGovern. Yet, as the Watergate episode proved, Nixon was not one to take any election for granted.

So Patterson and his wife and their two daughters appeared at the White House for what was essentially a photo opportunity. The meeting between the president and the former heavyweight champion lasted just seven minutes, sandwiched between other meetings on a busy White House calendar. Nixon was awkward during the session, as he usually was in situations that required small talk. He called Patterson "champ" and attempted to chat with the Patterson daughters: "All little girls are shy." Floyd and Nixon talked a bit about Clifford Evans, a longtime reporter and Nixon friend. Then, surprisingly, Nixon blurted out that he'd never seen a prizefight. "I mean, I've followed professional sports for many, many years," Nixon said. But the president did manage to talk a bit about Archie Moore and Joe Louis. Nixon wound down their brief conversation by telling Patterson he'd been a "great credit to the sport."[31] Patterson and his family departed, and Nixon returned to matters of state. If Patterson's first visit to the Oval Office a decade earlier had been big news, this visit was anticlimactic and, ultimately, meaningless. No one in the press cared much about it. Boxing was slipping in importance as a sport, and as the years progressed, presidents would find little to value in a professional fighter visiting the Oval Office. Floyd was one of the last to do so, although the sensational champion Manny Pacquiao received a White House invitation to meet with President Barack Obama in February 2011, reviving the practice of Oval Office visits by boxers.

Ali's return to boxing had been nothing short of remarkable. While his draft-evasion conviction worked its way through appeals courts, efforts began to find an American location that would be willing to host an Ali fight. Finally, in 1970, the city of Atlanta granted him a license to box. A match was made with Jerry Quarry, which Ali won in three rounds. Shortly thereafter, the New York State Supreme Court lifted Ali's ban from boxing. Allowed to fight in New York once more, Ali eventually signed to fight Joe Frazier for the world heavyweight championship. Hyped as the "fight of the century," the Madison Square Garden contest occurred on March 8, 1971.[32] Though Ali dominated the first three rounds, Frazier took command of the fight, knocked Ali down in the final round, and won a solid unanimous decision. Ali put together seven victories in a row following his loss to Frazier. Yet another title shot for Ali seemed remote at the time. And Floyd had been written off as a potential champion long ago.

So Ali-Patterson II was greeted by yawns at best from the moment it was announced. Fans expecting histrionics from Ali were disappointed. The press conference at which the contract was signed was a subdued affair, with Murray Chass of the *New York Times* writing that Ali acted as if he'd just finished a dual course with Amy Vanderbilt and Dale Carnegie. In fact, Ali used the occasion to show his respect for Patterson. "I thought he was finished," Ali said. "But like a ghost, he keeps coming back. It's something to see him still going like he is. He came back after Johansson, he came back after Liston, he came back after Quarry, he came back after me. Now he's in the lights of Madison Square Garden again.

"If Floyd Patterson whups me, Joe Frazier will look like nothing to him. Floyd Patterson is a better boxer than Frazier. He's a scientific boxer. He'd be like a schoolteacher to Frazier."

Even the old issue surrounding Ali's name failed to provoke him. "He still says Clay," Ali said, "but I can't even get mad at him, he's so nice. Everybody else calls me Muhammad and he calls me Clay. He's the only one who can get away with it."[33]

Oddsmakers wouldn't even touch the contest. They provided no betting line on the fight, a rarity in the world of betting. In at least one influential corner, though, Ali's making a match with Patterson elicited outrage. Howard Cosell went on the air to say the fight should not be sanctioned. Not only was Patterson beyond his prime, Cosell said, but even in his prime, Patterson was no match for Ali. Cosell reiterated his long-held belief that their first fight lasted as long as it did only because Ali had carried Patterson.

Madison Square Garden used Cosell's remarks as part of its PR campaign for Ali-Patterson II: Patterson intended to "show the Cosells of the world."[34] Ali predicted that the fight would go all the way, last all twelve rounds. But surely few of the 17,378 who showed up at the Garden actually bought into that, even though they did give more cheers to Patterson than they did to The Greatest.

The genial nature of the prefight activities could be explained, at least in part, by the reason the fight even took place. Much was made in the prefight publicity about how Patterson had earned $8 million in the ring, which was more than any other boxer in history had earned up to that point. Speculation held that he'd managed to keep up to $4 million of that, which was certainly a sizable fortune by 1972 standards. But the reality was that Patterson was anything but rich at the time, a fact that shocked Cosell when he learned about it.

In a private conversation between Ali and Cosell, Ali promised he would not harm his old boyhood hero in the ring. He said he had agreed to the fight only to help Floyd out. Patterson needed money, Ali told Cosell. Cosell found that hard to believe, given Floyd's reputation for managing his money well. "No," Ali said. "His taxes were all mixed up and the Internal Revenue has got all of it."[35] Surprised by this revelation, Cosell contacted Bob Arum, Ali's tax attorney at the time and later famous as a fight promoter. Arum confirmed to Cosell what Ali had said: Patterson was broke. The bout was built on Ali's desire to help Patterson — not exactly a situation that would boil the blood of either combatant.

Ali outweighed Patterson by almost thirty pounds. Compared to the Ali of the 1960s, the Ali of the early 1970s looked overstuffed and wooden, his footwork significantly slower than it was at his prime. Still, Floyd was no match for him. There was one key blow, a sixth-round straight right that ripped open a deep cut above Patterson's left eye. Patterson somehow hung on for the rest of the round and through the next one, although wobbly with blurry vision. The fight doctor examined Patterson and decided he should not continue. Referee Arthur Mercante awarded Ali a seventh-round knockout.

Afterward, Ali insisted to reporters that Patterson was a better fighter now than he'd been seven years earlier when the two fought for the first time. The judges' scorecards had given some of the early rounds to Patterson. Still, Patterson looked like a used-up boxer. If he won some of the early rounds, it was due more to Ali's own lackadaisical performance than to any dominance on Patterson's part. The whole affair ended with an air "more conducive to pathos than a prizefight," in the words of sportswriter Dave Anderson.[36] But the fight accomplished what its enablers set out to do in the first place: Ali took a step toward regaining his lost title, and Patterson took home a generous purse for a one-time great now on his last legs — $100,000 guaranteed against 20 percent of the total receipts.

Afterward, Floyd had little meaningful to say about his future. He retreated to the upstate New York home he shared with Janet and went into training, as always, though he had no matches lined up. "The thing about Floyd," said veteran New York sportswriter Vic Ziegel, "is that he never exactly retired. He just stopped fighting. For years people kept waiting to see if he would box again."[37]

Patterson did, in fact, come close to boxing once more. Five years after battling Ali at the Garden, Ali's people approached him about the possibility of yet another rematch. Ali had regained the title in 1974. But by 1977, Ali, a bloated parody of "The Greatest" of all time, desperately needed a fight against a challenger who was unlikely to give him too hard a time in the ring. Floyd, now in his forties, just might fit the bill. But in the end, Floyd said no. Ali instead fought Leon Spinks, an Olympic champion with just seven pro fights behind him — and he failed to win one of those. It was reminiscent of Patterson-Rademacher, with one huge difference: Spinks rather easily defeated Ali.

The handful of people who knew about Ali's offer to Patterson had to sit back and marvel about the fight's outcome. What if Floyd had agreed to battle Ali? What if Floyd instead of Spinks had been the one to emerge victorious? If that had happened, Floyd would have become both the youngest and the oldest man to win the championship, not to mention the first man to win the title three times.[38] But it was all only the stuff of dreams and speculation.

Floyd's battles in the ring were behind him.

Floyd's career may have ended, but he never left boxing. Like Voltaire's Candide, he settled in to "cultivate his garden." Floyd's garden was New Paltz, less than fifteen miles from Wiltwyck, in the Hudson Valley region that Patterson considered a kind of paradise. He opened the gym on his property to other fighters and began training boxing prospects from the area. All sorts of people worked out at his gym, but Floyd focused his efforts on teenagers, especially those who were poor or troubled — in his own way, carrying on the legacy of Wiltwyck. He attempted to instill in the kids the old-fashioned virtues he valued: He did not drink or take drugs. He was committed to fitness, as he had been throughout his boxing career. He ran with a passion, becoming a marathoner. The boxers he trained also logged many miles. In the gym, he sparred with the kids himself, often more than twenty rounds a day. Floyd didn't even bother to wrap his hands. He just slipped on some old gloves and climbed into the ring.[39]

In 1979 Floyd's belief that boxing could redeem a kid with troubles led him and Janet to adopt one of the boys who showed up at the gym, Tracy Harris. Tracy was fourteen at the time and had been training at Floyd's gym since he was eleven. Floyd was forty-four at the time, perhaps a little old to be adopting a boy Tracy's age. But Patterson imparted all the fighting knowledge he could to his adopted son, and Tracy thrived in the ring with Floyd as his manager. Fighting as Tracy Harris Patterson, he won two New York Golden Gloves titles before turning pro in 1985. In 1992 Tracy became a world champion, winning the International Boxing Federation's super-featherweight title. It was a first in the world of boxing — a world-champion father who trained and managed a world-champion son.[40] But the relationship between Floyd and Tracy deteriorated as Tracy questioned his father's management decisions. Finally, Tracy split with Floyd, only to reconcile shortly before Floyd's death.

About the time Floyd and Janet adopted Tracy, Floyd was making amends with the man who had been something of a surrogate father to him thirty years earlier. After he left the city, Cus D'Amato had settled in Catskill, New York, not far from Floyd's home in New Paltz. The two men began to see each other at amateur boxing events and over time started to warm to each other. In 1985 Cus's health declined, and Patterson went to visit his old manager as D'Amato lay dying of pneumonia in a New York City hospital. During a bedside confession, Floyd finally told D'Amato that it had been the Jim Jacobs television deal that caused him to make the final break with Cus. Floyd said he believed at the time that Cus had betrayed him. D'Amato looked relieved once he heard the explanation. "It's all right, Floyd," the old man said. A week later, D'Amato was dead. Floyd thereafter said that firing Cus was the biggest mistake he'd made.[41]

Floyd had no compelling reason to rekindle any sort of relationship with Ingemar Johansson. Ingo had said many negative things about Patterson during the time of their rivalry. But the 1980s found Johansson on hard times. He had fallen out of the limelight, had been through a divorce, and had allowed his money to slip away. Ingo lived in a rundown Florida motel he operated with his son, far from the life of lobster and champagne he'd known as heavyweight champ. No longer a pretty boy, Johansson weighed more than 300 pounds. Floyd reconnected with Ingo, and the two men developed into fast friends. Patterson encouraged Johansson to take up running to get back in shape, and Floyd and Ingo made news when they ran in a marathon together. Even after Johansson returned to Sweden, he and Floyd made transatlantic flights to visit each other.

Perhaps it was Patterson's Catholic faith that compelled him to reach out to those who had offended him the most. Without question, he was devout. He became a Eucharistic minister, giving Communion to New Paltz shut-ins. He was a mainstay in the town's Knights of Columbus activities as well. As a Christian, Floyd found it important to present himself as a decent person. At times, during his boxing career, an air of penitence seemed to hang around him. Howard Cosell, for one, thought it was a fraud designed to win Floyd public approval. But it persisted after Patterson left the ring, which suggests it was not an act. Floyd's finances during his years in New Paltz were often tight, contrary to what sports columnists reported, in large part because of his generosity. "Floyd never could say no to a cause he thought was worthy," said his longtime upstate friend Bill O'Hare.[42]

Floyd had to feel fortunate as the years passed by when he compared his own life to the fates of some of his rivals: Sonny Liston died in Las Vegas with heroin in his blood. Eddie Machen was sleepwalking when he fell to his death in San Francisco. Tommy "Hurricane" Jackson became a cab driver and died from injuries inflicted when he was struck by a car as he washed his taxi. Jerry Quarry died of dementia pugilistica, a malady boxers can develop from taking too many blows to the head. Oscar Bonavena was shot to death after engaging in an affair with the wife of the owner of a Nevada brothel. Jimmy Ellis was spotted aimlessly wandering the streets of Louisville, another victim of dementia pugilistica. Floyd's great rival Johansson wound up spending months in a Swedish nursing home before he died of either Alzheimer's disease or dementia pugilistica or both. Muhammad Ali lived on, eventually settling in Arizona, but Parkinson's disease, which he undoubtedly developed after taking too many blows to the head, had largely silenced the Marvelous Mouth.

For years, it seemed that Floyd would escape such a destiny. He served twice on the New York State Athletic Commission, the last time as chairman. During his term as chairman, however, it became apparent that Floyd was experiencing some sort of mental decline. Thomas Hauser, an attorney and author, spoke to Patterson at a reception in 1995. Hauser had interviewed Patterson for a Muhammad Ali biography a few years earlier, but Floyd seemed to have changed between the time of the interview and the night of the reception. "Floyd had become one of those guys who could talk about things that happened years ago but couldn't remember what he ate for breakfast," Hauser said.[43] Hauser believed that as time went on, the athletic commission office functioned incompetently because of Floyd's diminished state.[44]

Floyd's cognitive difficulties became painfully apparent in 1998. As the commission's chairman, Patterson was giving a videotaped deposition concerning mixed martial arts contests, which were banned in New York at the time. As the attorneys representing the MMA interests grilled him, Floyd's memory collapsed. Among other lapses, Patterson couldn't remember beating Archie Moore for the championship in 1956. Floyd couldn't even remember his secretary's name. Patterson blamed his miserable performance on lack of sleep, but it was obviously something much more serious than that. The damage was done. Patterson had to resign his post. He retreated to New Paltz, where an Associated Press reporter tracked him down a few months later. Patterson refused to discuss the disastrous deposition with the reporter, "but his face crumples when the subject is raised. Friends say what hurts him the most is the feeling that he let the governor [conservative George Pataki, who appointed Floyd to the post] down."[45]

Floyd steadily became further lost in dementia's fog as the old millennium played out and the new one began. Prostate cancer also afflicted him. The old champ who prided himself on being the boxer who got back on his feet more than any other was finally floored for good on May 11, 2006. He was seventy-one years old.

Patterson's death received significant coverage. Most accounts eulogized him as a gentleman in a sport in which gentlemen are rare indeed, noted the rivalry with Ali, the Liston disasters, the triumph over Johansson. But some commentators mined his contributions more deeply. One was Gregory Kane, an African American sports columnist for the *Baltimore Sun*. Kane weighed in on the accusations that Floyd exhibited Uncle Tom–like behavior. He wrote that Patterson's decision to fight Sonny Liston had showed he was "a man of integrity, not an Uncle Tom. It sounds like a man who would stand for what is right, not just what's convenient. That sounds like a man we should have more of these days . . . I'd wager Ali appreciates him now."[46] Others argued that Patterson's boxing skills were underappreciated, none more so than

Floyd's friend light-heavyweight champion José Torres, who said in an NPR interview, "You know, he knew that he was a good fighter, but he never spoke about it. And if he was champion, he had to know that he was the best."[47] The man who had to know he was the best was laid to rest in the New Paltz Rural Cemetery, his headstone engraved with "A Champion Always."

---◆---

Invisible Champion

O N A JULY NIGHT in 1997, over-the-hill former heavyweight champion Larry Holmes bested a little-known boxer with a checkered record named Maurice Harris. The fight meant little, but as chairman of the New York State Athletic Commission, the governing body for the match, Floyd Patterson attended. Afterward, Floyd stepped out of Madison Square Garden and moved through the summer night toward a waiting automobile. Fans milling on the sidewalk quickly surrounded him, asking for autographs. Floyd, happy to be recognized, obliged, then climbed into the car. The fans dispersed, the last one calling out, "Good night, Mr. Patterson." In his gentle voice, Floyd said, "Call me Floyd." Then he sped off into the darkness.[1] By the late 1990s, Floyd Patterson's name was still familiar. As a trainer, manager, and commission member, he remained a public figure in the years after he stopped fighting. But certainly few people on that sidewalk knew much about his career, other than that he'd been one of Muhammad Ali's foils. His achievements as a heavyweight title holder were lost to them. He was, for all practical purposes, an invisible champion.

Behind that cloak of invisibility lay the accomplishments of a significant American boxing champion. They included no small number of important firsts: For decades Patterson held the distinction of being the youngest heavyweight in history; he was the first to win the title twice; he fought in the first championship bout in Las Vegas, which shortly thereafter became the mecca of bigtime boxing; he was the first heavyweight with lightweight hand speed; he was the first world champion who trained and managed a world-champion son. Most important, he was the first black heavyweight champion to use the prestige of his title to speak out against bigotry and to demand that seating at his fights not be segregated by race.

In addition to those firsts, Patterson gave Archie Moore, one of boxing's all-time greats, a sound thumping, and he defeated contenders like Eddie Machen, George Chuvalo, Henry Cooper, Roy "Cut 'n Shoot" Harris, Brian London, Tommy "Hurricane" Jackson, and Oscar Bonavena. Floyd likely should have been awarded victories over Joey Maxim and Jimmy Ellis, both world champions, and Jerry Quarry, a top contender, as well. Without question, Patterson was a solid champion. "Floyd, like Sonny [Liston]," said *Sports Illustrated*'s Mark Kram, "was the real thing. No stranger or more interesting figure ever worked the landscape of sports."[2] The "stranger" aspect of Floyd's career came to overshadow all those firsts. He came to be remembered more for the fake beard, the covert nighttime escape, the fumbling to help an opponent recover a mouthpiece, the ring embraces, and the time he kissed Ingemar Johansson. And he was remembered for the seven-knockdown loss to Johansson. Finally, more than anything else, he was remembered as Muhammad Ali's rival.

Ali ranks with Joe Louis as the best heavyweight boxer of all time. As a media idol, Ali towers above everyone. In addition to his unassailable greatness in the ring, Ali was a remarkably effective self-promoter — no one has ever been better. He had the ability to compose doggerel on the fly — or, at an opportune moment, recite doggerel thought up by others and make it seem like his own. He had leading-man good looks and sex appeal and a one-of-a-kind voice. His sense of humor was uncanny and effective. Yet he had a way of making poignant statements about serious matters, always delivered at just the right moment. He was all those things, yet that never seemed to be enough for an American public that once vilified him, then later became obsessed with all things Ali. A bloated mythology inflated around him, obscuring other worthies such as Floyd Patterson, rendering them invisible except to students of boxing history. Ironically, much of that mythology is dependent on the likes of Patterson.

When the cloud of Ali mythology is removed, Floyd stands as a distinctive and important champion. Few have attempted to pull him into focus in the years since he left the prizefighting ring. David Remnick shined some much needed light on Floyd in the modern classic *King of the World.* Gerald Early did the same in books like *The Culture of Bruising* and *Tuxedo Junction.* But theirs is only an incomplete portrait of a compelling figure. A more thorough study has long been needed. Hence, this book.

It was Early who wrote, "Cultural observers are wrong who say that Muhammad Ali was the most complex of American heroes, although he was surely one of the most luminous; Patterson, during his days as an active fighter, was the most disturbed and disturbing black presence in the history of American popular culture."[3] A key word here is *hero.* Floyd was one.

When he was young, black culture in America valued achievement and status. Patterson certainly achieved — he won titles, he made a lot of money, he became famous. He had status. He lived out the Horatio Alger dream at a time when it was still credible, with nice homes in classy neighborhoods and expensive cars. He never let go of those values, even as black Americans began to question them shortly after Floyd won the heavyweight title for a second time. By the time he was thirty-five, he was perceived by many as a living, breathing anachronism. To his benefit, Floyd didn't seem to care much. He stuck by his principles, thus becoming Early's disturbing presence. He was a staunch anti-Communist, supported the war in Vietnam, believed in Martin Luther King Jr.'s nonviolent approach to social change while younger, more revolutionary blacks thought that the time to pick up the gun had arrived. As a result, many politicized young black Americans joined Muhammad Ali in attacking Floyd as an Uncle Tom.

It was an absurd slander. An Uncle Tom would not have sent money to support integration efforts in Fort Smith, Arkansas. An Uncle Tom would not have demanded desegregated seating for the audience at a title fight in Miami. An Uncle Tom wouldn't have braved the violence of Birmingham, Alabama, in 1963. But Patterson did all these things and more. After he retired, he occasionally addressed students at the State University of New York branch in New Paltz, urging them to adopt moderate political stances. Most of the students he spoke to had nothing but disdain for his positions. But Floyd held his ground, always with class. Heroically.

His eyes looked into the eyes of presidents, a pope, and a Nobel laureate. He viewed foreign capitals and the Great Sphinx in the Egyptian desert. He saw himself basking in victory. He saw himself hiding in shame. He was a truant, a thief, a reformed juvenile delinquent, a great athlete, a record setter, a national hero, a role model, a fallen knight, a scorned has-been, and a respected gentleman. He was also a family man, a churchman, a social reformer, and a public servant. And he was an important boxer whose story demands telling.

"When I was small," Floyd once said, "I could never look people in the eye. When I tried to look them in the eye, it always seemed that they could read my mind. There was nothing on my mind, but it seemed they could read it anyway. I tried very hard, and then one day I woke up and I could look people in the eye. It had kind of sneaked its way in."[4]

The story of Floyd Patterson's life is in that statement. At first he couldn't, and then he could. He tried very hard, and things kept sneaking their way into his life until he had accomplished much more than even the most fanciful of dreamers could have envisioned. Patterson, the invisible champion, could well have been trapped in the world of the Invisible Man. Like the narrator of Ellison's novel, he could have ended up at exactly the spot where he began — in Floyd's case, the mean streets of Bedford-Stuyvesant. But Floyd found a way out of the circle. His escape route involved leather gloves tied on his hands, a padded mat, and a roped-off square curiously called a ring. "My career has shaped my life," Floyd once said, "and I have learned much. I have met people from all over the world, the highest to the most humble. The finest of these people accept a man for what he is."[5]

It's easy to accept Floyd for what he was. He began life with nothing. Through determination and hard work, he reached the pinnacle of his field. Some people close to him thought that he could have put his work ethic into a safer endeavor. "It broke my heart," Gay Talese said, "that someone I cared about that much did what he had to do for his career. He had the capacity to do any number of things. I never understood it. Why boxing?"[6] But Floyd never lost his love of his chosen field, the field that defined him. For everything else he was, in the end, the invisible champion was a boxing man through and through, with a fascinating back story and a significant place in American popular culture — and one hell of a left hook.

ACKNOWLEDGMENTS AND SOURCES

◆

For a number of reasons, writing this book turned out to be particularly difficult. To say that the material concerning Floyd Patterson is voluminous and often contradictory is an understatement. So there was much that I had to sort out. Compounding matters, the book was written during a particularly stressful time, both at my day job and in my personal life. In the midst of the project, I had to contend with some health problems that, while not life threatening, posed more than a distraction. Several friends died as I worked on this book, some of them shockingly young. Family members dealt with various crises that required my attention. At times I felt completely bogged down, both in my life and in my writing. My more than capable editor Jenna Johnson helped me get back on the road, along with the help of her adept assistant Johnathan Wilber and the rest of the good folks at Houghton Mifflin Harcourt. My thanks go out to them and to everyone who had a hand in making this book a reality. I'd like to give a special shout-out to my agent, David McCormick. I feel blessed to have McCormick & Williams representing me. This is my third book with David, and I hope there are many more in our future.

Several people important to the Floyd Patterson story died during my work on this book: Ingemar Johansson, George Kimball, Norman Mailer, Budd Schulberg, Edwin "Bud" Shrake, José Torres, and

Vic Ziegel. May they rest in peace. When I was young, Shrake was one of my writing heroes; I learned much about how to write nonfiction from studying his *Sports Illustrated* and *Harper's* articles. Kimball and I communicated for the last time just days before he succumbed to cancer. There are too few souls like Kimball's in this dreary world. A poet, novelist, one-time political radical, anthologist, and hail-fellow well met at the legendary Lion's Head back in the day, he was also a great sports columnist and was recognized by many as the best boxing journalist of his generation. He was not at a loss for projects during the last few months of his life, yet he took the time to read my manuscript; I'll always be grateful.

I want to single out the assistance of my good friend John Schulian. John has many accomplishments as an author, sports columnist, magazine writer, screenwriter, pop culture critic, and TV writer and producer. Like George Kimball (his sometime collaborator), John is one of the finest boxing writers of our time, respected and beloved by many; with his enthusiastic approval to do so, I dropped his name numerous times to open doors for this project. John led me to Dave Kindred, another outstanding sportswriter, and Dave's assistance proved invaluable early on. I owe them both special kudos. But John also provided me with essential help when this project was stuck in the mud. Without his help, I never would have gotten it back on its way again. For that, I'll be forever in his debt.

I'd like to recognize Tom Dodge and Bob Compton for their continuing support of my projects, especially this one. My day-to-day existence is not exactly literary in nature, and I continue to look up to my longtime friends Jesse Sublett, David Marion Wilkinson, Jan Reid, Tom Zigal, and, in absentia, Christopher Cook, as examples of what being a writer is all about. Jan Reid in particular stands as an inspiration, and he gave significant help to me for this book. R. Lord's Boxing Gym in Austin seems to be connected to everything in the world by no more than the proverbial six degrees of separation. Contacts I've made at the gym certainly benefited this project, and I'm thankful to Richard Lord, his wife, Lori — they are among my best friends — and Richard's parents, Doug and Opal Lord, as well as the whole boxing gym crowd. In particular, I want to thank Jésus, Anissa, Armando, Johnny C., "Mad Dog" Marvin, King, Eddie V., El Gallito, Gabe, David, José,

Josea, Phil, Steve, Julian, Don, Jake, Morgan, Chuy, Sam, and, in particular, Joe Bernal, for the ring lessons they've given me over the years. It was through R. Lord's Boxing Gym that I met James "Gentleman Jim" Brewer, professional boxer, film and television actor, and entrepreneur — and my good friend. Jim knew the Hollywood side of Floyd and provided meaningful insight.

In undertaking this project, I was fortunate to have access to a considerable body of outstanding writing about Patterson, most of it in the form of newspaper and magazine pieces. As a young reporter on the *New York Times* in the 1950s and '60s and as an innovative magazine writer for *Esquire* in the 1960s, Gay Talese wrote thousands of impeccably crafted words about Floyd Patterson; collected in a volume, his four dozen or so bylined *Times* pieces about Patterson plus the articles from *Esquire* would have in themselves made for an insightful book. In addition, Talese was generous in sharing his time with me at a period during which he faced his own pressing deadlines. I want to express a special thanks to him.

Another part of my good fortune was being able to draw from the mostly superb, although at times self-serving, Patterson autobiography, *Victory over Myself,* coauthored by the late Milton Gross. I want to thank Milton Gross's children, Michael and Jane, for their help with this project. The late W. C. Heinz took an interest in Floyd Patterson, and his writings about him, collected in *Once They Heard the Cheers* and elsewhere, are golden; Bill Heinz was great at that, spinning literary gold. I want to thank his daughter Gayl for her help with this project. The late Mark Kram composed prose poems about boxing — his account of the Ali-Frazier Thrilla in Manila fight remains the best boxing essay I've ever read — for *Sports Illustrated* and other magazines. Just as Gayl Heinz went through her father's papers prospecting for any unpublished Patterson tidbits I could use, Mark Kram Jr. did the same with the material his father left behind, all of it disorganized and stored away in boxes, some of it notes scribbled on bar napkins or matchbook covers. I thank Mark Kram Jr. for his digging through that on my behalf.

As a writer living in the greater Austin area, I'm fortunate to have access to the libraries and collections of the University of Texas, in particular the Harry Ransom Center and the Dolph Briscoe Center for

American History. The staffs at both did their usual stellar jobs when I came requesting help for my research on Patterson. As always, I was amazed at what I found in their collections. For instance, who might have guessed that the morgue (clip file) for the late, great *New York Herald Tribune* would be in the Center for American History deep in the heart of Texas? The Norman Mailer Collection at the Harry Ransom Center was a gold mine. Of course, no one could take on this sort of project without the assistance of the staff of the New York Public Library, who were helpful and courteous. Likewise, I received much help from the staffs of the Franklin D. Roosevelt Presidential Library and Museum, John F. Kennedy Presidential Library and Museum, the Nixon Library and Museum, and the Ronald Reagan Presidential Foundation and Library. Finally, my special thanks to Archival Television Audio Inc., from which I was able to obtain rare audio tracks of Patterson fights as well as of appearances of Patterson and his contemporaries on programs aired during TV's golden era.

SOURCES

The following people acted as sources for this book, either through interviews for citations, through background interviews, or by providing suggestions, contact information, or other valuable material, or by providing advice and offers of help. The interviews and contacts were either in person, by telephone, by e-mail, or by traditional mail: Lonnie Ali, Cliff Arnesen, Joe Louis Barrow Jr., Michael Barson, Julian Bond, Jim Brewer, Hillary Cosell, Anthony M. Cucchiara, Peter De Pasquale, Liz Darhansoff, Ginny Foat, Phil Gries, Jane Gross, Michael Gross, the Reverend Mark Hallihan SJ, Roy "Cut 'n Shoot" Harris, Thomas Hauser, Gayl Heinz, Paul Hemphill, Montieth Illingworth, Kathryn James, Jeanie Kahnke, Dave Kindred, Mark Kram Jr., Jim Lehrer, J. Michael Lennon, Ron Lipton, Doug Lord, A. J. Lutz, Patricia Moore, Bill O'Hare, Geri D'Amato Olbermann, Dwayne Raymond (Prickett), Jan Reid, Ron Rich, Sara Rosen, Andrew Schott, John Schulian, John Shoonbeck, Edwin "Bud" Shrake, Jessica Sims, David Smith, Gay Talese, Jen Tisdale, Kim Vidt, Zach Vowell, Scott Waxman, Marc Weingarten, and Vic Ziegel.

PERIODICALS

American Weekly, Atlanta Magazine, Atlantic Monthly, Baltimore Sun, Berkshire Evening Eagle, Billings Gazette, Boxing Illustrated, Bridgeport Post, Chicago Sun-Times, Chicago Tribune, Corpus Christi Times, Ebony, Esquire, Florence Morning News, Harper's, Inside Sports, Jet, Life, Look, Los Angeles Times, Lowell Sun, Miami Herald, Miami News, Modesto Bee, Montana Standard, New York Daily Mirror, New York Daily News, New York Herald Tribune, New York Journal-American, New York Magazine, New York Post, New York Times, The New Yorker, Newsday, Newsweek, Nugget, Philadelphia Inquirer, Playboy, Ring Magazine, Sarasota Herald-Tribune, Saturday Evening Post, Sport Magazine, Sports Illustrated, Stars & Stripes, Time, and *Tucson Daily Citizen.*

VIDEO

Muhammad Ali: The Whole Story. Turner Home Entertainment, 1996.
Sonny Liston: The Mysterious Life & Death of a Champion. HBO Home Video, 1995.

WEBSITES

BoxRec, a reliable website containing information on fights and boxers' records, was a godsend. The same is true of YouTube, which contains many videos of significant fights. Other websites consulted were Ancestry.com, the Civil Rights Digital Library (http://crdl.osg.edu), ESPN, the International Coalition of Sites of Conscience, and Newspaper Archive.

BOOKS

Ali, Muhammad, with Richard Durham. *The Greatest: My Own Story.* New York: Random House, 1975.

Arkush, Michael. *The Fight of the Century: Ali vs. Frazier March 8, 1971.* Hoboken, NJ: Wiley & Sons, 2008.

Ashe, Arthur R. Jr. *A Hard Road to Glory: A History of the African American Athlete.* New York: Amistad/Warner Books, 1988.

Asinof, Eliot. *People vs. Blutcher: Black Men and White Law in Bedford-Stuyvesant.* New York: Viking, 1970.

Atlas, Teddy, and Peter Kaminsky. *Atlas: From the Streets to the Ring; A Son's Struggle to Become a Man.* New York: Ecco, 2006.

Baldwin, James. *The Fire Next Time.* New York: Dial Press, 1963.

———. *The Price of the Ticket: Collected Nonfiction 1948–1985.* New York: St. Martin's, 1985.

Berger, Phil. *Blood Season: Tyson and the World of Boxing.* New York: Morrow, 1989.

Berkow, Ira. *Red: A Biography of Red Smith.* New York: Times Books, 1986.

Boyd, Herb, with Ray Robinson II. *Pound for Pound: A Biography of Sugar Ray Robinson.* New York: Amistad/HarperCollins, 2005.

Brenner, Teddy, as told to Barney Nagler. *Only the Ring Was Square.* Englewood Cliffs, NJ: Prentice-Hall, 1981.

Brown, Claude. *Manchild in the Promised Land.* New York: Macmillan, 1965.

Butterfield, Fox. *All God's Children: The Bosket Family and the American Tradition of Violence.* New York: Knopf, 1995.

Callahan, Tom. *The Bases Were Loaded (And So Was I): Up Close and Personal with the Greatest Names in Sports.* New York: Crown, 2004. Also published under the title *Dancin' with Sonny Liston.*

Cannon, Jimmy. *Nobody Asked Me, But... The World of Jimmy Cannon.* Edited by Jack Cannon and Tom Cannon. New York: Holt, Rinehart and Winston, 1978.

Cavanaugh, Jack. *Tunney: Boxing's Brainiest Champ and His Upset of the Great Jack Dempsey.* New York: Random House, 2006.

Cleaver, Eldridge. *Soul on Ice.* New York: McGraw-Hill, 1968.

Cohen, Janet Langhart, with Alexander Kopelman. *From Rage to Reason: My Life in Two Americas.* New York: Kensington, 2004.

Conrad, Harold. *Dear Muffo: 35 Years in the Fast Lane.* New York: Stein and Day, 1982.

Cooper, Henry. *H for 'Enry: More Than Just an Autobiography.* London: Collins, 1984.

Cosell, Howard, with Mickey Herskowitz. *Cosell.* Chicago: Playboy Press, 1973.

Crouch, Stanley. *The Artificial White Man: Essays on Authenticity.* New York: Basic Civitas, 2004.

Dearborn, Mary V. *Mailer: A Biography.* Boston: Houghton Mifflin, 1999.

De Pasquale, Peter. *The Boxer's Workout: Fitness for the Civilized Man.* New York: Fighting Fit, 1988.

Dundee, Angelo, with Mike Winters. *I Only Talk Winning.* Chicago: Contemporary Books, 1985.

Dundee, Angelo, with Bert Randolph Sugar. *My View from the Corner: A Life in Boxing.* New York: McGraw-Hill, 2008.

Early, Gerald. *Tuxedo Junction: Essays on American Culture.* New York: Ecco, 1989.

———. *The Culture of Bruising: Essays on Prizefighting, Literature, and Modern American Culture.* Hopewell, NJ: Ecco, 1994.

———, ed. *The Muhammad Ali Reader.* Hopewell, NJ: Ecco, 1998.

Ezra, Michael. *Muhammad Ali: The Making of an Icon.* Philadelphia: Temple University Press, 2009.

Fitzgerald, Mike. *The Ageless Warrior: The Life of Boxing Legend Archie Moore.* Champaign, IL: Sports Publishing, 2004.

Fraser, Raymond. *The Fighting Fisherman: The Life of Yvon Durelle.* Garden City, NY: Doubleday, 1981.

Freeman, Lucy. "A Twenty-Cent Bag of Candy." In *Celebrities on the Couch: Personal Adventures of Famous People in Psychoanalysis,* edited by Lucy Freeman, 122–72. Los Angeles: Price/Stern/Sloan, 1970.

Fried, Ronald K. *Corner Men: The Great Boxing Trainers.* New York: Four Walls Eight Windows, 1991.

Gorn, Elliott J., ed. *Muhammad Ali, the People's Champ.* Urbana: University of Illinois Press, 1995.

Hamill, Pete. *A Drinking Life: A Memoir.* Boston: Little, Brown, 1994.

———. *Irrational Ravings.* New York: Putnam, 1971.

———. *Piecework: Writings on Men and Women, Fools and Heroes, Lost Cities, Vanished Friends, Small Pleasures, Large Calamities, and How the Weather Was.* Boston: Little, Brown, 1996.

Hauser, Thomas. *A Beautiful Sickness: Reflections on the Sweet Science.* Fayetteville: University of Arkansas Press, 2001.

———. *The Black Lights: Inside the World of Professional Boxing.* New York: Simon & Schuster, 1991.

———. *Muhammad Ali: His Life and Times.* New York: Simon & Schuster, 1991.

———. *The View from Ringside: Inside the Tumultuous World of Boxing.* Wilmington, DE: Sport Media, 2004.

Haygood, Wil. *Sweet Thunder: The Life and Times of Sugar Ray Robinson.* New York: Alfred A. Knopf, 2009.

Heinz, W. C. *Once They Heard the Cheers.* Garden City, NY: Doubleday, 1979.

———. *The Professional.* Cambridge: Da Capo Press, 2001. Originally published in 1958.

———. *What a Time It Was.* Cambridge: Da Capo Press, 2001.

Heinz, W. C., and Nathan Ward, eds. *The Book of Boxing.* Kingston, NY: Total/Sports Illustrated Classics, 1999. Updated edition.

Heller, Peter. *"In This Corner . . . !": Forty World Champions Tell Their Stories.* New York: Simon & Schuster, 1973.

———. *Bad Intentions: The Mike Tyson Story.* New York: New American Library, 1989.

Illingworth, Montieth. *Mike Tyson: Money, Myth, and Betrayal.* New York: Birch Lane Press, 1991.

Jacobson, Mark. *Teenage Hipster in the Modern World: From the Birth of Punk to the Land of Bush; Thirty Years of Millennial Journalism.* New York: Grove Press, 2005.

Johansson, Ingemar. *Seconds out of the Ring.* London: Stanley Paul, 1959.

Jones, LeRoi (Amiri Baraka). *Home.* New York: William Morrow, 1966.

Kahn, Roger. *A Flame of Pure Fire: Jack Dempsey and the Roaring '20s.* New York: Harcourt Brace, 1999.

———. *Into My Own: The Remarkable People and Events That Shaped a Life.* New York: Thomas Dunne Books/St. Martin's, 2006.

Kearns, Jack, as told to Oscar Fraley. *The Million Dollar Gate.* New York: Macmillan, 1966.

Kimball, George. *Manly Art: (They Can Run but They Can't Hide).* Ithaca, NY: McBooks Press, 2011.

Kindred, Dave. *Sound and Fury: Two Powerful Lives, One Fateful Friendship.* New York: Free Press, 2006.

Kram, Mark. *Ghosts of Manila: The Fateful Blood Feud between Muhammad Ali and Joe Frazier.* New York: HarperCollins, 2001.

Layden, Joe. *The Last Great Fight: The Extraordinary Tale of Two Men and How One Fight Changed Their Lives Forever.* New York: St. Martin's, 2007.

Levy, Alan H. *Floyd Patterson: A Boxer and a Gentleman.* Jefferson, NC: McFarland & Company, 2008.

Liebling, A. J. *A Neutral Corner: Boxing Essays.* San Francisco: North Point Press, 1990.

———. *The Sweet Science.* New York: Viking, 1956.

Mailer, Norman. *Advertisements for Myself.* New York: Putnam, 1959.

———. *Norman Mailer's Letters on "An American Dream," 1963–1969.* Edited by J. Michael Lennon. Shavertown, PA: Sligo Press, 2004.

———. *The Presidential Papers.* New York: Putnam, 1963.

Mailer, Norman, and John Buffalo Mailer. *The Big Empty: Dialogues on Politics, Sex, God, Boxing, Morality, Myth, Poker, and Bad Conscience in America.* New York: Nation Books, 2006.

Malcolm X, with Alex Haley. *The Autobiography of Malcolm X.* New York: Grove Press, 1965.

Manso, Peter, ed. *Mailer, His Life and Times.* New York: Simon & Schuster, 1985.

Maraniss, David. *Rome 1960: The Olympics That Changed the World.* New York: Simon & Schuster, 2008.

Marqusee, Mike. *Redemption Song: Muhammad Ali and the Spirit of the Sixties.* London: Verso, 1999.

McIlvanney, Hugh. *The Hardest Game.* Chicago: Contemporary Books, 2002. (Updated version of *McIlvanney on Boxing*, 1982.)

Mercante, Arthur, with Phil Guarnieri. *Inside the Ropes.* Ithaca, NY: McBooks, 2006.

Montgomery, Robin Navarro. *Cut 'N Shoot, Texas: The Roy Harris Story.* Austin, TX: Eakin Press, 1984.

Moore, Archie, and Leonard B. Pearl. *Any Boy Can: The Archie Moore Story.* Englewood Cliffs, NJ: Prentice-Hall, 1971.

Murphy, Jack. *Damn You, Al Davis: The Sporting World of Jack Murphy.* San Diego: Joyce Press, 1979.

Nagler, Barney. *Brown Bomber.* New York: World Publishing, 1972.

———. *James Norris and the Decline of Boxing.* Indianapolis: Bobbs-Merrill, 1964.

Newcombe, Jack. *Floyd Patterson: Heavyweight King.* New York: Bartholomew House, 1961.

Newfield, Jack. *Only in America: The Life and Crimes of Don King.* New York: William Morrow, 1995.

Oates, Joyce Carol. *On Boxing.* Garden City, NY: Dolphin/Doubleday, 1987.

O'Connor, Daniel, ed. *Iron Mike: A Mike Tyson Reader.* New York: Thunder's Mouth Press, 2002.

Olson, Jack. *Black Is Best: The Riddle of Cassius Clay.* New York: Putnam, 1967.

Patterson, Floyd, with Bert Randolph Sugar. *The International Boxing Hall of Fame's Basic Boxing Skills: A Step-by-Step Illustrated Introduction to the Sweet Science.* New York: Skyhorse, 2007. Originally published in 1974 as *Inside Boxing*.

Patterson, Floyd, with Milton Gross. *Victory over Myself.* New York: B. Geis; distributed by Random House, 1962.

Plimpton, George. *Shadow Box.* New York: Putnam, 1977.

Raab, Selwyn. *Five Families: The Rise, Decline, and Resurgence of America's Most Powerful Mafia Empires.* New York: Thomas Dunne Books/St. Martin's, 2006.

Rampersad, Arnold. *Jackie Robinson.* New York: Alfred A. Knopf, 1997.

Remnick, David. *King of the World: Muhammad Ali and the Rise of an American Hero.* New York: Random House, 1998.

Roberts, Randy. *Papa Jack: Jack Johnson and the Era of White Hopes.* New York: Free Press, 1983.

Ross, Barney. *Fundamentals of Boxing.* Chicago: Little Technical Library, 1942.

Rotella, Carlo. *Cut Time: An Education at the Fights.* Boston: Houghton Mifflin, 2003.

Schulberg, Budd. *Loser and Still Champion: Muhammad Ali.* Garden City, NY: Doubleday, 1972.

———. *Ringside: A Treasury of Boxing Reportage.* Chicago: Ivan R. Dee, 2006.

———. *Sparring with Hemingway: And Other Legends of the Fight Game.* Chicago: Ivan R. Dee, 1995.

Schulian, John. *Writer's Fighters and Other Sweet Scientists.* Kansas City, MO: Andrews and McMeel, 1983.

Sheed, Wilfrid. *Muhammad Ali: A Portrait in Words and Photographs.* New York: Thomas Y. Crowell, 1975.

Shropshire, Kenneth L. *Being Sugar Ray: The Life of Sugar Ray Robinson; America's Greatest Boxer and First Celebrity Athlete.* New York: Basic Civitas, 2007.

Sullivan, Russell. *Rocky Marciano: The Rock of His Times.* Urbana: University of Illinois Press, 2002.

Talese, Gay. *The Gay Talese Reader: Portraits and Encounters.* New York: Walker & Company, 2003.

———. "Origins of a Nonfiction Writer." In *Beyond the Godfather: Italian American Writers on the Real Italian American Experience,* edited by A. Kenneth Ciongoli and Jay Parini, 74–96. Hanover, NH: University Press of New England, 1997.

———. *A Writer's Life.* New York: Alfred A. Knopf, 2006.

Torres, José. *Fire and Fear: The Inside Story of Mike Tyson.* New York: Warner Books, 1989.

Torres, José, with Bert Randolph Sugar. *Sting Like a Bee: The Muhammad Ali Story.* New York: Abelard-Schuman, 1971.

Tosches, Nick. *The Devil and Sonny Liston.* Boston: Little, Brown, 2000.

United States Treasury Department, Bureau of Narcotics. *Mafia.* New York: HarperCollins, 2007.

Vecsey, George. *A Year in the Sun: The Games, the Players, the Pleasures of Sports.* New York: Times Books, 1989.

Von Hoffman, Nicholas. *Citizen Cohn.* Garden City, NY: Doubleday, 1988.

Wiley, Ralph. *Serenity: A Boxing Memoir.* New York: Henry Holt, 1989.

Wright, Richard. *Black Boy.* New York: Harper & Brothers, 1945.

Zirin, Dave. *What's My Name, Fool?: Sports and Resistance in the United States.* Chicago: Haymarket Books, 2005.

NOTES

PROLOGUE: NOTHING SHORT OF MIRACULOUS

1. Budd Schulberg, *Ringside: A Treasury of Boxing Reportage*, 43.
2. Lewis Burton, "The Lowdown: Lamb Stew on Friday's Menu," *New York Journal-American*, September 3, 1952.
3. Red Smith, "The Once and Future Floyd Patterson," *New York Times*, July 17, 1972.
4. Joyce Carol Oates, "Floyd Patterson: The Essence of a Competitor," 1988 Summer Olympics Viewer's Program.
5. Thomas Hauser, *Muhammad Ali: His Life and Times*, 326.

1. I DON'T LIKE THAT BOY!

1. North Carolina birth records as well as US Census and Social Security Death Index data list his actual name as Thames Patterson, but he seemed to prefer Thomas, and his son Floyd referred to him that way.
2. Her name has been spelled variously as "Annabelle" and "Anabelle." The Social Security Death Index lists her as "Annabelle," so I use that spelling.
3. Floyd Patterson, with Milton Gross, *Victory over Myself*, 11.
4. Lucy Freeman, "A Twenty-Cent Bag of Candy," in *Celebrities on the Couch: Personal Adventures of Famous People in Psychoanalysis*, ed. Lucy Freeman, 122.
5. Jimmy Breslin, "The Title Is the Champ's Life," *New York Journal-American*, June 27, 1960.
6. Freeman, "A Twenty-Cent Bag of Candy," 122.
7. Patterson's accounts of his youth were sometimes inconsistent. In *Victory over Myself*, he said it was not a case but a few bottles of soda in a paper bag. And he claimed he didn't steal them; the culprit was some other kid, who ran off after

giving the bag to Floyd, leaving Floyd to take the rap. But a few years later, in an interview with author Lucy Freeman published in *Celebrities on the Couch*, Patterson admitted to being the thief. He also told Freeman it was the soda-theft incident that led to his being sent to reform school, which is at odds with how he describes events in *Victory over Myself*.

8. Patterson, *Victory over Myself*, 19.
9. Freeman, "A Twenty-Cent Bag of Candy," 129.
10. Author interview, Cliff Arnesen.
11. International Coalition of Sites of Conscience, *The Wiltwyck School*, February 28, 2010, http://www.sitesofconscience.org/sites/eleanor-roosevelt/how-is-it-remembered/the-wiltwyck-school.
12. Patterson, *Victory over Myself*, 37.

2. TAKEN UP WITH BOXING

1. Floyd Patterson, with Milton Gross, *Victory over Myself*, 39.
2. Frank and Billy Patterson never established careers as professional boxers. Billy Patterson fought a few pro fights, but a detached retina ended his days in the ring. Frank was more of a natural boxer than Floyd and won a Golden Gloves championship but failed to become a successful pro.
3. Author interview, Geri D'Amato Olbermann.
4. Gay Talese, "Suspicious Man in the Champ's Corner," *New York Times*, September 23, 1962.
5. His real name was Gerardo, Anglicized to Gerald, though he was popularly called Gerry.
6. Talese, "Suspicious Man in the Champ's Corner."
7. Robert Friedman, "Raging Calf," *Inside Sports*, August 1981.
8. "In the pocket" is a boxing term meaning that an attacking boxer has minimized the space between himself and an opponent and is fighting very close in. Typically a boxer does not want to remain in the pocket for too long. Fighting in the pocket is sometimes called fighting "in the phone booth" because of the space constraints.
9. Friedman, "Raging Calf."
10. Barney Ross, *Fundamentals of Boxing*, 27. Ross won the world lightweight, junior welterweight, and welterweight titles and is widely considered one of the best prizefighters of all time. Published in 1942, *Fundamentals of Boxing* has become a kind of classic among boxing manuals.
11. Robert H. Boyle, "Svengali Returns!" *Sports Illustrated*, April 12, 1965.
12. Patterson, *Victory over Myself*, 47.
13. George McGuane, "Eight 'Gloves' Titles on Block," *Lowell Sun*, March 19, 1951.
14. Patterson, *Victory over Myself*, 52.

3. FLOYD PATTERSON IS OUT OF THIS WORLD

1. Floyd Patterson, with Milton Gross, *Victory over Myself*, 37.
2. Sometimes he threw a straight punch accompanied by a leap. This punch was also called a "gazelle."

3. The Olympic weight divisions differed somewhat from their American amateur boxing counterparts. The Olympic middleweight class was divided into two categories: heavy-middleweight (165 pounds) and light-middleweight (156 pounds).

4. "Patterson Steals Show in Ring Tryouts in Albany," *Berkshire Evening Eagle,* May 27, 1952.

5. Patterson, *Victory over Myself,* 66.

6. Murray Rose, "U.S. Fighters Should Capture Four Titles," *Corpus Christi Times,* July 11, 1952 (Associated Press article).

7. Ibid.

8. W. C. Heinz, "The Floyd Patterson His Friends Know," *Sport,* November 1960.

9. A portion of Smith's article is reprinted in Patterson's *Victory over Myself,* page 68.

10. Even though the fight lasted just twenty seconds, Patterson was warned twice during that brief time for rules violations, which suggests that he was correct in being concerned about the impartiality of the judging if the fight ended in a decision.

11. The 1952 Olympic boxing team was the best America fielded until the 1976 team matched its gold-medal wins.

12. Joseph M. Sheehan, "Eighty More Olympians Return, Including Five Boxing Champions," *New York Times,* August 8, 1952.

4. CUS ANSWERS THE QUESTIONS

1. Cus D'Amato, "The Two Battles of Floyd Patterson," *Look,* June 23, 1959.

2. Peter Heller, *Bad Intentions: The Mike Tyson Story,* 26.

3. Floyd turned to Charles Schwefel to look over the document, and Schwefel assured Patterson it was on the square. Schwefel also did some snooping into D'Amato's background and reported to Patterson that he could be trusted.

4. Floyd Patterson, with Milton Gross, *Victory over Myself,* 71.

5. "Reputed Front Man Silent," *Sarasota Herald-Tribune,* June 16, 1960 (Associated Press article).

6. Selwyn Raab, *Five Families: The Rise, Decline, and Resurgence of America's Most Powerful Mafia Empires,* 104.

7. Patterson, *Victory over Myself,* 85.

8. Milton Gross, Speaking Out, *New York Post,* September 23, 1953.

9. Raymond Fraser, *The Fighting Fisherman: The Life of Yvon Durelle,* 87. Newspaper accounts and other records of the fight show Durelle weighing as much as 171 pounds. But Durelle told novelist Raymond Fraser that his actual weight was just 158.

10. Caswell Adams, "Beaten Durelle Brings Out Patterson's Ring Failings," *New York Journal-American,* February 16, 1954.

11. To ensure that bigtime boxers would sign contracts, promoters typically provided "guarantees" in writing against a draw of "the gate" (ticket sales) and from other sources of revenue the promoters might have set up for the fight, such as radio and television broadcast rights.

12. Robert Friedman, "Raging Calf," *Inside Sports,* August 1981.

13. Patterson, *Victory over Myself,* 110.

5. DO I HAVE TO FIGHT FLOYD?

1. Raymond Fraser, *The Fighting Fisherman: The Life of Yvon Durelle*, 92.
2. Budd Schulberg, *Ringside: A Treasury of Boxing Reportage*, 46.
3. Paul O'Neil, "Meet the Next Heavyweight Champion," *Sports Illustrated*, January 30, 1956.
4. Ibid.
5. W. C. Heinz and Nathan Ward, *The Book of Boxing*. The 1999 "Total *Sports Illustrated* Classics" edition includes an authoritative list of heavyweight championship bouts from 1892 through March 1999, including weights of the boxers. It is printed on the reverse side of the book's dust jacket.
6. Some lists had Jackson as the number two contender, behind Archie Moore.
7. Moore was the undisputed best in the light-heavyweight ranks at the time. Between fights, his weight typically swelled up to more than 200 pounds (he also went through a grueling weight-loss regimen to prepare for a fight). Because of this, he had designs on moving up in weight to box as a heavyweight.
8. Floyd Patterson, with Milton Gross, *Victory over Myself*, 131.

6. YOUNGEST KING OF THE MOUNTAIN

1. According to columnist Jack Murphy, Moore called himself "the Mongoose," an animal known for its agility, sharp-sightedness, and speed. As Moore progressed in age, some sportswriters referred to him as "Old Man River." The two nicknames eventually came together as "the Old Mongoose."
2. Floyd Patterson, with Milton Gross, *Victory over Myself*, 136.
3. Archie Moore and Leonard B. Pearl, *Any Boy Can: The Archie Moore Story*, 87.
4. Budd Schulberg, *Sparring with Hemingway: And Other Legends of the Fight Game*, 80.
5. Author interview, Gay Talese.
6. "Word of the Week," *Jet*, June 18, 1959.
7. Frank Mastro, "Moore to Get $200,000," *Chicago Tribune*, November 30, 1956.
8. Jim Jennings, "B'klyn Claims Floyd as Own," *New York Daily Mirror*, undated clipping from the Center for American History, University of Texas.
9. Light-heavyweight champion José Torres was close to both Muhammad Ali and Patterson and observed them when both men were at their respective career peaks. He believed that Patterson, at the time he beat Moore, was the one heavyweight who might have successfully challenged Ali in his prime.
10. Mike Fitzgerald, *The Ageless Warrior: The Life of Boxing Legend Archie Moore*, 134.
11. Ibid., 135.
12. Moore, *Any Boy Can*, 156.
13. Arthur Daley, "Post Bellum Musings," Sports of the Times, *New York Times*, December 3, 1956.
14. "Floyd Patterson: Fighter of the Year," *The Ring*, February 1957.

7. A BLACK CHAMPION IN AMERICA

1. Floyd Patterson, with Milton Gross, *Victory over Myself,* 144.
2. Author interview, Gay Talese.
3. Gay Talese, "Origins of a Nonfiction Writer," in *Beyond the Godfather: Italian American Writers on the Real Italian American Experience,* ed. A. Kenneth Ciongoli and Jay Parini, 74.
4. "Jackson in Hospital with Bruised Kidney Suffered in Fight with Patterson," *New York Times,* July 31, 1957.
5. Ibid.
6. Hurricane Jackson fought only one other fight of any significance, then gave up the ring in 1961 after a series of fights in out-of-the-way venues. The one-time top heavyweight contender then eked out a living shining shoes. He died in early 1982 after being struck by an automobile a few weeks earlier as he was polishing his cab in New York.
7. John Lardner, "A Summer Dream," *Newsweek,* August 26, 1957.
8. Dale Wright, "Champ Avoids Bright Lights," *Jet,* February 6, 1958.
9. The Wrigley Field in Los Angeles opened in 1925. The more famous Wrigley Field in Chicago is an older ballpark; first known as Weeghman Park and then as Cubs Park, in 1926 it received its current name. Both were named for chewing-gum magnate William Wrigley Jr., who owned the Chicago Cubs and the now-defunct minor-league Los Angeles Angels (not to be confused with the current Major League Baseball team of the same name). A handsome stadium with Spanish architectural flourishes, the Los Angeles Wrigley Field was demolished in 1966.
10. Martin Kane, "You Watch Out, Ali!" *Sports Illustrated,* November 14, 1966.
11. Joe David Brown, "A Tall Texan Tale," *Sports Illustrated,* August 18, 1958.
12. Author interview, Roy "Cut 'n Shoot" Harris.
13. John De La Vega, "Patterson Eyes Another Title Defense in '58," *Los Angeles Times,* August 20, 1958.
14. Gene Ward, "Floyd Wants Sept. Bout, But Who Will He Fight?" *New York Daily News,* August 20, 1958.
15. Author interview, Roy "Cut 'n Shoot" Harris.
16. Steve Springer, "A Lone Star Memory; Harris, from Cut N' Shoot, Texas, Hasn't Forgotten Title Bout He Lost to Patterson 45 Years Ago in LA," *Los Angeles Times,* June 16, 2003.
17. Jimmy Cannon, column, *New York Journal-American,* August 20, 1958.
18. Red Smith, "Morning After," *New York Herald Tribune,* August 19, 1958.
19. Finding challengers to Patterson's crown had become a somewhat desperate pursuit for D'Amato. There were even negotiations around this time for Patterson to fight Oklahoma's Danny Hodge, a three-time NCAA national champion wrestler and Olympic silver medalist who had begun a professional boxing career. Hodge had won a national Golden Gloves title as a boxer before he turned pro, and he'd won eight of ten professional fights, but he was in no way an appropriate challenger for the heavyweight championship. Hodge went on to become one of the early stars of televised professional wrestling. In some quarters, there was speculation that Patterson would go down in weight to fight the great Sugar Ray Robinson, but nothing ever came of such talk.

20. "Title Fight Discussed," *New York Times*, November 25, 1958.
21. Cooper was knighted in 2000 for his boxing career.
22. The Lonsdale Belt was awarded to British boxing champions between 1909 and 1987. It was named for the award's patron, Hugh Lowther, Fifth Earl of Lonsdale.
23. William J. Briordy, "British Heavyweight Drilling in Gym on East Side," *New York Times*, April 16, 1959.
24. Martin Kane, "The Two Faces of Cecil Rhodes," *Sports Illustrated*, April 27, 1959.
25. "Talkative Challenger Says It's Great to Be a Fighter," *New York Times*, April 17, 1958 (Associated Press article).
26. Janet Langhart Cohen, with Alexander Kopelman, *From Rage to Reason: My Life in Two Americas*, 28.
27. "Patterson and London Floor Spar Mates," *Chicago Daily Tribune*, April 20, 1959 (Associated Press article).
28. "Comic Opera," *Time*, May 11, 1959.

8. LIGHTNING AND TOONDER

1. Floyd Patterson, with Milton Gross, *Victory over Myself*, 180.
2. "Ingo Meets His Match," *Sports Illustrated*, June 8, 1960.
3. Ingemar Johansson, *Seconds out of the Ring*, 51.
4. Ibid., 58.
5. Sanders, an enlisted man in the Navy, began fighting professionally after his tour of duty was complete. Badly battered in his ninth pro fight, he died of his injuries three days later.
6. Al Buck, "Working Press," *New York Post*, June 1959.
7. Patterson, *Victory over Myself*, 35.
8. Patterson, as champion, used the permanent dressing room of the Yankees beneath the stands instead of the virtual tent out on the grass.
9. Howard Cosell, with Mickey Herskowitz, *Cosell*, 155.
10. Floyd Patterson as told to W. C. Heinz, "I Was a Champion," *American Weekly*, May 15, 1960.
11. Johansson, *Seconds out of the Ring*, 173.
12. Patterson as told to Heinz, "I Was a Champion."
13. John Lardner, "As Advertised, It Came," *Newsweek*, July 6, 1959.
14. Cosell, *Cosell*, 158.
15. Patterson, *Victory over Myself*, 187.
16. Ibid.
17. Joseph M. Sheehan, "Loser Ruefully Admits Failure to See Punch That Began End," *New York Times*, June 27, 1959.
18. Ibid.

9. NOT THE TIME TO QUIT

1. Floyd Patterson, with Milton Gross, *Victory over Myself*, 191.
2. Ernie Prevatte, column, *Florence Morning News*, June 28, 1959.

3. "Tunney Praises Swedish Champ," *Montana Standard*, June 28, 1959 (Associated Press article).
4. Milton Gross, "Floyd Tells How Ingemar 'Tricked Me with Right,'" *New York Post*, June 29, 1959.
5. Howard Cosell, with Mickey Herskowitz, *Cosell*, 158–59.
6. Arnold Rampersad, *Jackie Robinson*, 363.
7. Letter to Floyd Patterson from Archie Moore, date unknown, reprinted in Patterson, *Victory over Myself*, 194.
8. Harry Grayson, "Tunney, Others Called Turn on Built Up Patterson," *Modesto Bee*, July 9, 1959 (NEA article). The Cardiff Giant Grayson mentions was a hoax that received national attention in the 1800s. The Cardiff Giant was supposed to have been the petrified remains of a ten-foot-tall giant unearthed in Cardiff, New York. In fact, the "giant" recently had been created and planted by a New York tobacconist named George Hull. Though the hoax was rather quickly dismissed as a fake by archaeologists, promoters were successful in charging people to see it, enough so that P. T. Barnum created an imitation. The expression "There's a sucker born every minute" came into use as a result of the Cardiff Giant affair.
9. Author interview, Jan Reid. Reid is a novelist and journalist who has written extensively about boxing.
10. The plot was built around the death of the white commander of a Marine rifle platoon who, with his dying words, puts a black sergeant, played by Poitier, in charge. Thus the film's conflict involves Poitier and the white Marines under his command more than the war between the Americans and the North Koreans — a touch of irony, given the racial implications of Johansson's defeat of Patterson.
11. Oddly enough, Johansson failed to win a similar honor in Sweden, where sportswriters polled selected soccer player Agne Simonsson as the nation's top athlete for 1959.
12. Johansson, as it turned out, would be the last white man to be considered the undisputed heavyweight champion of the world. Later, a few white men — in particular the Ukrainian Klitschko brothers in the early 2000s — would rise to dominance in the heavyweight ranks, but by that time, the alphabet soup of sanctioning organizations made determining an undisputed champion virtually impossible.
13. IBC president Jim Norris was found guilty of violating antitrust laws in 1957; that conviction was upheld by the nation's highest court two years later. Frankie Carbo went down in 1959 on charges of conspiracy, undercover management of boxers, and undercover matchmaking. He was sentenced to two years. Almost immediately after his release from prison he was brought up on federal racketeering charges; convicted, he was sentenced to twenty-five years at Alcatraz.
14. Montieth Illingworth, *Mike Tyson: Money, Myth, and Betrayal*, 29–30, and author interview, Montieth Illingworth.
15. Cosell, *Cosell*, 159.
16. Lucy Freeman, "A Twenty-Cent Bag of Candy, in *Celebrities on the Couch: Personal Adventures of Famous People in Psychoanalysis*, ed. Lucy Freeman, 133.

17. Jimmy Breslin, "Trainer's Tip Made Champ Big Fighter," *New York Journal-American*, June 28, 1960.

18. Arthur Daley, "Sports of the Times: Continued Story," *New York Times*, April 11, 1960.

19. Charles Schwefel, who had served as Floyd's major financial adviser, died unexpectedly on August 21, 1956. With his passing, Patterson turned to others for advice on financial matters, among them, of course, D'Amato. But by the time of the second Johansson fight, attorney Julius November had become Patterson's foremost business adviser.

20. Jimmy Breslin, untitled clipping, *New York Journal-American*, June 26, 1960, from the Center for American History, University of Texas.

21. Jimmy Breslin, "His Boss? No, It's Floyd," *New York Journal-American*, June 29, 1960.

22. Patterson, *Victory over Myself*, 212.

23. Red Smith, "Behind the Words," *Pacific Stars & Stripes*, undated clipping from the Center for American History, University of Texas (syndicated article from the *New York Herald Tribune*).

24. Frank M. Blunk, "Louis Will Advise Patterson on Title Fight," *New York Times*, May 17, 1960.

25. Howard M. Tuckner, "Champion's Pre-Fight 'Retreat' Proves to Be Television Show," *New York Times*, June 20, 1960.

26. James F. Lynch, "For D'Amato the Bell Doesn't Toll," *New York Times*, June 12, 1960.

27. Howard M. Tuckner, "Melee Broken Up by Police Detail," *New York Times*, June 21, 1960.

28. Milton Gross, column, *New York Post*, June 21, 1960.

29. Ingemar Johansson vs. Floyd Patterson (video of closed-circuit TV broadcast), 1960. Retrieved July 6, 2010, from http://www.youtube.com/watch?v=O68Z7 DJxXbo&feature=related.

30. Cosell, *Cosell*, 160.

31. George Plimpton, *Shadow Box*, 298.

32. Robert Lipsyte, "Patterson Takes Title to PS 614," *New York Times*, June 25, 1960.

33. "It Was a Victory for Us!" *Ebony*, August 1960.

34. A. J. Liebling, *A Neutral Corner: Boxing Essays*, 164.

10. STANDING AT THE PEAK

1. David Maraniss, *Rome 1960: The Olympics That Changed the World*, 286.

2. Ibid.

3. Thomas Hauser, *Muhammad Ali: His Life and Times*, 37.

4. Robert H. Boyle, "Hail, Hail, the Gang's All Here," *Sports Illustrated*, February 20, 1961.

5. Ibid.

6. Gay Talese, "Portrait of the Ascetic Champ," *New York Times Magazine*, March 5, 1961.

7. Ibid.

8. Ibid.

9. Ibid.
10. A. J. Liebling, *A Neutral Corner*, 134.
11. Ibid., 141.
12. Florida rules required a mandatory eight-count following a knockdown. So while Patterson was up at two, he had to wait until the referee reached the count of 8 before the fight could resume.
13. Liebling, *A Neutral Corner*, 143.
14. Johansson's camp claimed that the referee had mismanaged the count in the sixth round, that Patterson should not have been awarded the knockout. But the ref's ruling stood.
15. Floyd Patterson, with Milton Gross, *Victory over Myself*, 241.
16. Howard Cosell, *Cosell*, 160.
17. Jimmy Cannon, "Floyd Wins 'Hands Down' at Making Safe Landings," *New York Journal-American*, May 16, 1961.
18. Dick Schaap, "How to Succeed in Publishing without Really Publishing," *New York Times Book Review*, August 13, 1967.
19. Robert Cromie, "The Bystander," *Chicago Tribune*, September 30, 1962.

11. CAMELOT DENIED

1. Martin Kane, "A Question of Violence," *Sports Illustrated*, November 13, 1961.
2. Deane McGowen, "Loser's Verdict: Floyd Can Punch," *New York Times*, December 5, 1961.
3. Presidential appointment book page, January 12, 1962, John F. Kennedy Presidential Library.
4. Floyd Patterson, letter to Robert F. Kennedy, January 20, 1962, John F. Kennedy Presidential Library.
5. Drew Pearson, "Reds Say Only Gagarin and Titov Sent into Space," *Billings Gazette*, April 7, 1962 (syndicated column).
6. Gay Talese, "Liston's Plight Shocks Patterson," *New York Times*, April 28, 1962.
7. Red Smith, "Behind the Words," *Pacific Stars & Stripes*, undated clipping from the Center for American History, University of Texas (syndicated article from the *New York Herald Tribune*).
8. Thomas A. Bolan, "Patterson in Egypt," *The Ring*, July 1962.
9. "Ghana Runnerup in Cairo Boxing Tournament," *Jet*, April 12, 1962.
10. Bolan, "Patterson in Egypt."
11. Robert Cromie, "The Bystander," *Chicago Tribune*, September 30, 1962.
12. Ibid.
13. Brian O'Doherty, "Telephone Interview with Busy Poet Produces Her Views on Baseball, Floyd Patterson, and Verse Style," *New York Times*, November 15, 1962.
14. Gay Talese, "A Fighter with Fear," *New York Times*, June 24, 1962.
15. Jim Murray, "Victory for Floyd," *Los Angeles Times*, May 20, 1962.
16. Author interview, Michael Gross. Though long out of print and mostly unknown to the generations of readers since 1962, *Victory over Myself* stands as one of the dozen or so best books written about boxing. It is a flawed book. There are occasional factual mistakes. It is at times a self-serving book as well,

particularly in its sanitized portrayal of Floyd and Sandra's relationship in the early 1960s. Some events are portrayed in ways that are inconsistent with how Floyd described them elsewhere. But its merits far outweigh its shortcomings. Patterson's emotionally naked self-portrait provides deep insight into the inner workings of an athlete's mind.

17. Robert Cromie, "The Bystander."
18. Michael Leahy, "Floyd Patterson: His Own Man," *Sports Illustrated,* June 1, 1992.
19. David Remnick, *King of the World: Muhammad Ali and the Rise of an American Hero,* 294.
20. *Sonny Liston: The Mysterious Life & Death of a Champion,* directed by Jeff Lieberman (HBO Home Video, 1995).
21. Nick Tosches, *The Devil and Sonny Liston,* 34.
22. "Liston Now Ready to Sign," *New York Herald Tribune,* March 3, 1962.
23. James Baldwin, "The Fight: Patterson vs. Liston," *Nugget,* February 1963. Reprinted as an afterword in Gerald Early, *Tuxedo Junction: Essays on American Culture,* 325.
24. Ibid.
25. Ibid., 330.
26. Ibid., 332.
27. Ibid., 333.
28. Ibid., 333.
29. Author interview, Edwin "Bud" Shrake.
30. Daniel M. Daniel, "Odds Won't Win It"; and James J. Braddock as told to Lester Bromberg, "Patterson Will Win!" *The Ring,* July 1962.
31. Norman Mailer, "Ten Thousand Words a Minute," *Esquire,* February 1963; reprinted in his *The Presidential Papers,* 237.
32. Ibid., 240.
33. Jack R. Griffin, "Floyd 'Froze' before Fight — Triner," *Chicago Sun-Times,* February 4, 1963.
34. Just two heavyweight championship fights had taken less time to resolve: Tommy Burns knocked out Jem Roche in one minute, twenty-eight seconds in 1908; Joe Louis knocked out Max Schmeling in two minutes, four seconds in 1938.
35. Baldwin, "The Fight: Patterson vs. Liston," in Early, *Tuxedo Junction,* 334.

12. CONFRONTING A CERTAIN WEAKNESS

1. Norman Mailer, *The Presidential Papers,* 263.
2. Mary V. Dearborn, *Mailer: A Biography,* 186.
3. Harold Conrad, *Dear Muffo: 35 Years in the Fast Lane,* 150.
4. Milton Gross, "Floyd Makes Lonely Trip Home Incognito," *Chicago Daily Tribune,* September 29, 1962 (originally appeared as a copyrighted article in the *New York Post,* September 28, 1962).
5. Leonard Lewin, "Liston'll Fight Me: Floyd," *New York Daily Mirror,* April 11, 1963.
6. David Remnick, *King of the World: Muhammad Ali and the Rise of an American Hero,* 36.

7. "Floyd Patterson Speaks on Rights," *New York Times*, February 26, 1962 (UPI article).

8. WSB-TV newsfilm clip of former heavyweight boxing champion Floyd Patterson speaking to a reporter about the civil rights movement in Birmingham, Alabama, May 9, 1963. The Civil Rights Digital Library, May 24, 2010.

9. Howard Cosell, with Mickey Herskowitz, *Cosell*, 159.

10. Mable Roberson, telegram to President Kennedy, September 22, 1963, John F. Kennedy Presidential Library.

11. Howard Kleinberg, "600 Show Up to 'Floor' Floyd," *Miami News*, March 10, 1963.

12. Pat Putnam, "Laughing Boy Floyd Buries His Despair," *Miami Herald*, March 4, 1963.

13. William Nack, "O Unlucky Man," *Sports Illustrated*, February 4, 1991.

14. Budd Schulberg, *Sparring with Hemingway: And Other Legends of the Fight Game*, 130.

15. Norman Mailer, letter to Pete Hamill, July 5, 1964, Norman Mailer Collection, Harry Ransom Center, University of Texas.

16. Undated, handwritten note, Norman Mailer Collection, Harry Ransom Center, University of Texas.

17. Melvin Durslag, "Floyd No Longer a Neurotic Wreck," *Philadelphia Inquirer*, June 29, 1963.

18. Undated, handwritten note, Norman Mailer Collection, Harry Ransom Center, University of Texas.

19. Jimmy Burns, "Floyd Knows One Thing Sure: 'Never Show Signs of Fear,'" *Miami Herald*, March 17, 1963.

20. Cosell, *Cosell*, 162.

21. Remnick, *King of the World*, 74.

22. Melvin Durslag, "Has Floyd Lost Desire to Fight?" *Philadelphia Inquirer*, July 27, 1963.

23. "The Patterson Comeback: Where Is It Headed?" *Boxing Illustrated*, April 1964.

24. "America's 100 Most Influential Negroes," *Ebony*, September 1963.

13. A TITLE FOR AMERICA

1. Gay Talese, "The Loser," in *The Gay Talese Reader*, 66. Originally published in *Esquire*, March 1964.

2. Ibid.

3. Author interview, Jane Gross.

4. Pete Hamill, "Floyd's Fight to Save His Pride," *Saturday Evening Post*, June 27, 1964, reprinted in *Irrational Ravings*, 341.

5. The part of Yonkers in which the Pattersons lived was very close to Scarsdale. Their house was serviced by the Scarsdale Post Office, so their mailing address was Scarsdale. Sometimes the Pattersons were referred to as living in Scarsdale, though they actually were in Yonkers.

6. Talese, "The Loser," in *The Gay Talese Reader*, 69.

7. Ibid., 77.

8. Robert H. Boyle, "Svengali Returns!" *Sports Illustrated,* April 12, 1965.

9. Ibid.

10. Hamill, "Floyd's Fight to Save His Pride," *Irrational Ravings,* 339.

11. Arthur Daley, "Road to Nowhere," Sports of the Times, *New York Times,* July 2, 1964.

12. Hamill, "Floyd's Fight to Save His Pride," *Irrational Ravings,* 337.

13. Floyd Patterson, with Milton Gross, "I Want to Destroy Clay," *Sports Illustrated,* October 19, 1964.

14. Hamill, "Floyd's Fight to Save His Pride," *Irrational Ravings,* 342.

15. James Baldwin, *The Fire Next Time,* 21.

16. Patterson, with Gross, "I Want to Destroy Clay." Indeed, Ali did eventually deliver a segregationist speech at a Ku Klux Klan rally.

17. José Torres, with Bert Randolph Sugar, *Sting Like a Bee: The Muhammad Ali Story,* 143.

18. Some newspapers listed him as the number four contender.

19. Bob Waters, "Man on the Way Back," *Newsday,* January 23, 1965.

20. Gay Talese, "Patterson Fumes but Disdains Exchanging Insults with Clay," *New York Times,* January 22, 1965.

21. Ibid.

22. Floyd Patterson, with Gay Talese, "In Defense of Cassius Clay," *Esquire,* August 1966.

23. Jesse Abramson, "Poet Cassius Digs Floyd," *New York Herald Tribune,* November 20, 1965.

24. Gerald Eskenazi, "Cassius the Prophet a Loss as a Bus Driver," *New York Times,* January 20, 1965.

25. Floyd Patterson vs. George Chuvalo — Fight of the Year 1965 (video of closed-circuit TV broadcast). Retrieved May 30, 2010, from http://www.youtube.com/watch?v=EmIE5oDGtak.

26. Ibid.

27. Tex Maule, "Okay — But Don't Bring on Clay," *Sports Illustrated,* February 8, 1965.

28. Though most experts on the scene believed Patterson won, each round was closely fought. United Press International reported it would have called the fight a draw. The Canadian Press's reporter scored it 6-5-1 in favor of Patterson.

29. Jesse Abramson, "What Can Boxing Do for Encore?" *New York Herald Tribune,* February 3, 1965.

30. Most reports list the knockdown as occurring at 1:42 of the first round; however, Maine boxing officials said it took place at the 1:00 mark. However, in the confusion that followed, the knockout was not declared until either 2:15 or 2:17 of the first round; again, the precise time was in dispute.

31. Accounts vary about precisely when and where the conversation between Patterson and Liston occurred. I've chosen to include Patterson's own telling of it.

32. Floyd Patterson, interviewed in *Sonny Liston: The Mysterious Life & Death of a Champion,* directed by Jeff Lieberman (HBO Home Video, 1995).

33. In the popular mind, LA was perceived in the mid-1960s as a city of oppor-

tunity, with plenty of jobs and a thriving economy. It was a clean place where people of any color seemed to be able to reinvent themselves. In fact, beneath its gleaming exterior, LA had a long history of bigotry and suppressed rage, as the Watts riots revealed.

34. Muhammad Ali, with Richard Durham, *The Greatest: My Own Story*, 219.
35. LeRoi Jones (Amiri Baraka), *Home*, 156.
36. Malcolm X, with Alex Haley, *The Autobiography of Malcolm X*, 313.
37. Eldridge Cleaver, *Soul on Ice*, 91.
38. Floyd Patterson, with Jack Mahon, "Cassius Clay Must Be Beaten," *Sports Illustrated*, October 11, 1965.
39. Patterson, with Talese, "In Defense of Cassius Clay."
40. Author interview, Joe Louis Barrow. At the time, Patterson was hardly alone in declining to use the name "Muhammad Ali." Ali was unpredictable, and many boxing writers of the 1960s believed his infatuation with the Black Muslims might be no more than a youthful lark. His adopted name might not last — so they continued to refer to him as Clay. It was the editorial policy of magazines such as *Sports Illustrated* to call him Clay. On order of the publisher, the *New York Times* did so as well, saying Clay had not gone through the court mechanics to legally change his name to Muhammad Ali. It was a specious stance for the paper to take. I asked Joe Louis Barrow Jr., son of the great champion Joe Louis, born Joseph Louis Barrow, if his father had ever legally changed his name. He said he didn't know that he had. Yet the *Times* had no problem referring to the champ as Joe Louis. Likewise it had no problem referring to Walker Smith Jr. as Sugar Ray Robinson or Archibald Lee Wright as Archie Moore.
41. "Clay Says He Will Punish Patterson for His Remarks," *New York Times*, November 2, 1965.
42. Ronald K. Fried, *Corner Men: The Great Boxing Trainers*, 291.
43. Ibid., 306.
44. Howard Cosell interview with Muhammad Ali, *Wide World of Sports*, January 29, 1966.
45. Ibid.
46. David Remnick, *King of the World: Muhammad Ali and the Rise of an American Hero*, 282.
47. Ali's trainer, Angelo Dundee, was also perplexed by why Ali had not knocked out Patterson. Dundee shouted from ringside during the final rounds, imploring Ali to put Patterson away. The crowd, too, was angered by Ali's refusal to go for the kill.
48. Robert Lipsyte, "Clay Knocks Out Patterson in the 12th and Keeps Heavyweight Championship," *New York Times*, November 23, 1965.
49. "Sickening Spectacle in the Ring," *Life*, December 3, 1965.
50. In the days immediately following the fight, some sports columnists roundly criticized Floyd for not canceling because of his back injury.
51. Author interview, Gay Talese.
52. Floyd Patterson with Gay Talese, "In Defense of Cassius Clay."
53. Ibid.

14. A BOXING MAN

1. Gay Talese, *The Gay Talese Reader: Portraits and Encounters*, 70.
2. Author interview, Gay Talese.
3. Sandra found success working in real estate in her new hometown, becoming well known in Springfield business and social circles; she was the first African American to serve on the city's Board of Realtors.
4. Bobbie Barbee, "Seeking 3rd Heavyweight Crown," *Jet*, September 12, 1968.
5. "Floyd Patterson Obtains Divorce," *Tucson Daily Citizen*, August 23, 1966 (Associated Press article).
6. Barbee, "Seeking 3rd Heavyweight Crown."
7. "Marriage 'No Secret,' Says Floyd Patterson," *Bridgeport (CT) Post*, July 11, 1968 (United Press International article).
8. Barbee, "Seeking 3rd Heavyweight Crown."
9. Ali was still known as Cassius Clay at the time.
10. Robert Lipsyte, "Clay Weighs 'Summit Meeting' with Patterson," *New York Times*, September 24, 1966.
11. The World Boxing Association (WBA) and the New York State Athletic Commission first withdrew their recognition of Ali as champion in 1964 because he opted to fight Liston in a rematch rather than abide by the rules those organizations had in place to determine the next challenger. After Ali defeated Ernie Terrell in early 1967, he was briefly recognized as universal champion. Then, after his refusal to be inducted into the Army later that year, Ali's title was stripped by the WBA, the New York State Athletic Commission, and the World Boxing Council (WBC); several other less significant sanctioning bodies followed suit.
12. Ray Belford, "Patterson May Shun Title Tourney," *Pacific Stars & Stripes*, July 5, 1967.
13. Mark Kram, "The Brawler at the Threshold," *Sports Illustrated*, June 16, 1969.
14. California boxing rules allowed officials to give extra weight to knockdowns when scoring a fight. Patterson was knocked down twice; Quarry, just once. Though Patterson clearly outboxed Quarry through most of the fight, Quarry partisans pointed to the knockdowns as justification for the draw.
15. "US Could Learn Racial Lesson in Vietnam," *Pacific Stars & Stripes*, July 5, 1967 (United Press International article).
16. Mark Kram, "The Brawler at the Threshold."
17. Rebecca Burns, "Funeral: An Oral History," *Atlanta Magazine*, April 2008.
18. "Transcripts of Prayer, Tribute and Eulogy Delivered at Services for Dr. King," *New York Times*, April 10, 1968.
19. Harold Conrad, *Dear Muffo: 35 Years in the Fast Lane*, 178.
20. Ibid.
21. During Ali's three-year ring absence, Dundee trained and managed Jimmy Ellis.
22. Conrad, *Dear Muffo*, 179.
23. Arthur Mercante, with Phil Guarnieri, *Inside the Ropes*, 190.
24. Conrad, *Dear Muffo*, 180.
25. Howard Cosell, *Cosell*, 165.
26. Author interview, Charles Valan. Boxing expert Harold Lederman, famil-

iar to many HBO viewers as the "unofficial official" during the network's fights, concurs with Charles Valan. He says Harold Valan was in fact afraid that Patterson wouldn't give him work once Floyd became a member of the New York State Athletic Commission in the 1970s. "But Floyd never even thought about it. Floyd used Harold Valan as if nothing ever happened. I think Harold was shocked by that, but that was Floyd's nature. He held no grudges against you." (Kieran Mulvaney, "Patterson An All Time Great outside the Ropes," *Boxing*, espn.com, originally published May 12, 2006.)

27. Cosell, *Cosell*, 165.
28. Author interview, Doug Lord.
29. Author interview, Edwin "Bud" Shrake.
30. Red Smith, "Patterson Gains Decision over Bonavena at Garden," *New York Times*, February 12, 1972.
31. Tape recording of Floyd Patterson's visit to the White House, August 8, 1972. Nixon Presidential Library and Museum.
32. This fight occurred at the fourth incarnation of Madison Square Garden, which opened in 1968 atop Pennsylvania Station on Eighth Avenue between Thirty-First and Thirty-Third Streets.
33. Murray Chass, "Ali-Patterson Is Set for Garden August 28," *New York Times*, July 7, 1972.
34. Cosell, *Cosell*, 166.
35. Ibid., 222.
36. Dave Anderson, "Ali Seventh-Round Victory over Patterson," *New York Times*, September 21, 1972.
37. Author interview, Vic Ziegel.
38. Author interview, Andy Schott. Schott was a young amateur training under Patterson in New Paltz, New York, at the time the negotiations took place for a possible third Ali-Patterson bout.
39. Author interview, Andy Schott.
40. Floyd managed and trained other professional fighters, including, briefly, Donovan "Razor" Ruddock. Following the death of Cus D'Amato, Floyd offered to train D'Amato's last boxing discovery, Mike Tyson. Patterson's offer was turned down.
41. Michael Leahy, "Floyd Patterson: His Own Man," *Sports Illustrated*, June 1, 1992.
42. Author interview, Bill O'Hare. O'Hare and his brother, Dan (a Catholic priest), were among Floyd's closest friends.
43. Author interview, Thomas Hauser.
44. In fact, in boxing circles, there was talk of Floyd's decline for several years before New York Governor Pataki appointed Patterson to chair the athletic commission. Michael Katz, a one-time sports editor of the *International Herald Tribune*, related a story about Floyd's trip to Pas-de-Calais, France, in December 1992 for Tracy Patterson's title fight against Daniel Zaragoza. Spotted in Paris by an old acquaintance, Patterson was asked, "Floyd, what are you doing in France?" A befuddled Patterson responded, "I'm in France?"
45. The Associated Press, "Losses Still Haunt Former Champ," August 2, 1998.

46. Gregory Kane, "A Champ at Living a Life of Grace and Dignity," *Baltimore Sun*, May 13, 2006.

47. "Fellow Champ Torres Remembers Patterson," *Weekend Edition*, NPR, May 13, 2006.

EPILOGUE: INVISIBLE CHAMPION

1. Carlo Rotella, *Cut Time: An Education at the Fights*, 220.

2. Mark Kram, *Ghosts of Manila: The Fateful Blood Feud between Muhammad Ali and Joe Frazier*, 122.

3. Gerald Early, *The Culture of Bruising*, 33.

4. W. C. Heinz, "The Floyd Patterson His Friends Know," *Sport*, November 1960.

5. W. C. Heinz, *Once They Heard the Cheers*, 62.

6. Author interview, Gay Talese.

FLOYD PATTERSON'S BOXING RECORD

---◆---

55 (40 KOs)-8-1

Date	Patterson's Weight	Opponent	Opponent's Weight	Opponent's Record	Fight Location	Win/Loss for Patterson	Outcome	Round Fight Ended	Rounds Scheduled
9/20/1972	188½	Muhammad Ali	218	38-1-0	Madison Square Garden, New York	L	TKO	7	15
7/14/1972	193½	Pedro Agosto	196	20-3-0	Singer Bowl, Flushing, New York	W	TKO	6	10
2/11/1972	191¾	Oscar Bonavena	206	47-7-1	Madison Square Garden, New York	W	UD	10	10
11/23/1971	195	Charlie Harris	218½	8-13-1	Portland, Oregon	W	KO	6	10
8/21/1971	189	Vic Brown	198	22-17-0	Peace Bridge Arena, Buffalo	W	UD	10	10
7/17/1971	190	Charley Polite	222	14-18-3	Erie Arena, Erie, Pennsylvania	W	UD	10	10
5/26/1971	190½	Terry Daniels	188½	24-2-1	Arena, Cleveland	W	UD	10	10
3/29/1971	192	Roger Russell	185	11-8-2	Arena, Philadelphia	W	TKO	9	10

Date	Weight	Opponent	Opp. Weight	Record	Location	Result	Method	Round	Rounds
1/16/1971	192¾	Levi Forte	199¼	19-22-2	Convention Hall, Miami Beach	W	KO	2	10
9/15/1970	186	Charley Green	184	13-6-0	Madison Square Garden, New York	W	KO	10	10
9/14/1968	188½	Jimmy Ellis	198	26-5-0	Solna Fotbollsstadium, Stockholm	L	PTS	15	15
10/28/1967	195½	Jerry Quarry	195	24-1-4	Olympic Auditorium, Los Angeles	L	MD	12	12
6/9/1967	194	Jerry Quarry	193	23-1-3	Memorial Coliseum, Los Angeles	D	MD	10	10
3/30/1967	197	Bill McMurray	209½	22-16-2	Civic Arena, Pittsburgh	W	KO	1	10
2/13/1967	200¾	Willie Johnson	183½	14-20-1	Auditorium, Miami Beach	W	KO	3	10
9/20/1966	193	Henry Cooper	191¾	33-12-1	Empire Pool, Wembley, London	W	KO	4	10x3
11/22/1965	196¾	Muhammad Ali	210	21-0-0	Convention Center, Las Vegas	L	TKO	12	15
5/14/1965	196½	Tod Herring	212	26-3-0	Johanneshov, Stockholm	W	TKO	3	10

KO=knockout; TKO=technical knockout; SD=split decision; UD=unanimous decision; RTD="retired," meaning the referee stops the fight after a round when both boxers are in their respective corners (similar to a TKO and counts toward a boxer's knockout total); PTS="points," meaning the fighter wins on judges' points; MD=majority decision, meaning two of three judges score the fight for the winner, and the third scores it a draw.

Date	Patterson's Weight	Opponent	Opponent's Weight	Opponent's Record	Fight Location	Win/Loss for Patterson	Outcome	Round Fight Ended	Rounds Scheduled
2/1/1965	197¼	George Chuvalo	208	29-8-2	Madison Square Garden, New York	W	UD	12	12
12/12/1964	197	Charlie Powell	213	25-9-3	Hiram Bithorn Stadium, San Juan	W	KO	6	10
7/5/1964	192½	Eddie Machen	198½	47-4-2	Råsunda, Solna, Sweden	W	PTS	12	12
1/6/1964	192	Santo Amonti	191	47-4-3	Johanneshov, Stockholm	W	TKO	8	10
7/22/1963	194½	Sonny Liston	215	34-1-0	Convention Center, Las Vegas	L	KO	1	15
9/25/1962	189	Sonny Liston	213	33-1-0	Comiskey Park, Chicago	L	KO	1	15
12/4/1961	188½	Tom McNeeley	197	23-0-0	Maple Leaf Gardens, Toronto	W	KO	4	15
3/13/1961	194¾	Ingemar Johansson	206½	22-1-0	Convention Hall, Miami Beach	W	KO	6	15

Date	Weight	Opponent	Opp. Weight	Record	Venue	Result	Method	Round	Rounds
6/20/1960	190	Ingemar Johansson	194¾	22-0-0	Polo Grounds, New York	W	KO	5	15
6/26/1959	182	Ingemar Johansson	196	21-0-0	Yankee Stadium, Bronx	L	TKO	3	15
5/1/1959	182½	Brian London	206	22-4-0	Fairgrounds Coliseum, Indianapolis	W	KO	11	15
8/18/1958	184½	Roy Harris	194	23-0-0	Wrigley Field, Los Angeles	W	RTD	12	15
8/22/1957	187¼	Pete Rademacher	202	0-0-0	Sick's Stadium, Seattle	W	KO	6	15
7/29/1957	184	Tommy Jackson	192½	29-5-1	Polo Grounds, New York	W	TKO	10	15
11/30/1956	182¼	Archie Moore	187¾	159-20-8	Chicago Stadium, Chicago	W	KO	5	15
6/8/1956	178	Tommy Jackson	193½	27-4-1	Madison Square Garden, New York	W	SD	12	12
4/10/1956	183	Alvin Williams	176	49-12-6	Memorial Hall, Kansas City	W	KO	3	10
3/12/1956	183	Jimmy Walls	192	19-40-2	New Britain, Connecticut	W	TKO	2	10
12/8/1955	178½	Jimmy Slade	180	32-15-5	Olympic Auditorium, Los Angeles	W	TKO	7	10

Date	Patterson's Weight	Opponent	Opponent's Weight	Opponent's Record	Fight Location	Win/Loss for Patterson	Outcome	Round Fight Ended	Rounds Scheduled
10/13/1955	175	Calvin Brad	174½	8-5-1	Olympic Auditorium, Los Angeles	W	KO	1	10
9/29/1955	175½	Dave Whitlock	181	34-14-2	Winterland Arena, San Francisco	W	KO	3	10
9/8/1955	177	Alvin Williams	172	48-11-6	Moncton, New Brunswick	W	TKO	8	10
7/6/1955	170¾	Archie McBride	186¼	24-9-0	Madison Square Garden, New York	W	KO	7	10
6/23/1955	170	Yvon Durelle	170	55-12-1	Newcastle, New Brunswick	W	RTD	5	10
3/17/1955	169	Esau Ferdinand	174	44-12-8	Auditorium, Oakland	W	TKO	10	10
1/17/1955	168	Don Grant	166¾	15-1-0	Eastern Parkway Arena, Brooklyn	W	TKO	5	10
1/7/1955	166	Willie Troy	162	30-2-0	Madison Square Garden, New York	W	TKO	5	8
11/19/1954	169¼	Jimmy Slade	175	28-11-5	Madison Square Garden, New York	W	UD	8	8
10/22/1954	170¼	Joe Gannon	174	32-3-0	Madison Square Garden, New York	W	UD	8	8

Date	Weight	Opponent	Opp. Weight	Record	Venue	Result	Method	Round	Sched.
10/11/1954	169¼	Esau Ferdinand	166	43-11-8	St. Nicholas Arena, New York	W	UD	8	8
8/2/1954	169	Tommy Harrison	176¾	22-9-2	Eastern Parkway Arena, Brooklyn	W	TKO	1	8
7/12/1954	164¾	Jacques Royer Crecy	166	39-15-1	St. Nicholas Arena, New York	W	TKO	7	8
6/7/1954	168	Joey Maxim	177	79-21-4	Eastern Parkway Arena, Brooklyn	L	UD	8	8
5/10/1954	165½	Jesse Turner	172½	36-14-5	Eastern Parkway Arena, Brooklyn	W	UD	8	8
4/19/1954	167	Alvin Williams	172¾	43-10-6	Eastern Parkway Arena, Brooklyn	W	UD	8	8
3/30/1954	167	Sammy Brown	168½	6-1-0	Turner's Arena, Washington, DC	W	TKO	2	10
2/15/1954	167	Yvon Durelle	158	47-6-1	Eastern Parkway Arena, Brooklyn	W	UD	8	8
12/14/1953	168	Dick Wagner	177	33-19-5	Eastern Parkway Arena, Brooklyn	W	TKO	5	8
10/19/1953	166½	Wes Bascom	175¾	16-7-1	Eastern Parkway Arena, Brooklyn	W	UD	8	8

Date	Patterson's Weight	Opponent	Opponent's Weight	Opponent's Record	Fight Location	Win/Loss for Patterson	Outcome	Round Fight Ended	Rounds Scheduled
6/1/1953	165	Gordon Wallace	163	23-3-1	Eastern Parkway Arena, Brooklyn	W	TKO	3	8
4/13/1953	166½	Dick Wagner	175½	33-18-5	Eastern Parkway Arena, Brooklyn	W	SD	8	8
1/28/1953	163½	Chester Mieszala	160	19-7-1	Chicago Stadium, Chicago	W	TKO	5	6
12/29/1952	167½	Lalu Sabotin	175	21-6-0	Eastern Parkway Arena, Brooklyn	W	TKO	5	8
10/31/1952	165	Lester Johnson	163	0-0-0	Madison Square Garden, New York	W	TKO	3	6
10/6/1952	166	Sammy Walker	161¼	35-32-7	Eastern Parkway Arena, Brooklyn	W	TKO	2	6
9/12/1952	164½	Eddie Godbold	163	5-13-1	St. Nicholas Arena, New York	W	KO	4	6

INDEX

Abramson, Jesse, 177
Action Sports Inc., 193
Adams, Caswell, 45
Agaganian, Hranoush, 49
Agosto, Pedro, 246
Ahlquist, Edwin, 89, 96, 97, 98, 99, 197
Alan, Mickey, 144, 155, 157
Alexander Hamilton Vocational High
    School, FP attends, 28
Ali, Muhammad, 182, 193, 209, 214–15
    vs. Bonavena, 202
    boxing abilities of, 185
    conversion and name change, 174
    Henry Cooper almost defeats, 191
    and Cosell, 201
    Gerald Early on, 215
    and Ellis, 197
    and FP, xiii–xiv
      Ali's criticism of, 175, 176, 215
      Ali's praise of, 204–5
      confrontation with, 176–77
      fight against (first), 183–84,
        185–88, 241nn.47,50, 247
      fight against (second), 203, 204–6,
        246
      FP attends Ali-Liston fight, 180–81
      and FP as rival, 213, 214
      FP's criticism of, 173, 174, 203

      FP's defense of, 187–88
      FP's obsession with, 172
      and FP's marriage to white woman,
        190
      rematch discussed, 192
      third fight proposed, 206–7
    and Archie Moore, 64
    and name change from "Clay," 176,
      241n.40
    predicts Chuvalo victory over FP, 176
    return of after end of suspension, 204
    vs. Leon Spinks, 207
    stripped of title, 193, 242n.11
    See also Clay, Cassius Marcellus, Jr.
Ali-Liston fight (first), 172
Ali-Liston fight (second), 180–81
All the Young Men (movie), Johansson
    in, 111
Amateur Athletic Union boxing
    championships, 23, 28
American Boxing Association, heavy-
    weight rankings of, 84
Amonti, Santo, 248
Anderson, Dave, 206
Anthony, Tony, 30, 31
Aragon, Art, 83
Arcel, Ray, 41, 184
Armstrong, Henry, 49–50, 72, 184

Arnesen, Cliff, 10–11
Arum, Bob, 205–6
Atlanta, as venue for Quarry fight, 204
Aurora Downs, Liston training camp
    in, 149

Baer, Max, 49, 111
Baker, Bob, 79, 85
Baldwin, James, 150–53, 155, 173–74
Baraka, Amiri, 182
Barrodale, Barry, 29, 30, 33
Bascom, Wes, 251
Basilio, Carmen, 83
Battling Battalino, 36
Battling Siki, 49
Bear Mountain Inn, FP's training at, 22
Bedford-Stuyvesant, Brooklyn, 2, 5
    escape from for FP family, 58
    social services lacking in, 7
Bengtsson, Olle, 95
Besmanoff, Willi, 85
Bethea, Wayne, 79
Bimstein, Whitey, 95, 100, 123, 127, 128,
    184
Birmingham
    civil rights demonstrations in (1963),
       159–62
    young girls killed in church bombing
       in, 166
Black, Charley, 113, 114
Black Muslims, 162, 174, 188, 203,
    241n.40
    FP's fear of, 184
Bolan Al, 156
Bolan, Tom, 141
Bonavena, Oscar "Ringo," 197, 202, 209,
    214, 246
Boston Garden
    FP wins AAU championship at, 28
    as planned site for McNeeley fight,
       137
Boxing
    D'Amato on, 18
    diminished importance of (1970s),
       204
    "in the pocket," 230n.8
    integration of, 14
    lighter-weight vs. heavyweight
       divisions in, 54

organized crime in control of, 37–39
and regaining of heavyweight
    championship, 120
as sole major sport for blacks, 13
title vacancy after Ali stripped,
    193–94
Brad, Calvin, 250
Braddock, James J., 60, 111, 153–54
Brando, Marlon, 49, 196
Brenner, Teddy, 40, 46, 165, 197
Breslin, Jimmy, 4, 116, 117
Brooklyn, Bedford-Stuyvesant, 2, 5
    escape from for FP family, 58
    social services lacking in, 7
Brown, David, 85
Brown, James, 182
Brown, Jim, 196, 198
Brown, Sammy, 251
Brown, Vic, 246
Brown v. Board of Education of Topeka,
    61, 75
Buck, Al, 98
Bunche, Ralph, 154
Burton, Lewis, xii

Callahan, Mushy, 87
Cannon, Jimmy, 56–57, 88, 91, 100,
    132–33, 134
Canzoneri, Tony, 36, 49–50
Capone, Al, 38
Carbo, Frankie (Paolo Giovanni), 38–39,
    55, 80, 147, 235n.13
Cardiff Giant, 110, 235n.8
Carlton Avenue YMCA, 13–14, 16
Carnegie, Dale, and Ali's demeanor
    (Chass), 204
Carnera, Primo, 49, 111, 133
Carroll, Diahann, 160
Carson, Johnny, FP interviewed by,
    200
Carter, Harold, 27–28, 79
Cassady, Neal, 49
Chamberlain, Wilt, 196
Charles, Ezzard, 21, 60, 62, 120, 154
Chass, Murray, 204
Chocolate, Kid, 50, 65
Chuvalo, George, 175–76
    Ali on, 176
    Bonavena defeats, 202

in fight with FP, 175, 178–79, 214, 248
in tournament of contenders, 194
Cicala, Freddie, 139
Civil rights
  beginnings of movement toward, 61
  Birmingham demonstrations (1963),
    159–62
  Father Delaney in, 75
  and FP, xiii
    in Birmingham demonstration,
      159, 160, 161–62, 215
    criticized as Uncle Tom, 175,
      182–83, 203, 210, 215
    and early experience of segregated
      arena, 76
    and King assassination, 196
    lauded for participation in, 165–66
    on trip to Mississippi, 160
  and FP's family in Brooklyn, 2
  in Freedom Summer (1964), 174
  NAACP, 2
  and social turbulence, 195–96
  and Watts riots, 182
  See also Race relations and racism
Clay, Cassius Marcellus, Jr., 126–27, 174
  FP celebratory poem by, 125
  FP idolized by, 177
  Johansson embarrassed in sparring
    with, 127–28
  as leading contender, 170
  and Liston in Las Vegas, 164
  at 1956 Olympics, 126, 127
  See also Ali, Muhammad
Clay, Rudolph Valentino, 126
Cleaver, Eldridge, 183
Cleveland, Patterson-Daniels fight in,
  201
Cohen, William, 92
Cohn, Roy, 117–18, 128
Cokes, Curtis, 201
Cold War, and Rademacher win over
  Soviet fighter, 80
Comiskey Park, Patterson-Liston fight
  in, 148
Connor, Eugene "Bull," 159
Conrad, Harold, 127, 128, 145, 149, 150,
  197, 198, 200
Conrad, Robert, 198
Cooper, Clarence, 7–8

Cooper, Henry, 88, 89, 191–92, 214, 247
Corbett, James J., 120
Cosby, Bill, at MLK funeral, 196
Cosell, Emmy (wife), 114, 164
Cosell, Howard, 100–101
  and Ali on fight with FP, 186
  Ali as new interest of, 201
  and FP, 101
  on FP before second Liston fight, 164
  FP discarded by, 200–201
  and FP vs. Johansson, 120, 132
  and FP on rats in training facility, 114
  on FP's air of penitence, 209
  on FP's financial plight, 205–6
  on Patterson-Ali fights, 205
  and Patterson-Ellis fight, 199, 200
  at second Patterson-Johansson fight,
    123
  visits to help with FP's depression,
    108–9
Cosell, Jill (daughter), 107
Costen, Vivian, 9–10, 18–19, 33, 47
Crecy, Jacques Royer, 251
Crispus Attucks High School,
  Indianapolis, 91–92
Culture of Bruising, The (Early), 215
Cut and Shoot, Texas, 83–84

Dade, Harold, 21
Daley, Arthur, 71–72, 171
D'Amato, Cus (Constantine), xii, xiii,
  16–18, 37
  James Baldwin on, 151
  and Cassius Clay offer, 127
  on Cohn operations, 118
  and Cosell, 101
  and Eastern Parkway, 40
  and Gramercy Gym, 15
  and Graziano, 35
  and IBC/organized crime, 39, 42,
    46–47, 73, 79, 112–14, 121, 179
    battles with as impoverishing, 169
    and FP fights outside New York, 53
    and Weill, 82
  and Jim Jacobs, 145
  and Lavelle, 35, 51–52 (see also
    Lavelle, Frank)
  loses NY boxing license, 113, 116, 179,
    192

D'Amato, Cus (Constantine) (*cont.*)
  and Mathis, 192–93
  retires upstate, 193
  Talese on, 68
  and Torres, 114, 169, 179–80, 192
  AND FP'S CAREER, 16, 18–19, 25, 39
  and age controversy, 42–43
  D'Amato's complaints against FP and
    legal action, 168–69
  and D'Amato's confidence, 18, 23
  and D'Amato as spokesman, 33
  and deal for TV retrospective, 145
  in early amateur fights, 20
  end of relationship as manager, 114,
    116, 117, 169
  and exhibition tour between
    Johansson fights, 115
  as failing to line up contenders, 137
  and fights around country to build
    reputation, 53
  and FP as pro, 26–27
  on FP's abilities, 179–80
  and FP's age, 42–43
  in FP's autobiography, 142
    and rejected manuscript, 134
  and FP's depression following
    Johansson defeat, 108
  golden crown presented to FP, 110
  as hanger-on at training before third
    Johansson fight, 128, 131
  and Harris fight (title defense),
    82–83, 113
  and heavyweight championship, 60
  and intimations of homoerotic
    feelings, 67–68
  irregularities in negotiations over
    London fight, 90–91, 114
  and Jackson title defense, 74, 78–79
  and Johansson fight (first), 89, 98,
    102, 103, 104
  and Johansson fight (second), 110,
    116, 121
  Liston confrontation with over
    chance to fight FP, 148
  and Liston fight, 141
  and Liston rematch, 163
  and London fight, 89, 90–91
  and Mailer on FP's loss to Liston, 156
  management of title defense, 79, 81

  and McNeeley fight, 137–38
  and Archie Moore fight, 67, 69, 70
  peek-a-boo stance taught, 20
  pro contract signed, 35
  psychological support in early
    training, 18–19
  reconciliation, 208
  and Schulberg on McBride fight, 56
  versatility developed in FP, 28
D'Amato, Damiano (father), 17
D'Amato, Elizabeth (mother), 17
D'Amato, Gerry (brother), 17
D'Amato, Nick (brother), 19
D'Amato, Tony (brother), 17
Daniel, Daniel M., 153
Daniels, Terry, 201–2, 246
Darren, James, 111
Daugherty, Duffy, 137
Davis, Miles, 151
Deauville Hotel, Miami, FP training at,
  130
Dee, Ruby, 160
Delaney, Samuel J., 75, 76
Dempsey, Jack, 60, 72, 103
  Johansson compared with, 118
  racist glorification of, 111
  vs. Tunney, 149
  as unable to regain title, 120, 169
DeWolf, L. Harold, 196–97
Downtown Athletic Club, 19
Du Bois, W. E. B., 2
DuMont Television Network, 40
Duncan, John, 139
Dundee, Angelo, 127–28, 172, 173, 191,
  198
Dundee, Chris, 127
Durelle, Yvon, 44–45, 46, 53–54, 56,
  250, 251
Durslag, Melvin, 165
Dynamite Payne, 65

Early, Gerald, 215
Eastern Parkway Arena, 40, 44–45, 46,
  48
Ebony magazine
  FP as one of "100 Most Influential
    Negroes," 165
  on FP victory over Johansson, 125
Eckstine, Billy, 57–58, 182

Edward J. Neil Memorial Plaque, 72
Egypt, FP's trip to, 141–42
Elgin, Illinois, FP trains at, 149
Ellis, Jimmy, 195, 197–200, 209, 214, 247
Ellison, Ralph, quoted, ix
Empire Sports Club, 19
Esquire magazine, 150
  article on Ali in, 188
  FP profile in, 167, 170
  Mailer covers Patterson-Liston fight for, 150
Evans, Clifford, 203
Evers, Medgar, 166

Far Rockaway, Queens, 61
Faubus, Orval, 75
Fear, D'Amato on, 18
Feature Sports Inc., 118
Ferdinand, Esau, 250, 251
Fire Next Time, The (Baldwin), 173
Fisher, Eddie, 163
Fitzsimmons, Bob, 120
Fleischer, Nat, 180, 202
Flood, Curt, 160
Florio, Dan, 35–36, 51
  death of, 184
  and first Johansson fight, 102, 104
    in entourage, 98
    and FP's depression in aftermath, 109
  on FP vs. Marciano, 59–60
  and FP's training for Moore fight, 68
  and FP's training for second Johansson fight, 115, 116, 117
  and Moore fight celebration, 70
  and prejudice on southern tour, 74
  at third Johansson fight, 131
  on trip to Egypt, 141
Florio, Nick, 36, 100, 131
Floyd Patterson Cup, 142
Floyd Patterson Enterprises, 80–81, 87, 90
Floyd Patterson House, 133, 140
Floyd Patterson Trophy, 99
Folley, Zora
  Bonavena's victory over, 202
  as candidate for FP bout, 79

as contender, 84, 88, 137, 140
  Cooper's victory over, 89, 191
  Johansson contrasted to, 111
  Machen fight, 171
  Patterson-Harris fight as overshadowing, 83
  in tournament of contenders, 194
Foreman, George, FP compared with, xiii
Fort Smith, Arkansas
  FP confronts racism in, 75–76
  FP supports integration leader in, 76, 215
"Fourth of July Kid" (Archie Moore ring name), 65
Fowler, Ernest, 157
FP. *See* Patterson, Floyd
"Frank Sinatra Has a Cold" (Talese), 187
Frazier, Joe
  and Ali on FP, 204–5
  Ali loses to, 204
  and Bonavena, 202
  and D'Amato on Mathis, 192
  FP compared with, xiii
  FP's desire to fight, 202
  in Olympics, 192
  at Patterson-Quarry fight, 194
  as proposed match for Ellis, 197
  and tournament of contenders, 193
Freedom Summer (1964), 174
Fugazy, Bill, 118, 128, 129
Fuller, Peter Davenport, 138

Gallico, Paul, 21
Gannon, Joe, 250
Gans, Joe, 14
Garvey, Marcus, 2
Gaston Motel, Birmingham
  bombing of, 161
  FP and Jackie Robinson stay at, 161
Gavilán, Kid, 50
"Gazelle punch," 27, 86, 230n.2 (ch.3)
Geis, Bernard, 133–34, 143
Ghana, FP's ceremonial robe from, 125
Gibson, John, 22
Gladson, Gordon, 29
Gleason, Jackie, 110–11
Godbold, Eddie, xii, 252

Golden Gloves championship
  FP's son Tracy wins, 207–8
  Rademacher winner in, 80
Golden Gloves championship (1951)
  FP in, 21–23
  Johansson in, 96
Golden Gloves championship (1952), FP in, 27–28
Goldman, Charley, 36
Goldstein, Ruby, 78, 100, 103, 119
Grady, Sandy, 152
Gramercy Gym, 15–16, 23, 35, 90, 101
Gramercy Park Hotel, FP given job at, 28, 34
Grant, Don, 51, 51–52, 250
Grayson, Harry, 110, 111
Graziano, Rocky, 35, 50, 184, 185
Great Migration of black Americans, 1, 146
Great Neck, FP home in, 189
"Great white hope," 88, 184
Green, Charley, 247
Greenwood Lake, NY, FP's training at, 73
Gross, Jane, 168
Gross, Milton, 42, 108, 134–35, 142, 143–44, 168, 172–73
Grossinger's, Johansson training at, 94–95, 120
Guerrero, Richard, 22, 23

Haley, Alex, 183
Hamill, Pete, 154, 171, 173
Ham Pounder, 65
Hanson, Ted, 168
Harder They Fall, The (Schulberg), 55
Harris, Big Henry, 84, 87, 88
Harris, Charlie, 246
Harris, Maurice, 213
Harris, Roy "Cut 'n Shoot," 83–85
  and FP as easy knockdown, 186
  FP fights, 82, 83, 86–88, 214, 249
    and Black, 113
    social conflict symbolized in, 85–86
  and Johansson, 100
  Liston fights, 137
  as possible contender, 140
Harris, Tracy (adopted son of FP), 207–8

Harrison, Tommy, 36–37, 251
Hauser, Thomas, 209–10
Heinz, W. C., 80, 101, 102, 183
Helfand, Julius, 82
Helsinki, FP at Olympics in, 30
Herring, Tod, 247
Hicks, Sandra Elizabeth, 23–25, 26, 46, 47, 51, 56
  and FP's conversion to Roman Catholicism, 24–25
  marries FP, 58
  See also Patterson, Sandra Hicks
Hidden Well Ranch, FP training at, 163, 164
Highland Mills, FP training camp in, 143, 158, 167
Hill, Richie, 21
Hiss, Alger, and Cohn, 118
Hodge, Danny, 233n.19
Holden, William, 101–2
Holman, Johnny, 79
Holmes, Larry, 213
Hunt, Lamar, 118
Hurley, Deacon Jack, 80, 83
Huston, John, 140
Hyde Park (Roosevelt estate), 11

Illingworth, Montieth, 114
International Boxing Club (IBC), 38, 40, 42
  and D'Amato, 39, 42, 46–47, 73, 79, 112, 179
    battles with impoverishing, 169
    and fights outside New York, 53
    and Weill, 82
  demise of, 112
  Marciano controlled by, 55, 59
  and Joey Maxim, 46–47
  and Archie Moore guarantee, 69
  and Vitale, 147
International Boxing Guild, 39
Invisible Man (Ellison), ix

Jackson, Tommy "Hurricane," 61, 233n.6
  as black heavyweight contender, 60–61
  death of, 209, 233n.6
  as defeated contender, 214

FP fights (first), 60, 62–63, 67, 74, 214, 249
  and race relations, 60–61
FP fights (second), 74, 76–77, 78–79, 214, 249
  as sparring partner, 50
Jacobs, Jim, 145, 208
Jeffries, Jim, 120, 184
Johansson, Ingemar, 88–89, 95–98, 208
  and aftermath of first FP fight, 107–8
  as contender, 79
  death of, 209
  as example for FP, 130, 133
  fights FP (first), 98–100, 102–5, 249
    FP's training for, 94
    Louis's analysis of, 119
  fights FP (second), 118, 119–25, 249
    and Rosensohn, 112
    training for, 114–16
  fights FP (third), 131–32, 248
    training camp for, 128–29, 130–31
    writers' criticisms of, 132–33
  and FP as easy knockdown, 186
  FP's hatred of, 112, 115–16, 120
  glorification of in U.S., 110–11, 115
  Machen upset by, 170, 171
  Archie Moore's critique of, 109–10
  on Patterson-Liston fight, 154
  at Patterson-London fight, 92, 93
  training routine of, 94–95
    for third FP fight, 127–28
John XXIII (pope), 124–25, 127, 129
Johnson, Charley, 23
Johnson, Jack, 55, 85, 184
Johnson, Lester, 252
Johnson, Walter (Wiltwyck director), 11, 47
Johnson, Willie, 247
Johnston, Charley, 69, 71
Jones, Doug, 171
Jones, LeRoi, 182
Jones, Washington, 29

Kahn, Irving B., 82, 128
Kane, Gregory, 210
Kane, Martin, 91
Karadag, Ehsan, 50, 90, 94
Kearns, Jack, 154

Kefauver, Estes, and Kefauver Committee
  and D'Amato, 113–14
  and Liston as challenger, 141
Keiter, Les, 101
Kennedy, Jacqueline, 196
Kennedy, John F., 136, 139, 149, 154, 159
  assassination of, 166
Kennedy, Robert, 140, 196
Kid Chocolate, 50, 65
Kid Galahad (film), 185
Kid Pocahontas, 65
King, A. D., 161, 196
King, Martin Luther, Jr., 61, 159, 215
  assassination of, 196
  "I Have a Dream" speech of, 166
King of the World (Remnick), 215
Kram, Mark, 194, 195, 214
Kramer, Edith, 9
Krim, Seymour, 150
Ku Klux Klan, in East Texas, 85

Ladd, Alan, 111
LaMotta, Jake, 50, 184
Langhart, Janet, 92
Lardner, John, 80, 103
Las Vegas
  Patterson-Ali fight in, 181, 184
  Patterson-Liston fight in, 162–63, 214
Lavelle, Frank, xii, 14
  FP discovered by, 14, 16, 23, 35, 52
  in FP's entourage, 15, 19, 20, 23, 51
  FP's relationship with curtailed under D'Amato, 35, 51–52
Lee, Norvel, 96
Lence, Emil, 40, 73, 74, 79, 81
Leonard, Benny, 55, 72
Lewiston, Maine, Ali-Liston fight in, 180
Liebling, A. J., 125, 130–31, 132, 155
Life magazine, on Patterson-Ali fight, 186–87
Lipsyte, Robert, 186
Liston, Charles "Sonny," 137, 138, 145–49, 162
  Ali's defeat of (first), 172
  Ali's defeat of (second), 180–81
  in Ali's/FP's plans for exhibition tour, 187

Liston, Charles "Sonny" (*cont.*)
  Baldwin on, 152–53
  death of, 209
  FP compared with, xiii
  and FP as easy knockdown, 186
  FP fights (first), 143, 148–49, 154–55,
      248
    FP's escape after, 156–59
    and FP's integrity (Kane), 210
    JFK's concern over, 139
    journalists' coverage of, 149–50
    postfight press conference, 156
    predictions of FP win, 153–54
  FP fights (second), 159, 164–65,
      248
    FP's defeatist attitude in, 164
    and FP's downslide, 165–66
    FP's feelings in aftermath of,
      167–68
    FP's public pronouncements on,
      162, 164
    FP's training, 163–64
    in Las Vegas, 162–63, 214
  FP's criticism of, 173
  Kennedys opposed to, 139
    and ties to organized crime, 139,
      140
  Machen fights, 171
  New York boxing license denied to,
      140
  Shrake interview with, 153
  in tournament of contenders, 194
Liston, Helen, 146
Liston, Tobe, 146
London, Brian
  Cooper's victory over, 191
  FP fights, 89, 92–93, 100, 214,
      249
    Clay watches, 126
    and D'Amato, 90–91, 114
  and Johansson on FP, 99
  in Archie Moore's letter, 109
  Pastrano knocked out by, 88
London, Jack, 55
London, Patterson-Cooper fight in,
      191
"Long Ride Home, The" (Gross
      column), 134
Lonsdale Belts, 89, 234n.22

Lord, Doug, 201
Los Angeles
  FP on tour in, 57–58
  Patterson-Quarry fights in, 194, 195
  Watts riots in, 181–82
Los Angeles Wrigley Field, 233n.9
  Patterson-Harris fight at, 82, 83,
      86
"Loser, The" (profile of FP in *Esquire*),
      170
Loughran, Tommy, 81, 185
Louis, Joe, 13, 44, 60
  as African-American hero, 44, 124
  FP compared/contrasted with, 29,
      72, 88, 106, 214
  as FP consultant, 118–19
  as FP hero, 108, 125
  FP presented trophy by, 43–44
  Big Henry Harris as proposed
      opponent for, 84
  and Liston, 162
  and Madison Square Garden, 21
  and name change, 241n.40
  in Nixon's conversation, 203
  and racial prejudice, 74
  vs. Schmeling, 149
  and self-managership, 116
  title defenses of, 79
  as unable to regain title, 120
  and weight, 60
  vs. white challengers, 88–89
Lundgren, Birgit, 95, 100, 111, 120
Lynching
  in East Texas, 85
  of Emmett Till, 61, 85

Machen, Eddie, 79, 170–71
  as contender, 84, 88, 137
  death of, 209
  FP fights, 170, 172, 214, 248
  Johansson's celebrity contrasted with,
      111
  Quarry beaten by, 194
Madame Bey's (training camp),
      49–50
Madison Square Garden, 21, 243n.32
  Ali-Frazier fight in, 204, 243n.32
  Golden Gloves tournament in, 21,
      22, 27

as IBC-controlled, 46, 48, 55

Norris family majority interest in, 38

Patterson-Ali fight in, 205

Patterson-Bonavena fight in, 202

Patterson-Chuvalo fight in, 176, 179

Paterson-Jackson fight in, 60, 62

Patterson-McBride fight in, 56

Madrid, Spain, FP escapes to, 159

Madriguera, Enric, 114

Mailer, Norman, 150, 154, 156, 163

Malcolm X, 162, 174, 180, 182–83
widow of, 196

Mann, Arthur, 134

Marciano, Rocky, 36, 54–55, 58–60
and D'Amato's plans for FP, 50
downplaying of as champion, 111
and Edward Neil Memorial Plaque, 72
and IBC/organized crime, 55, 59
on Johansson's right, 103
and Johansson's training companion, 95
Moore in title fight with, 66–67
FP studies films of, 68
retirement of, 59–60, 80, 202
attempt to lure out of, 81–82
and self-managership, 116
and weight, 60

Marrone, Frank, 39

Marshall, Marty, 147

Martin, Leotis, 194, 197

Mathis, Buster, 192–93

Maule, Tex, 178

Maxim, Joey (Giuseppe Antonio Berardinelli), 21, 46–48, 171, 214, 251

McBride, Archie, 55–57, 250

McCarthy, Joseph, and Cohn, 118

McGovern, George, 203

McMurray, Bill, 247

McNeeley, Tom, 137–39, 248

Media
and Clay-Ali name change, 241n.40
and FP, 48–49
and Boyle article on FP training camp, 128–29
at first pro fight, xii–xiii

FP's criticism of, 151–52
and Talese, 77–78
New Journalism, 150, 170
See also Breslin, Jimmy; Cannon, Jimmy; Cosell, Howard; Gross, Milton; Hamill, Pete; Heinz, W. D.; Lardner, John; Liebling, A. J.; Mailer, Norman; Shrake, Edwin "Bud"; Smith, Red; Talese, Gay

Mello, Pete, 29, 30, 31, 33

Mercante, Arthur, 199, 206

Miami, third Patterson-Johansson fight in, 126, 130–31, 166

Midtown Gym, Chicago, 41

Mieszala, Chester, 41, 252

Mildenberger, Karl, 202

Miller, Alex, 26

Miller, Freddie, 36

Mirisch Company, Patterson-Johansson broadcast sponsored by, 101

Montgomery County, Texas, 83–84, 85

Moore, Archie, 47, 65–67, 232n.1 (ch.6)
as black heavyweight contender, 60–61
on civil rights trip to Mississippi, 160
Durelle fights, 45
FP fights, 63, 64, 69–71, 157, 214, 249
and birth of FP's baby, 65
and Cosell, 101
delay, 50–51
FP fails to remember, 210
FP's training for, 67, 68, 149
Johansson's celebrity contrasted with, 111
prefight insults from Moore, 64–65
and suspect financial arrangements by IBC, 69
FP receives encouragement and advice from, 109
Marciano fights, 58–59
in Nixon's conversation, 203
picks FP over Liston, 154
rape allegation against, 71

Moore, Marianne, praises *Victory over Myself*, 143

"Mr. Gray" (Mafia chief of IBC), 38–39, 40, 55

Muhammad, Elijah, 173, 180, 183

Mukhin, Lev, 80

Murder Inc., 39

Murray, Jim, 143

NAACP, 2
  and denial of license to Liston, 140, 141
  FP addresses, 160
  FP cochairs fundraising drive for, 133
  FP as member of, 76, 154
  See also Civil rights

Nasser, Gamal Abdel, 141–42

Nation of Islam, 173–74, 193, 203

New Brunswick, Patterson vs. Durelle in, 53

Newcombe, Don, 134

New Frontier, FP as symbol of, 136

New Journalism, 150, 170

Newman, Paul, 185

New Paltz, New York
  FP speaks to students at university in, 216
  FP's home and training gym in, 190, 207, 208, 210
    FP buried near, 211
    and FP as Eucharistic minister, 209

Newtown training camp, 114, 117, 119

New York Boxing Writers Association
  FP named fighter of year by, 72
  FP named Ring Rookie of the Year by, 43–44

New York City
  as scene of FP's first professional fight, xi
  See also Gramercy Gym; Madison Square Garden

New York State Athletic Commission
  Ali title stripped by, 242n.11
  and D'Amato's license, 113
  FP's service on, 209, 210, 213
  and Valan, 243n.26

Frazier recognized as champ by, 197
Liston denied license by, 140

New York State Supreme Court, Ali's ban lifted by, 204

New York Times, and Clay-Ali name change, 241n.40

New York Times Magazine, FP profile in, 129–30

Nixon, Richard, 196, 203–4

Norris, James, 38–39, 59, 80, 112, 235n.13

North American Boxing Federation, 202

November, Julius, 116
  and D'Amato, 117
  and D'Amato's claims against FP, 169
  FP fires, 201
  and Liston fight (first), 141
  and Liston rematch, 158–59
  in *Sports Illustrated* article, 128–29
  on trip to Egypt, 141
  and *Victory over Myself*, 142
  selection of coauthor for, 134

Nugget magazine, 150

Oates, Joyce Carol, xiii

O'Donnell, Kenneth, 139

O'Hare, Bill, 209

Of Mice and Men (Steinbeck), 62

Olympic championship (1956), Rademacher wins, 79, 80

Olympic championship (1960), FP as spectator at, 126

Olympic competition (1952), 27, 28–33
  Johansson in, 97

Olympic competition (1964), Mathis in, 192

On the Waterfront (film), 55

Organized crime
  and boxing, 37–39
  D'Amato's involvement with, 112–14, 121
  and Eastern Parkway Arena, 40
  and Graziano management, 35
  and Liston, 147, 148
    as challenger, 140
  and Joey Maxim, 47

and Rosensohn, 112–13, 118
and Lou Viscusi, 84
See also International Boxing Club
Owen, J. T., 29
Owens, Jesse, 27, 162

Pacquiao, Manny, 204
Page, Patti, 182
Palermo, Blinky, 147
Papanek, Ernst, 10, 47
Parker, William, 181
Parks, Rosa, 61
Parnassus, George, 83
Pastrano, Willie, 79, 85, 88, 89, 179
Pataki, George, 210
Patterson, Annabelle (mother of FP), 1,
    3, 7, 34
Patterson, Billy (brother of FP), 3
    and boxing, 13–14, 15–16, 230n.2
        (ch.2)
    and FP's prefight run, 19–20
Patterson, Floyd
    achievements of, 215, 216
    as African-American hero, 91, 92,
        106, 215
        after Johansson victory, 124–25
        on "100 Most Influential Negroes"
            list, 165
    and Ali (Clay), 127, 176–77
        Ali's criticism of FP, 175, 176, 215
        and Ali's draft refusal, 193
        Ali's praise of FP, 204–5
        and "Clay" as name, 176, 183, 205,
            241n.40
        confrontation with, 176–77
        FP attends Ali-Liston fight,
            180–81
        FP obscured by Ali mythology,
            214–15
        FP as rival, 213, 214
        FP's criticism of Ali, 173, 174, 203
        FP's defense of Ali, 187–88
        and proposal for third fight,
            206–7
        rematch discussed, 192
    autobiography of (*Victory over
        Myself*), 3, 134–35, 142–44,
        237–38n.16
    birth of, 1

childhood and adolescence of
    delinquency, 6–7
    emotional disturbances of, 3–4,
        11–12
    fantasy escapes, 5
    and FP's dreams for his children,
        58
    home conditions of, 2–3, 34
    in public school, 4–6, 15, 26
    romance with Sandra Hicks,
        23–25, 46 (*see also* Hicks, Sandra
        Elizabeth)
    in vocational school, 27, 28
    at Wiltwyck School, 7–12, 15, 19
and civil rights, xiii, 215 (*see also* Race
    relations and racism)
    in Birmingham demonstration,
        159, 160, 161–62, 215
    criticized as Uncle Tom, 175, 182–
        83, 203, 210, 215
    and early experience of segregated
        arena, 76
    and King assassination, 196
    lauded for participation in, 165–66
    on trip to Mississippi, 160
death of, 210
marriage and family (first), 58, 106
    birth of first child (Seneca), 69,
        70
    boxing takes toll on, 107, 143–44,
        189–90
    divorce, 190
    opposing personalities in, 190
    racism in Yonkers, 144–45, 168
    and Seaquist, 144
marriage and family (second),
    190–91
    son adopted, 207–8
and media, 48–49 (*see also* Media)
    and Boyle article on FP training
        camp, 128–29
    and Cannon, 57, 88, 132–33
    at first pro fight, xii–xiii
    FP's criticism of, 151–52
    and Talese, 77–78
mental deterioration of, 209–10,
    243n.44
operates training facility for
    neighboring youth, 207

Patterson, Floyd (*cont.*)
  personal characteristics of, 210
    articulate, xiii
    Baldwin on, 151, 152
    celebrity status uncomfortable for,
      72
    compassion toward opponents, 88,
      100, 123, 132, 192
    depression after losing, 48, 108–10
    fear of flying, 168
    generosity, 31, 58, 209
    hip look, 49
    running, 23, 207, 208
    self-declared cowardice, 159
    spending habits, 58
  and politics (*see also* Civil rights)
    as Kennedy follower, 136
    Mailer on, 154
    meets JFK and Bobby, 139, 140
    meets with Nixon, 203–4
    on trip to Egypt, 141–42
  and religion, 208–9
    vs. Ali, 173
    converts to Catholicism, 24–25
    gains audience with John XXIII,
      227
    and racial equality, 130
  BOXING CAREER OF, xiiii–xiv, 213–14,
    216–17
  and Ali, xiii, 172, 175, 215 (*see also* Ali,
    Muhammad)
  as corporation, 80–81
  cutthroat attitude lacking, 41, 48
  D'Amato's tutelage of, 18–19, 25, 28,
    39 (*see also* D'Amato, Cus)
  dedicated to training program, 23, 73
    roadwork, 23
  distinctive achievements of, 213–14
  earnings from, 205
  eye contact at beginning of fights
    avoided, 100
  on feeling of being knocked out,
    167–68
  as flawed, 88, 91, 107, 132–33, 171
    easily hit, 191
    as easy knockdown, xiv, 81, 186
  and Florio brothers, 36 (*see also*
    Florio, Dan)
  foot speed of, 86

  Hamill on Patterson-Liston fights as
    legacy, 171
  hand speed of, 49, 59, 185, 214
  injuries suffered, 62, 63, 106, 185, 187
  and Lavelle, 14, 15, 35, 51–52 (*see also*
    Lavelle, Frank)
  as life ambition, 26
  never quitting, 173
  opponents treated with fairness and
    compassion, 41, 64, 88, 100, 123,
    132
  peek-a-boo stance of, 20, 21, 192
  as public figure in after-boxing years,
    213
  Red Smith's tribute to, 31
  as spectator at Johansson's Olympic
    bout, 97
  Torres on, 210–11, 232n.9
  BOXING CAREER OF (EVENTS AND MILE-
    STONES; CHRONOLOGICAL)
  first taste of boxing at Wiltwyck,
    11–12, 14
  beginning of training, 13–16, 18
  beginning of relationship with
    D'Amato, 16
  first amateur fights, 19–20
  in Golden Gloves tournament (1951),
    20–22, 23
  in Amateur Athletic Union champi-
    onship, 23, 28
  in Golden Gloves tournament (1952),
    27–28
  in Olympics (1952), 27, 28–33
  transition to professional status,
    34–36
  first professional fight, xi–xiii, xiv, 39
  preparatory professional fights,
    40–42, 46, 48
  named Ring Rookie of the Year by
    boxing writers, 43–44
  training as professional, 50
  fights outside New York to evade IBC,
    53–54, 57–58
  first heavyweight fight (McBride),
    55–57
  Marciano retirement as opportunity,
    59–60
  as youngest-ever heavyweight
    champion, 71–72

named *Ring* magazine fighter of year, 72

exhibitions as heavyweight champ, 74

first heavyweight defense (Jackson), 76–77, 78–79, 214, 249

aftermath of first Johansson fight, 106–10, 111–12

as own manager, 116–17

and D'Amato's deal for TV retrospective, 145

end-of-career fights, 189

end of, 206, 207

BOXING CAREER OF (MAJOR FIGHTS; CHRONOLOGICAL)

Durelle fight (first), 44–45, 46, 56, 251

Maxim fight, 46–48, 214, 251

Durelle fight (second), 53–54, 250

McBride fight, 56–57, 250

Jackson fight (first), 60, 62–63, 67, 74, 214, 249

and race relations, 60–61

Moore fight, 63, 64, 69–71, 157, 214, 249

and birth of baby, 65

and Cosell, 101

delay, 60–61

FP fails to remember, 210

FP's training for, 67, 68, 149

Johansson's celebrity contrasted with, 111

prefight insults from Moore, 64–65

and suspect financial arrangements by IBC, 69

Jackson fight (second), 74, 76–77, 78–79, 214, 249

Rademacher fight, 79, 81, 249

and FP as easy knockdown, 81, 186

Harris fight, 82–83, 86–88, 113, 214, 249

social conflict symbolized in, 85–86

London fight, 89, 92–93, 214, 249

Clay watches, 126

and D'Amato, 90–91, 114

Johansson fight (first), 98–100, 102–5, 249

FP's training for, 94

Louis's analysis of, 119

Johansson fight (second), 118–25, 249

and Rosensohn, 112

training for, 114–16

Johansson fight (third), 131–32, 248

training camp for, 128–29, 130–31

writers' criticisms of, 132–33

McNeeley fight, 137–39, 248

Liston fight (first), 143, 148–49, 154–55, 248

FP's escape after, 156–59

and FP's integrity (Kane), 210

JFK's concern over, 139

journalists' coverage of, 149–50

postfight press conference for, 156

predictions of FP win, 153–54

Liston fight (second), 159, 164–65, 248

FP's defeatist attitude in, 164

and FP downslide, 165–66

FP's feelings in aftermath of, 167–68

FP's public pronouncements on, 162, 164

FP's training, 163–64

in Las Vegas, 162–63

Machen fight, 170, 172, 214, 248

Chuvalo fight, 175, 178–79, 214, 248

Ali as TV commentator for, 177–78

Ali's antics to promote, 176–77

Ali fight (first), 185–88, 241nn.47,50, 247

and FP's slipped disc, 185, 187

Las Vegas as site of, 181

Malcolm X's view on, 182–83

religious/social disputes excite interest in, 183–84

Cooper fight, 89, 191–92, 214, 247

Quarry fight (first), 194, 214, 242n.14, 247

Quarry fight (second), 195, 214, 247

Ellis fight, 197–200, 214, 247

Daniels fight, 201, 246

Bonavena fight, 202, 214, 246

Ali fight (second), 204, 205–6, 246

Cosell's condemnation of, 205

and FP's need for money, 205–6

prefight rituals, 204–5

White House break in training for, 203

overall record with data, 246–52

Patterson, Frank (brother of FP), 3, 6
  and boxing, 13–14, 15–16, 18, 230n.2
    (ch.2)
Patterson, Janene (daughter), 201
Patterson, Janet Seaquist (wife of FP),
    190–91, 201, 207–8
Patterson, Jeannie (daughter), 168
Patterson, Jennifer (daughter), 201
Patterson, Raymond (brother of FP), 78,
    115, 141, 167, 197
Patterson, Sandra Hicks (wife of FP),
    65, 106, 242n.3
  divorces FP, 190
  with FP in intervention against bully-
    ing of daughter, 168
  and FP's depression after Johansson
    fight, 107, 108, 112
  and FP's escape from first Liston
    fight, 157, 158
  racial discrimination against, 129–30
  and *Victory over Myself*, 142
  on visit to Hurricane Jackson, 79
  See also Hicks, Sandra Elizabeth
Patterson, Seneca (daughter of FP), 69,
    70, 143–44
Patterson, Sherman (brother of FP),
    78
Patterson, Thomas (father of FP), 1–2,
    3, 34, 39
Patterson, Tracy Harris, 207–8
Peek-a-boo boxing stance, 20
  in Cooper fight, 192
  Archie Moore's refinement of, 66
Piano Man Jones, 65
Plimpton, George, 124
Poitier, Sidney, 111
Polier, Justine Wise, 10, 124
Polite, Charley, 246
Polo Grounds
  FP fights Jackson in title defense at,
    73–74, 78
  second Patterson-Johansson fight at,
    118, 120, 121, 124
Powell, Charlie, 247
Presidential Papers, The (Mailer), 163
Presley, Elvis, 49, 185
Press. *See* Media
Prevatte, Ernie, 107
Professional, The (Heinz), 80

PS 614
  FP attends, 15, 24, 26, 28
  and FP championship, 125
  FP revisits, 99
  and Schwefel, 28

Quarry, Jerry, 194
  Ali wins over, 204
  death of, 209
  Ellis wins over, 197
  FP fights (first), 194, 214, 242n.14,
    247
  FP fights (second), 195, 214, 247

Race elations and racism
  Birmingham church bombings, 166
  and black boxer as heavyweight
    champion, 61
  in Brooklyn vs. Wiltwyck, 8
  and Eckstine as role model, 57
  FP on, 130, 174
    vs. Ali, 173
    military seen as commendable,
      194–95
    on racial pride, 125
  and Patterson-Liston fight, 149
  and FP's demand for desegregated
    audience at Johansson fight, 130,
      166, 215
  FP's experiences of on tour, 74–76
  and FP's home in Yonkers, 130,
    144–45, 189
    discrimination against wife,
      129–30
    harassment of children, 168
  and FP's treatment in South, 45–46
  and Kennedy's election, 136
  Nation of Islam on, 173–74
  and Patterson-Harris matchup,
    85–86
  and public gloating over Johansson's
    victory, 110–11
  school segregation, 91
  and Watts riots, 181–82
  and white vs. black opponents, 88
  See also Civil rights
Rademacher, Pete, 79–81, 83, 100
  fights FP, 79, 81, 249
  and FP as easy knockdown, 186

Remnick, David, 215
Rickey, Branch, 124, 134
Ring, The (magazine)
  names Patterson-Chuvalo as fight of
    year, 179
  names FP fighter of year, 72
  ranks Cooper as contender, 191
Roaring Brook, NY, training camp, 114
Roberson, Mable, 162
Robertson, Oscar, 91–92
Robinson, Jackie
  as African-American hero, 124
  and Birmingham demonstrations,
    161
  civil rights meeting called by, 160
  on civil rights trip to Mississippi, 160
  and Mailer on FP, 154
  as NAACP fundraising cochair, 133
  visits to help with FP's depression,
    108–9
Robinson, Sugar Ray, 21, 37, 47, 58, 72,
    124
  vs. white challengers, 88–89
Rockville Centre
  FP's house in, 72
  racial discrimination against Sandra
    Patterson in, 129–30
Rodak, Leo, 21
Rogin, Gil, 128
Roosevelt, Eleanor, 10–11, 154
Roosevelt, Franklin, 44
Roosevelt Raceway as reported fight
    venue, 62
Rosenberg, Julius and Ethel, and Cohn,
    118
Rosensohn, Bill, 82, 83, 89, 99
  and organized crime, 112–13, 114,
    118
Ross, Barney, 20, 21
Ruby, Earl, 126
Runyon, Damon, xii
Russell, Roger, 246

Sabedong, Duke, 171
Sabotin, Lalu, 40–41, 252
Saddler, Sandy, 50
Safwat, Mahmoud, 141
Sahl, Mort, 111
St. Nicholas Arena, xi–xii, 39, 48

Salerno, Anthony "Fat Tony," 112–13,
    114, 118
Sanders, Ed, 97, 234n.5
Scalzo, Petey, 36
Scarsdale, and FP's residence, 130, 168,
    239n.5
Schaap, Dick, 133–34
Schenkel, Chris, 122
Schmeling, Max, 13, 44, 49, 111, 120,
    133, 149
Schulberg, Budd, xii, 55–57, 162–63, 163
Schwefel, Charles, 28, 34
Seaquist, Janet (later Mrs. Floyd
    Patterson), 144, 190–91
Shabazz, Betty, 196
Sharkey, Jack, 111, 133
Sherman Antitrust Act, and IBC, 112
Shore, Dinah, 110–11, 115
Shrake, Edwin "Bud," 153, 202
Silvani, Al, 184–85, 186
Sinatra, Frank
  and FP, 57, 182, 187
  and FP's Miami training site, 130
  and proposed Patterson-Marciano
    fight, 81–82
  and Silvani, 184
Slade, Jimmy, 249, 250
Smith, Red, 31, 88, 117, 141, 202
Smith, Wallace "Bud," 21
Somebody Up There Likes Me (film), 185
Soviet Union
  Rademacher's victory over fighter
    from, 79–80
  regimented training for boxers of,
    30–31
Spinks, Leon, 207
Sports Illustrated
  article on FP training camp in,
    128–29
  and Clay-Ali name change, 241n.40
  FP autobiography serialized in, 143
  FP essay in, 172–73
Sportsman's Park, FP trains at, 67, 68,
    101, 149
Stevenson, Adlai, 154
Stillman's Gym, 35, 36–37, 61, 62,
    184
Strode, Woody, 13
Sullivan, Ed, 110–11, 116, 124, 148

Summerlin, Johnny, 79
Summit, NJ, training facility, 49
Sweden
    FP's affection for, 129
    as venue for post-Liston fights, 170,
        172
        Paterson-Ellis fight, 197, 199

Talese, Gay, 77–78
    and Baldwin's entrée, 152
    on D'Amato-FP relationship, 67–68
    at FP press conference, 151
    FP profiles by (*Esquire*), 129, 167,
        170
    with FP protecting daughter from
        racial bullying, 168
    on FP's career, 216–17
    and FP's marriage, 189–90
    and Sinatra, 187
    on *Victory over Myself*, 143
Taylor, Elizabeth, 163
Texas Western, all-black basketball
    champions from, 32
Thomas, Ike, 92
Till, Emmett, 61, 85
Tita, Vasile, 32
Tocco, Johnny, 146
Tonight Show, The, Patterson
    interviewed on, 200
Toronto, as planned venue for McNeeley
    fight, 138
Torres, José, 114, 169, 179, 192, 210–11,
    232n.9
Triner, Joseph, 155
Troy, Willie, 250
Tunney, Gene, 21, 49, 95, 107–8, 111
Turner, Jesse, 251
Tuxedo Junction (Early), 215
TV
    closed-circuit, 82, 83, 120, 138, 184
    Ali as commentator for, 177–78
    in White House, 139
    and Eastern Parkway Arena fights,
        40
    FP in *Wild, Wild West* series, 198

Unitas, Johnny, 111
United Artists, Patterson-Johansson
    broadcast sponsored by, 101

United Kingdom
    fight offer from, 73
    Patterson-Cooper fight in London,
        191
United States
    political atmosphere of (1952),
        32–33
    political changes in (1960s), 203
    social turmoil in (1963), 166
    Vietnam War turmoil in, 195–96
    See also Civil rights; Race relations
        and racism

Valan, Charles, 200
Valan, Harold, 198, 199–200,
    243n.26
Valdes, Nino, 55
Val-Kill (Roosevelt home), 10–11
Vanderbilt, Amy, and Ali's demeanor
    (Chass), 204
Victory over Myself (FP autobiography),
    3, 134–35, 142–44, 237–38n.16
Vietnam War
    and Ali's draft refusal, 193
    FP's support of, 195, 203, 215
    visits troops on USO tour, 194
Viscusi, Lou, 84
Vitale, John J., 147

Wagner, Dick, 41–42, 251, 252
Wagner, Robert F., 124
Walcott, Jersey Joe, 36, 50, 60, 75, 120,
    138, 180
Walker, Sammy, 252
Walker, Wyatt Tee, 161
Wallace, George, 190
Wallace, Gordon, 252
Walls, Jimmy, 249
Washington, Kenny, 13
Watson, Buster, 51
    FP assumes name of in Madrid,
        159
    in FP's entourage, 51, 67, 115, 131
        in corner for first Ali fight, 185–86
    intercedes to prevent postfight
        brawl, 104
    on tour in Egypt, 141
    and racial discrimination in Kansas
        City, 74

Watts riots, 181–82
Wayne, John, and FP, 101, 103, 107
Weill, Al, 82–83
Weinberg, Joel, 134
Wembley Stadium, London, Patterson-Cooper fight in, 191
Westphal, Albert, 138
Westport, CT, FP training at, 114
What's My Line? (TV show), Johansson as guest on, 119–20
Whitlock, Dave, 250
Wild, Wild West, The (TV series), Patterson in, 198
Wilkins, Roy, 133
Williams, Alvin, 249, 251
Williams, Cleveland "Big Cat," 111, 137, 171
Williams, Edward Bennett, 169
Williams, Ike, 50
Williams, Tennessee, and Gross on FP's life, 143

Wiltwyck School for Boys, 7
    FP attends, 7–12, 14, 15, 18–19, 136
    FP's home near, 207
    FP sponsors halfway house for, 133, 140
    FP testimonial proceeds to, 124
    FP trains at, 47
    as publication party beneficiary, 143
Winters, Shelley, 154
World Boxing Association (WBA)
    Ali title stripped by, 242n.11
    FP ranked by, 191
World Boxing Council (WBC), Ali title stripped by, 242n.11

Yankee Stadium, Patterson-Johansson fight at, 94, 99
Yeats, William Butler (quoted), 196
Yonkers, FP home in, 144–45, 158, 189, 239n.5

Ziegel, Vic, 206